The
Kitchen
Consultant

The Kitchen Consultant

a common-sense guide to kitchen remodeling

Herrick Kimball

The Taunton Press

Cover photo by Scott Gibson

Text © 1998 by Herrick Kimball
Illustrations © 1998 by The Taunton Press, Inc.
All rights reserved.

Printed in the United States of America
10 9 8 7 6 5 4 3 2 1

The Taunton Press, Inc., 63 South Main Street,
PO Box 5506, Newtown, CT 06470-5506
e-mail: tp@taunton.com

Library of Congress Cataloging-in-Publication Data

Kimball, Herrick.
    The kitchen consultant : a common-sense guide to kitchen
remodeling / Herrick Kimball.
        p.   cm.
    "A fine homebuilding book" — T.p. verso.
    Includes index.
    ISBN 1-56158-247-6
    1. Kitchens—Remodeling.   I. Title.
TH4816.3.K58K56   1998
643'.4—DC21   97-46052
                                                      CIP

To three special women who have had a profound influence on my life:
Mary Kimball, my grandmother; Mary Murphy, my mother;
and Marlene Kimball, my wife.

Each of you has been a great blessing to me.

ACKNOWLEDGMENTS

My personal experience as a kitchen remodeler over the past 20 years has given me tremendous insight into the remodeling process, but not total knowledge of everything. Realizing that, I put a lot of effort into soliciting the insight, opinions, and experiences of many other people in the course of writing this book. It would be impossible to list all the organizations, manufacturers, craftsmen, and homeowners who contributed in some way to *The Kitchen Consultant,* but I do want to mention a few here.

First, my great thanks to Pam Bobinis, CKD, of PMB Designs in Cortland, New York, for taking such an enthusiastic interest in this project from the beginning and for reviewing each chapter as I wrote it. Pam, you are a tribute to your profession. The little smiley faces you put on the manuscript were great. And, as much as it vexed me at the time, all those red-ink criticisms were necessary and appreciated.

Laura Hunsinger, of Moravia, New York, for whom I have done remodeling work over the years, reviewed my first four chapters and didn't hesitate to point out flaws and shortcomings. Thanks, Laura, your frank critique was invaluable, and those chapters turned out all the better because of it.

My gratitude also goes out to the following people who reviewed individual chapters or provided me with specific information along the way:

Harvey Baker of Woodland Specialties, Syracuse, New York; Fred Beasley of Nashville Sash and Door Company, Nashville, Tennessee; David Brown, CKD, of Rynone Kitchen and Bath, Waverly, New York; Paul Compeau of Aspen Research Corp., St. Paul, Minnesota; Lawrin T. Ellis of Fantech, Sarasota, Florida; Ed Fenstermacher and Russ Sampson of Alpine Building Supply, Moravia, New York; Bill Furner of Pyramid Tile Company, San Francisco, California; John Iler of Edward Joy Lighting, Syracuse, New York; Leigh Keith of Class Act Kitchen and Bath Design Center, Cortland, New York; Paul Raymer of Tamarack Technologies, West Wareham, Massachusetts; Steve Sheinkoph of Yale Electric, Dorchester, Massachusetts; and Dawn Sroka of Tile and Carpet One, Auburn, New York.

I also want to extend special thanks to all the fine folks at The Taunton Press who had a hand in bringing this book to print, most notably my editor, Ruth Dobsevage.

CONTENTS

INTRODUCTION

Having your kitchen remodeled can be a satisfying experience that enriches your life or a bad experience that leaves you with regrets. The difference between the two lies not in chance or circumstance but in making wise decisions. And wise decisions come from knowledge properly applied. That's why I've written this book.

If this is your first remodel, you may not realize how complicated the process can be. Kitchen remodeling is a jungle. The choices that must be made regarding design, products, prices, suppliers, contractors, and work specifications are the equivalent of rushing streams, rickety rope bridges, sweltering heat, pestilence, and dense undergrowth. Some homeowners bushwhack their way through and somehow manage to survive, but the smart ones do their research, hire a guide, and confidently strike out for the treasure that awaits them.

So much for wild analogies; I think you get the idea. And if you do, this book can serve as your guide. It contains the basic information you'll need to make prudent decisions about how and where to spend your hard-earned dollars to get the kitchen of your dreams.

Talk, of course, is cheap, and many other books have been written about kitchen remodeling. What's so special about this one? I've been a remodeler for 20 years, and I've worked on literally hundreds of kitchens, including my own! So I know what it's like, as both a professional and a homeowner. You'll get the benefit of my hard-won experience from a professional and pragmatic perspective that few other books can match.

Don't be taken in by gaudy coffee-table books that feature sleek photos of esoteric or unconventional design schemes and outlandishly expensive product lines. Such extravagances may be entertaining to look at but not ultimately useful in planning your own kitchen remodel. I will discuss some products typically found in "high-end" kitchens but it will be with an eye toward value and performance. I won't waste your time and money on overblown ostentation or quirky style. Nor will I bore you with reams of tedious data. Should you wish to delve more deeply into different products or procedures, you can consult one of the numerous publications listed in Resources on pp. 194-197.

The Kitchen Consultant is a handbook of advice and information, and as such it has been organized for quick and easy reference. Each chapter is devoted to a particular aspect of the remodeling process. The information is geared to the homeowner who will be hiring a general contractor to do the work, but it will also be useful to you if you decide to act as your own general contractor, or even if you decide to do the hands-on work yourself. I will tell you what options are available and discuss their pros and cons. Along the way, I won't hesitate to make some professional recommendations of my own.

But enough of this talk; let's get down to business. Pick a subject, locate it on the contents page or in the index, and turn to the appropriate pages. See for yourself if this book meets your informational needs. I am confident that it will empower you to make the best decisions when you remodel your kitchen. Here's to your success.

CHAPTER 1

REMODELING OPTIONS

The kitchen is the place where food is prepared—from there, virtually anything goes. Depending on your lifestyle, your kitchen may also serve as the regular dining room. It may be the place where friends gather over a cup of coffee or the place you gab on the phone while cooking a meal. Much can happen at the kitchen table: dining, reading the paper, craftwork, homework, paying bills.

Kitchens evoke memories of childhood. As long as I live, whenever I smell hot cinnamon-pecan rolls, I will once again be a little boy in my grandmother Kimball's kitchen, pestering her with questions while she whips up some of the most delectable foods I have ever known. Her birch-plywood-door cabinets and green patterned Formica countertop were brand new and very modern in 1958, the year I was born. Today her kitchen looks the same, and though it's now old and dated, to me it is the most beautiful kitchen in the world.

Yes, I can certainly get sentimental about kitchens, and I imagine you can too, because in a home, kitchens are really more than places to prepare food. They are also places

where memories are made. This is where your kitchen remodeling should start—reflecting on your past experiences, as well as on your current and future needs and desires. You can be pragmatic later, but, for now, take some time to dream...

Okay, time's up. Now we can get down to the business at hand. Let's start with money.

Cost

Cost is the first concern of many people contemplating a kitchen remodel, and it is indeed a critical issue. Remodeling a kitchen is a lot more expensive than remodeling any other room in the house. If you've lived in your home for very long, you have probably put off doing much of anything with the kitchen for years, primarily because you dread the anticipated high cost. This is why kitchens are typically the last room in the house to get refurbished.

How much will a new kitchen cost? It's not an easy question to answer. New kitchens are a lot like new cars. How much does a new car cost? It depends. Are you talking foreign or domestic? Compact or luxury? Standard or automatic? Four-wheel drive? Leather seats? See what I mean?

Nevertheless, we can discuss averages. Each year the editors of *Remodeling*, a professional trade magazine, publish a cost vs. value report for 12 hypothetical home remodeling projects. I'll discuss what cost vs. value is and the findings as they relate to kitchens shortly, but for now, let's focus on two of the projects, a "minor" kitchen remodel and a "major" kitchen remodel, which are described as typical remodels in mid-range neighborhoods. After the definitions, we'll talk price.

■ MINOR KITCHEN REMODEL: "In a functional but dated 200-sq.-ft. kitchen with 30 lineal feet of cabinetry and countertops, refinish existing cabinets, install new energy-efficient wall oven and cooktop, new laminate countertops, new mid-priced sink and faucet, wall covering and resilient flooring, and repaint. Job includes new raised-panel wood doors on cabinets."

■ MAJOR KITCHEN REMODEL: "Update an outmoded 200-sq.-ft. kitchen with a functional layout of new cabinets, laminate countertops, mid-priced sink and faucet, energy-efficient wall oven, cooktop and ventilation system, built-in microwave, dishwasher, disposer, and custom lighting. Add new resilient flooring. Finish with painted woodwork and ceiling. Include 30 lineal feet of semi-custom-grade wood cabinets and counter space, including a 3-ft. by 5-ft. center island."

To determine an accurate price for these projects, *Remodeling* editors submitted each job description to three well-known publishers of construction estimating software and manuals that are used by remodelers nationwide. Each company "bid" on the projects, adjusting their numbers to reflect labor and materials costs in 60 cities in 50 states, which were divided into four regions of the country. In other words, *Remodeling* made an honest effort to determine the national average cost of an average kitchen remodel. The average costs for 1997-1998 are as follows: $8,395 for the minor kitchen remodel and $22,509 for the major kitchen remodel. For a full report, or an updated copy of *Remodeling* magazine's study and findings, see Resources on pp. 194-197.

Remodeling a kitchen is a lot more expensive than remodeling any other room in the house.

If at this point you're feeling sticker shock, that's good, because you really do need a realistic idea of costs if you are planning a remodel, and I believe these numbers are realistic. However, if you find them highly discouraging, don't toss this book aside in hopeless despair. Attractive and functional remodels can be done for less money (and maybe even much less). If you do your homework (i.e., read this book and follow its suggestions), shop around for materials and do some of the work yourself, you can save yourself a bundle.

Then again, if you're rolling in cash, the costs cited above might strike you as bargain-basement prices. I once read an article about a kitchen remodel that cost

$86,000. The kitchen was undoubtedly nice, and the article was interesting, but it failed to answer the biggest question in my mind, which was, what the heck did the homeowners do for a living that they could justify spending that much money on a kitchen? I could build a small house for $86,000! So price can certainly be relative, and the sky may be the limit—but not in this book, I assure you.

Financial payback

Besides getting a wonderful new kitchen, the good news is that the money you spend remodeling will more than likely add substantially to the value of your home. And if you intend to sell your house in the next few years, there is a statistically good chance you'll be able to recoup a sizable chunk of the money you parted with, if not all of it. Some people even walk away from the deal with a profit.

Q. Will the value of my home increase?

A. Yes, definitely...

You've probably heard the adage that the three most important things when it comes to selling real estate are location, location, and location. But when it comes to selling a home, your kitchen might be next on the list. Real-estate agents will tell you that a pleasant and modern kitchen can often be the deciding factor in a home's sale.

Remodeling magazine's latest annual cost vs. value report, which I referred to earlier, consulted with over 300 real-estate agents around the country and asked them how much each of the two kitchen remodeling projects would add to the value of a mid-priced house in an established neighborhood in their town. Then they divided the cost of remodeling by the value to figure the percentage of return, and again, they averaged the numbers out.

The payback for a major kitchen remodel ranged from 54% in Anchorage, Alaska, to 141% in New Haven, Conecticut, with the national average weighing in at a very decent 90%. However, what I find particularly interesting is that the payback for a minor kitchen remodel ranged up to 183% and averaged 102%. In fact, of the 12 remodeling categories in the report, the minor kitchen remodel has consistently taken top honors for several years, while a major kitchen remodel ranks high, but usually in third or fourth place.

What all of this means is that remodeling your kitchen can be a downright smart investment. Not only is the return of your money possible, but a new kitchen could also be the factor that helps you sell your home better and faster. However, let me remind you that these are only statistics, and certainly not a guarantee of anything when it comes down to your particular situation. There are many other variables that enter into the equation. For example, if other homes in your neighborhood that are similar to yours routinely sell for $75,000, it's not likely that yours will fetch significantly more, even with the new kitchen (but you might not get that much without it).

Defining the scope
of the work

A kitchen remodel can be anything from a quick cosmetic fix to a total reconfiguration. I like to break this range into four categories: budget, minor, major, and really major.

Budget remodeling is just a sprucing up of the kitchen—new curtains and a fresh coat of paint on the walls and ceiling. For an inexpensive new look, you might even paint the cabinets (there are also companies that specialize in painting cabinets). If budget remodeling is all your wallet will allow, then by all means get out the paint. (But don't go overboard—I once remodeled a kitchen whose previous owners had slathered the walls, ceiling, cabinets, tile backsplash, and even the refrigerator with a layer of lavender paint!) Repainted cabinets will probably look better than they used to, but nowhere near as nice as new or refaced cabinets.

Minor kitchen remodeling means working with the existing cabinetry. There are no substantial changes in the size and layout of the room. Countertops, flooring, and appliances are upgraded or modernized, and cabinetry is refaced by installing new doors and drawer fronts (see the sidebar on pp. 122-123 for details on this increasingly popular option).

Minor remodeling is an excellent option as long as the cabinet layout of the kitchen you're working with is well designed to begin with and as long as it will meet your needs. Be honest with yourself here; don't make substantial compromises that you'll regret later. Minor remodeling should not for a minute imply substandard quality. If you think that minor remodeling is nothing more than a cheap fix, you are missing the point.

In light of the fact that minor kitchen remodeling can be such a low-cost/high-value approach, it makes sense to consider this option seriously.

Q. Should we have the walls torn down or just get the room repainted?

A. You can do a little or a lot, depending on your needs and your budget.

Major remodeling means tearing everything old right on out of there, usually down to the wall and ceiling framing, and sometimes even the floor joists. Windows are often added or removed. New insulation might be added, and substantial reworking or upgrading of the electrical and plumbing lines is typical.

Really major kitchen remodeling includes everything that major remodeling involves, and then some—substantial rearranging of walls and doorways and stairways and that sort of thing. Building an addition to the house to accommodate the new kitchen would most definitely fall into this category.

Big-bang vs.
evolutionary remodeling

Once you've decided on the scope of your project, you must then decide how fast to have the job done. With minor or major remodeling, you can have the job done all at

Whatever the scope of your remodel, the kitchen will be off limits to the family, and you need to make some arrangements beforehand so your household can run smoothly, or at least continue to function.

First, pack up everything in the room and move it elsewhere—from major appliances such as stoves, refrigerators, and freezers right down to cookbooks, pots and pans, utensils, and of course, the food. Some people just cram everything into boxes, pile them helter-skelter about the house, and plan to eat out or order pizza for every meal. That approach may sound like fun, but it gets old fast. And it also gets expensive.

You can still use remodeling as an excuse to dine out more often, but when you start longing for a return to normalcy, you'll be a lot happier if you take the time to set up a camp kitchen away from the remodeling chaos. Here are some ways to cope with the disruption:

■ Start with a refrigerator, a good-sized table, and a garbage can. It's not as convenient to hook up a temporary stove as it is the refrigerator, so plan on using a microwave, a toaster, and maybe a hot plate. An outdoor propane gas grill is very useful, too.

■ Stock up on paper plates and cups and plastic utensils; washing dishes in the bathroom tub or sink can be a real bother.

■ Organize the dry and canned foods in boxes under the table.

■ Plan simple meals that don't require a lot of preparation or cleanup, such as sandwiches. Fruit and cookies make a good dessert.

■ Precook and freeze some meals that can be conveniently heated up. Lasagna and casseroles are two good choices.

■ Most kitchens have a phone, and you'll probably want to leave it there for the contractor to use. You will also want to have an extension phone set up outside the kitchen for your own use, since the kitchen will be sealed off from the rest of the house (see the sidebar on p. 61), and you will want to prevent construction dust from being tracked back and forth.

■ Plan to use another entry into the home besides the kitchen, and provide a place nearby for shoes, boots, hats, mittens, umbrellas, and other such gear.

once or gradually over time. The installment approach, sometimes called the "five-year plan," works best with minor remodeling and amounts to doing a little bit at a time as you get the money. For example, you might get a new dishwasher and stove this year, a countertop and a sink next year, the cabinet refacing the following year, and so forth.

Q. We don't have a lot of money—does everything have to happen all at once, or can the work be done in stages?

A. You can plan the work however you like.

Major remodeling on the installment plan can be a major pain because it takes a long time—often longer than expected—to get a normally functioning, completed kitchen. I know this from personal experience. When I first started out as a carpenter I built my own house (it's a great way to learn), so naturally I decided to build my own kitchen cabinets. I built and installed them without any problem, but, to my wife's disgust, three years passed before I got around to making the doors. It was even longer until I put down the vinyl flooring. And after 11 years, when we decided to do a complete minor remodeling, there were still several things I hadn't finished, and that's a typical do-it-yourself homeowner situation. The second time around, I did a minor remodeling of everything all at once (the big-bang approach). Needless to say, if you can afford it, this is the best way to go, and my wife seconds that.

Strategies for cutting labor costs

As you plan your multi-thousand-dollar project, you will want to do everything in your power to keep costs under control. Those of you who have done a little carpentry work in the past might jump at the chance to participate actively; others might be tempted to manage the project as general contractor, scheduling the delivery of materials and the flow of the work. You might even have relatives, friends, or neighbors in the trades who would be willing to do the work for less than the going rate. All of these options seem attractive at first glance, but I can't recommend them wholeheartedly without pointing out some of the drawbacks.

Doing the work yourself

Sweat equity can be a valuable asset, and one of the ways to reduce costs is by doing your own work. However, unless you are a professional remodeler or a serious do-it-yourself homeowner with past professional experience, you'd be nuts to take on an entire major remodeling job by yourself. A minor re-model might be more manageable (especially on the installment plan), but it would still be a big undertaking. That isn't to say that you can't tackle certain segments of your project, because, if you have the time and the inclination, I think you should. Saving money will not be the only benefit. You'll also come away from the experience with a great feeling of empowerment and self-satisfaction.

Above all, be honest about your abilities and limitations. An average homeowner with a little experience, a lot of determination, some basic tools, and good how-to information can certainly rip out old cabinetry, install replacement windows, work with ceramic tile, paint, and wallpaper, and even reface cabinets. More experienced and motivated individuals could successfully tackle more demanding tasks: installing new cabinets, making a plastic-laminate countertop, and performing minor electrical and plumbing work. If you're not sure about whether you should tackle a certain job, seek the counsel of your spouse or significant other. This person may not know a lick about remodeling, but will have an uncanny understanding of your track record, temperament, and time demands. The advice you get will be very wise (and brutally honest); take it seriously.

Q. Hiring a contractor will cost a bundle, and we'd rather spend our cash on high-quality materials and appliances. Can we manage the job ourselves?

A. Yes, but it's a lot of work! Think about it carefully before making your decision.

One good way to take an active part in remodeling your kitchen is to hire a professional to do most of the work and reserve a few tasks to do on your own. This kind of arrangement can work well as long as your part of the work doesn't interfere with what you hire the pro to do. For example, you gut and dispose of the old kitchen before the contractor installs the new kitchen; when that's done, you finish up with the wallpapering and painting. Or you reface your own cabinets and afterwards have a pro come and put in a new countertop and sink. When there are clear divisions of work responsibilities, things go more smoothly. Hiring a professional to redo the whole kitchen while you take care of all the plumbing work would not be a good arrangement because you would be directly involved with and interfering with what the professional would be doing.

Never, never try to help a contractor you hire. Customers who offer me this kind of assistance often have a pretty good understanding of how things are done and sincerely want to be useful. But the fact is that you will be more of a hindrance than a help. It's much better to allow the contractor to do the work without getting in the way.

Acting as your own general contractor

To save money, some homeowners consider acting as their own general contractor for a building or remodeling project, which is to say that they organize and run the whole show, lining up and coordinating materials and a variety of tradesmen who act as subcontractors. On a minor kitchen remodel, the scope of the job is small and manageable, and I see no reason why a homeowner who wants to shouldn't act as general contractor.

However, if your plans call for major or really major remodeling, I strongly suggest that you not be the general contractor. In my experience, homeowners rarely perform very well as a general contractor on a large, extensive project. Most who try it find this out the hard way, unfortunately. Let a competent professional take responsibility for orchestrating the project. General contractors are well worth their cost in this regard.

People are always trying to do things that they really don't know much about. Sometimes you can learn as you go along, but in remodeling, a little knowledge can indeed be a dangerous thing.

In your zeal to participate in the project and save yourself some money, you can wreak a lot of havoc if you don't really know what you're doing at the outset. You are setting yourself up for frustration and substandard quality; you might even be putting your life in danger.

Remodeling can call for knowledge of framing, plumbing, wiring, cabinetmaking, countertop installations, and flooring. Even if you're not planning to participate actively in the work, you'll want to know enough to make intelligent decisions. And if you plan to upgrade your appliances, you'll want to know how the different makes and models stack up against one another before you plunk down your hard-earned cash. Here's an overview of your sources for technical information; for my specific recommendations, see Resources on pp. 194-197.

BOOKS

Books are one of the best ways to get a well-focused, thorough treatment of a subject. I have assembled such an extensive how-to library that now, when I buy another book, my wife smiles and gives me that "do-you-really-think-you-should-be-spending-money-on-another-book" look. The answer is yes, absolutely! This is one way I can learn new things and stay current with my profession. (And besides, it's a business deduction.)

MAGAZINES

How-to magazines can be an excellent source of pertinent information, but you may have to do a little research to find out what you want to know. One way is to check classifications in the *Reader's Guide to Periodical Literature* at your library. You can also call the publication, ask to talk to an editor, and inquire about recent articles on the subject you're interested in. Then buy the back issue or get it at the library.

CLASSES AND SEMINARS

Vocational high schools in my area of the country offer evening classes for adults on topics such as plumbing, cabinetmaking, carpentry, and kitchen design. These hands-on classes usually meet once a week for a couple of months, and the teachers are often working professionals from the community. I've taught such classes, and they can be a great way for homeowners to learn the ropes from a professional craftsman.

Seminars are usually put on by lumberyards and home centers as a way to educate do-it-yourself homeowners and promote products. Manufacturers' representatives are on hand, and sometimes a professional craftsman. Seminars may last only an hour or so, or they may run all day and you can stop in at your leisure to ask questions. Generally speaking, such seminars are a great source of specialized information and well worth attending. Bring lots of questions—it's the people who participate actively in the discussion who benefit the most.

MANUFACTURERS

Manufacturers of building materials and kitchen appliances usually have instructional literature and spec sheets that are available to consumers on request. They typically provide hot lines or customer-service phone numbers. These exist for your benefit—most are toll free—so don't hesitate to use them. Generally speaking, I've found technical representatives to be knowledgeable and helpful. If you talk to someone like this, it's a good idea to jot down the person's name in case you have to call another time.

While we're on the subject of information from manufacturers, let's not overlook the instructions supplied with the product. This source of information may seem rather obvious, but it's amazing how many people don't read the directions. I like to read any instructions the night before I do a job. That way, when I'm at work, my progress isn't held up while I try to figure things out. There's another good reason for reading the instructions: If you fail to follow them, the manufacturer's warranty will probably be void. File this material when you're done with the installation; it may

also contain pertinent phone numbers, addresses, and a list of replacement parts.

THE INTERNET

The Internet can be a tremendous resource for how-to and product information. There are various construction and remodeling bulletin boards where you can post questions and get answers from professionals. Most companies that sell kitchen remodeling products have web pages where you can review product lines and compare prices; through e-mail, you can ask technical questions or request product literature. I relied on the Internet to do some of the research for this book and made contact with numerous industry professionals. There is no reason why you can't do the same. Even if you don't have a home computer, you can probably access the Internet at your local library; that's how I got started.

In the movie *The Money Pit,* a couple buy a house and decide to have it remodeled. When they ask the contractor how long the job will take, he replies offhandedly, "Two weeks." Over the next several months, the job turns into a nightmare. But every time the homeowners inquire how much longer the work will take, they get the same answer—two weeks.

There's a definite element of truth to this gag. Contractors are always optimists—whatever they tell you, add a week to be safe. If the work gets done sooner, you'll be pleasantly surprised.

However, if you have carefully figured the job specifications ahead of time (see Chapter 2) and don't make too many changes to them, and if you choose a reputable contractor (see Chapter 3), you should be given a realistic idea of how long the job should take.

Sometimes people want to remodel their kitchens in time for a special event, such as a wedding, when they expect to entertain many guests in their home. If you have an important deadline like that, make your plans, line up a contractor, and schedule the work long in advance—one year ahead of time is not too soon to get the wheels in motion.

Give your contractor 6 to 10 months of lead time to schedule your project, and specify a completion date that is well before the big event. You might also want a completion deadline spelled out in your work contract (see p. 51).

Hiring friends and relatives

Now here's an idea—hire your Uncle Joe, who has always been a handy guy, or one of your co-workers who does a little remodeling work on the side. It is an idea, all right, but it is not a good one. It's very convenient and tempting to hire someone you know and trust to do your work, but you may be inviting trouble if the person is not a full-time professional remodeler. Yes, I am showing some real prejudice here, but it's not without foundation. If you're going to hire someone to do a specialized job like kitchen remodeling, you may as well get a professional. A competent pro is worth every dollar.

Another risky arrangement is hiring a close friend or next-door neighbor who is a professional remodeler. Such people may be well qualified (and they may not), but there are many things (little things) that can go wrong, lead to hard feelings, and end what was once a good personal relationship. You aren't obligated to hire friends and relatives. I myself do work for close family, but I'm very reluctant to do work for friends and neighbors. Usually I ask them to find someone else. Trust me on this one: I've been around, and I've heard the stories.

If you disregard my advice and do hire a friend or relative, make sure that you handle any transactions in a strictly professional way. Have a clear job description and a signed agreement before any work begins (see pp. 47-52 for a discussion of what a work contract should include). And don't expect to get a price break on the work; if your friend or relative is a professional remodeler or tradesman, expecting work for less than the going rate would be taking advantage of the relationship.

Sometimes friends and relatives offer to work for you as a favor or in return for your help on a project of theirs. That's a different situation, and there's certainly nothing wrong with people helping each other out. After all, that's what family and friends are for.

Three advantages to hiring a pro

There's a lot to be said for hiring a professional to remodel your kitchen. First, a professional kitchen remodeler or a reputable general contractor will finish the job. (Had I hired a pro to build my first kitchen, it would not have had unfinished loose ends 11 years later.) Second, a pro will generally do a better job than you will. There is a lot to be said for experience (and I'll say more about it in Chapter 3). Third, a pro will get the job done at a professional pace, much sooner than you would if you did the work yourself. This is a major benefit because the kitchen is one of the most used rooms in the house, and you don't want it out of commission any longer than it has to be.

Exactly how long will it take a professional to remodel an average kitchen? That's hard to say, because there are so many variables. Since I don't know of any official studies or statistics on the subject, I'll have to wing it, based on my experiences as a professional kitchen remodeler working with one skilled assistant. An average minor kitchen remodeling takes me one to two weeks, and a major kitchen remodeling generally takes two to three weeks. With really major remodeling, the job could stretch into a couple of months.

Dealing with the stress and the mess

No matter how well you plan and prepare for the work, remodeling can be very stressful. All the decisions, the disruption of your routine, the mess, and any number of other elements will severely affect your lifestyle. There are several ways to deal with the situation. Above all, keep in mind that the mess and chaos are temporary conditions, and they will come to an end. If you roll with the punches and keep a smile on your face, you'll get through the remodeling just fine. Honest.

When complications arise, as they inevitably will, realize that it's par for the course. Don't be surprised. Don't get your feathers ruffled. Consult with the pros, weigh your options, deal with them reasonably, and move on. If you're doing work yourself and run into a particularly thorny problem, try to see it as a creative opportunity—that's what I tell myself when I run into a snag.

If you're not doing the work yourself, stay out of the house as much as you can. Absolutely do not take time off from work just to be home when contractors are doing their thing. Be available (give them your phone number at work and stop in regularly), but don't hang out because the process will seem so much more protracted. If you don't work outside the home, make plans to be away—go shopping, take day trips, visit friends, have fun. On a couple of occasions, I've worked for people who stayed around for a few days to make sure the job got off to a good start and then left for vacation. I don't know if I would recommend that, but, if you've done your planning well and hired a reputable pro, you really can (and should) take it easy.

CHAPTER 2

DESIGN AND PLANNING

Good design and planning are the foundation upon which every successful kitchen remodeling project is built. In those instances when remodeling goes awry, or turns out less wonderful than it could have been, the cause can very often be traced back to a homeowner who failed to take design and planning seriously. If you invest some time and effort (and perhaps a bit of money) here at the start, I guarantee you it will pay off. The job will progress more smoothly, you will get more value for your dollars, and you will be much more delighted with the results.

In this chapter you'll find out how you can go about getting the best new kitchen design, whether you do it yourself or have it done by a professional designer. Then you'll learn how to assemble your plans into specifications, which are a written description of the work to be done. Your specifications will inform bidding contractors what they should base their bids on. And when it comes time to do the work, this document will be a clear road map showing exactly where you want your remodeling project to go.

Think about design in terms of style and function. Style hits you the minute you walk into a room: the cabinet doors, moldings, countertops, colors, window treatments, and a whole array of other details blend together to give a room its style. Function is a more subtle concept. In a kitchen that functions well, the layout of cabinets, appliances, and work surfaces is conducive to organization, efficiency, and convenience; the kitchen may or may not look beautiful, but it is a pleasure to work in.

Having a well-designed kitchen is ultimately more important than having top-of-the line appliances and trendy countertops. You can spend a small fortune on the highest-quality products, but if you neglect to fit those items into a functional and cohesive design, your new kitchen will be a failure. On the other hand, if you remodel using much less costly materials but the layout and craftsmanship are sound, your kitchen will be a definite success.

Deciding on a style

The important first step to finding the design that is right for you is to find a style that appeals to you. I call this process "predesign." The style that you choose for your kitchen will be a reflection of your personality and interests, and it might even provide a glimpse of your alter ego. That is as it should be.

Options abound. I myself am fond of the spare country look, best described as Shaker. Some people prefer a warmer, more cluttered country style. Some have elegant, traditional tastes; others long for the clean lines and bright surfaces of a contemporary kitchen. Maybe you would prefer a commercial restaurant look, or the Craftsman style, which is currently in vogue. Classical Italian? Avant-garde? Bon vivant? Whimsical? Bohemian? The possibilities go on and on, and they are all fun to imagine and consider.

But descriptive words and mental images are not enough (what does a Bohemian-style kitchen look like, anyway?). To clarify your thoughts, you need to cast a wider net. I advise my clients to have a look at kitchen designs in books and magazines. Flooding the mind with all sorts of pictures will broaden your understanding of the design possibilities. If you try this, you will find certain design features that appeal to you.

Another important predesign step is to go window shopping. Check out the big home-center chain stores and the smaller kitchen and bath centers. You're not going there to buy (at least not yet); you're gathering ideas and information by looking at the displays, getting product literature, and talking to the salespeople. Make it a point to visit these stores on a weekday, when business is typically slow and the sales staff will have more time to talk. Ask questions about different products; ask about prices; ask for recommendations. Ask about the store's design service— what can it do for you when you get to that stage? If there are photos of kitchens the store has designed, give them a gander.

Do you find the salespeople knowledgeable? How do they make you feel? You will feel more comfortable at some places, and with some people, than with others. Trust your feelings. Collect business cards. Having done all of these things, you will be better informed and prepared to enter into the final design phase of your project.

Blending style with layout

With a style in mind, it's time to put your design together, and here you have two options. You can educate yourself by reading design information in kitchen-design books and magazine articles, or you can seek out the services of a professional kitchen designer.

If you like to figure things out for yourself, you can consult books on kitchen design (see Resources on pp. 194-197). Another option might be to use a kitchen planning kit, which a few cabinet manufacturers make available to homeowners for a nominal price.

There is no doubt that if you invest the time and effort to research the topic, you can come up with a great design without outside help. But for the best design, and especially if your kitchen will undergo major changes in layout, I recommend that you work, at least in part, with someone who is a specialist.

Designing a kitchen is like assembling a puzzle with many interlocking pieces. What makes this puzzle so challenging is that it has a variety of solutions. The task should be taken very seriously because you are spending a lot of money, and any poor decisions (choices you later regret) will not be easy to put behind you; they will be evident every time you cook a meal.

Designing a kitchen is like assembling a puzzle with many interlocking pieces. What makes this puzzle so challenging is that it has a variety of solutions.

Professional designers are trained and experienced puzzle masters. They work with you to come up with a logical and pleasing kitchen layout. Together, you craft a plan that will meet your expectations and conform to your budget—a harmonious blend of style, function, and practicality. If you decide not to work with a kitchen designer, I recommend that you at least have your final drawings reviewed by a pro. You will find the feedback to be quite constructive.

Finding a qualified kitchen designer

Good design is where you find it. A dust-covered carpenter with callused hands can come up with an idea that's as good as the advice from a squeaky-clean architect with a college degree. But, for the most part, there are qualities that distinguish talented design professionals from the multitude of wannabes. Those qualities are training, experience, and reputation.

Starting your search

Professional kitchen designers can be found among the ranks of architects, interior designers, retail cabinet salespeople, and residential remodeling contractors. You can also find independent designers who specialize in kitchens exclusively. It's impossible to say which of these avenues will be your best option. How then do you sort through the choices and find a talented designer? Here are three suggestions:

- Ask for recommendations from friends and acquaintances who have remodeled their kitchen.
- Look for a Certified Kitchen Designer (see the sidebar on p. 20).
- Look for independent kitchen designers. Independent designers are usually very experienced and good at their job.

Conducting an interview

Keep in mind that finding a talented designer is not enough; you also have to know if you want that person to do your design work. The best way to find the right designer for your project is to conduct an interview. Here are some key questions to ask:

- What are the designer's professional qualifications?
- How long has the designer been in the business?
- Will there be a charge for the designer's services? If so, how much will it be and what will the pay schedule be (more about this shortly).

CERTIFIED KITCHEN DESIGNERS

Certified Kitchen Designer (CKD) is a designation given by the National Kitchen and Bath Association (NKBA). To earn the title, designers must have at least seven years of experience in residential kitchen design or the equivalent in experience and education. They must supply letters of reference from past clients. And they must pass a day-long examination. New requirements established in 1997 require candidates to pass a National Council of Interior Design Qualification exam before they begin training for the CKD exam.

Over the years, I've talked to many CKDs about the qualification process. All the evidence I've seen points to the designation of CKD as being legitimate and truly a professional standard. Designers who are CKDs have specialized training in kitchen design, and have demonstrated a serious commitment to pursue that level of professional qualification. These are undoubtedly good things.

Don't confuse a CKD with someone who is a member of the NKBA; CKDs earn their designation, while members of the NKBA do not have to fulfill design training requirements. As I write this, there are currently more than 2,600 CKDs working in the United States and Canada. You can find out more about them or locate one near you by contacting the National Kitchen and Bath Association (see Resources on pp. 194-197).

■ Exactly what services will be provided? Some designers limit their work to space planning (the layout of cabinets and appliances), which is at the heart of the design process, but others may be able to help you select and coordinate lighting fixtures, colors schemes, and fabrics. Architects who are kitchen designers will be best qualified to draw up plans for you that include substantial structural work (on really major remodels, drawings stamped by an architect may be required for obtaining a permit). Any kitchen designer will be able to help you with your specifications, but a few will go so far as to draw up complete job specifications for bidding purposes and even act as a general contractor, if you so choose.

■ Does the designer have references? Every professional should be able to give you the names of some past clients. On pp. 38-39 is a discussion of how to check out a contractor's references, and much of what's said there can be applied to designers. Also ask to see pictures of kitchens the designer has designed. A picture is worth a thousand words, you know.

■ Are you and the designer going to be able to work together? This isn't a question to be asking during the interview, but one that should be in the back of your mind. Is the designer a good listener? Receptive to your ideas? Helpful? In short, do you like the person? Don't even consider hiring anyone you have no rapport with—no matter how highly recommended or well qualified the person may be.

Paying for design

At some stores where kitchen cabinets are sold, you can get kitchen design services for free. At others, you will be charged for any design work. The design fee you pay may be applied later toward your purchase of cabinets or it may be non-refundable. And then there is the option of hiring an architect or independent designer, in which case there will certainly be a charge for design services.

So what gives here? Why would you pay for design in one place when they can get it free somewhere else? Or, to put it another way, are free design services somehow inferior to design services that have a price tag? The answers to these questions can be found in your expectations—you need to understand what you will be getting in each case. Do you want a basic cabinet layout, or do you want custom space planning that caters to your personal lifestyle? Do you want a pedestrian design or one with flair and character? Do you want someone to spend several hours meeting with you to determine your needs and explain your options, or is that not important? Those are the sorts of questions that you need to ask yourself before you speak to specific designers about the services they offer. It may be that you can find exactly what you need from a free design service.

That said, let me make it perfectly clear that good design is worth paying for. Custom design, special details, and extraordinary service are the hallmarks of designers who put a premium on their skills. And when you pay for design, you become more than an average customer, you become a client. There is a difference.

The cost of design will depend on the demands you place on the designer and the value the designer places on his or her skills. The cost could range from a few hundred dollars to a few thousand. That's a big spread, and it's why you need to bring up the subject during the interviewing process.

Some designers charge a flat fee. I'm partial to this approach because you know your cost ahead of time and can budget accordingly. But if you hire a designer for a flat fee, make sure there is an understanding of how much you get for what you pay. For example, it's not reasonable to expect the designer to spend an unlimited number of hours drawing an unlimited number of different plans.

Other designers charge by the hour. If you choose this payment approach, it's a good idea to ask up front for a general idea of total cost. After discussing the time requirements typically involved, you could place a ceiling on the amount you want to spend for design. It's also a good idea to have the designer bill you in segments, say every 10 hours, so you can keep tabs on the cost along with the progress (and the designer will appreciate getting paid along the way). The invoice should include a general description of the work that was done for each hour.

Working with a designer

The designer you work with will come to your home to see your space, discuss your goals, and take measurements. Competent designers will ask questions to find out more about your lifestyle and how your family uses the kitchen. At this first meeting, share with the designer your predesign findings; now is the time to spread out the book and magazine pictures of kitchen designs that appeal to you.

After getting an idea of what you want to do, the designer should also be able to give you some ballpark prices for a kitchen of your size and style. These prices will typically be for materials only, but some designers can also give you a general idea of labor costs. Keep in mind that "ballpark" means a rough approximation. Estimated kitchen costs are always very general at the start, because the specifics of the design are not clearly defined. As elements of the design are clarified, more realistic prices will emerge. But you should already have a budget figure in your mind (see pp. 43-44 for a discussion of budgets), and it's only fair to let the designer know what it is—even if it too is a ballpark figure.

Armed with the measurements and other information, the designer will prepare one or more preliminary drawings. When this is done, you meet again to review the plans, discuss other ideas or options, and iron out the details. You also start getting a clearer idea of what materials will cost. You might meet a few more times before the designer is ready to put together the final drawing (or drawings).

The final drawing will be a floor plan showing the arrangement of walls, windows, doors, cabinets, and appliances (see p. 24 for an example). This working plan is what your remodeling contractor will depend on for guidance. However, a floor plan will only go so far toward helping you to visualize exactly what your finished room will look like. An elevation drawing (see p. 25) and a perspective drawing will give you a better idea of how the room will actually look.

Some designers will also render (at your request) a mechanical drawing that shows the position of lights, switches, electrical outlets, phone jacks, gas lines, smoke detectors, and other utility-related components. Other drawings a designer might do are a countertop plan and a soffit plan (a drawing that shows the boxed-in space above wall cabinets, which can be extended out as a design detail or to hide lighting).

A designer can help you make final choices about kitchen components and also can recommend some reputable contractors. Some designers can put together your job specifications and act as a general contractor, but most choose not to. They typically work with you to create a new kitchen layout. It then becomes your responsibility to see that the plans are incorporated into the job specifications and to hire a contractor to do the work. The contractor should also figure into the design process (see the sidebar on the facing page).

The importance of a written job description

Once the details of your design are nailed down, you need to make certain you have clear job specifications for the work you want done. This is not nearly as enjoyable and exciting as working out a design, but it is, nevertheless, a necessity.

In the event that you have a trusted contractor you are accustomed to working with and you don't intend to solicit bids from other contractors, then you needn't go to the trouble of drawing up a job description with specifications. You can have your contractor

Some people who want to remodel call a contractor first; others call a designer before they call a contractor. Which should you do? It doesn't matter. Both are necessary players in the design process, and each is essential to its success. The important thing is that they collaborate with you to help achieve a workable design.

It's possible that you could find a contractor who is also a qualified kitchen designer or who has a qualified designer on staff. However, that is seldom the case. Most contractors lack the training to deal with your design needs. They may be familiar with good design practices, but they are not usually well versed in overall kitchen planning. This doesn't mean that they can't contribute practical ideas and valuable suggestions. They certainly can.

A REALITY CHECK

The insight of a contractor can save you money and trouble, but only if you call on this expertise early in the planning stage. In most instances, the contractor's role in the design process will be to help you and your designer determine what you can and can't do, or should and shouldn't do. For example, let's say your design calls for moving the wall behind the sink. The contractor will be able to look at it and tell you, "I can remove that wall, but it won't be easy because the plumbing pipes and heat duct going to the upstairs bathroom are in it, and they will have to be rerouted." Translated, this means that it's going to cost you a whole lot more to move that wall than to leave it there. The contractor can give you an idea of how much of an added expense you're looking at. Then you can make an informed decision to pay the money or alter the design.

This isn't to suggest that kitchen designers are ignorant of construction. Experienced designers are keenly aware of the logistical problems that a kitchen remodel can entail. But most contractors have a better eye for these things because they do the actual work.

I recommend that you consult with a contractor during the design process sometime before the final drawings are put together. If your remodeling plans are complex, it might be a good idea to arrange a meeting with the designer and contractor at your home so all of you can go over the plans. The contractor you consult should be the contractor you expect to hire to do the work, but that isn't a necessity. You might invite a prospective contractor candidate and use the meeting as an opportunity to evaluate the contractor's acumen.

If you aren't sure of the feasibility of a particular course of action—such as removing a wall—it would be prudent to hire the contractor to cut out some sections of drywall and see just exactly what is in there. Similarly, a contractor venturing into a crawl space under the kitchen might discover other problems lurking out of sight. Complications are much easier to deal with if they are anticipated before the job begins.

DESIGNER'S FLOOR PLAN FOR A SAMPLE REMODEL

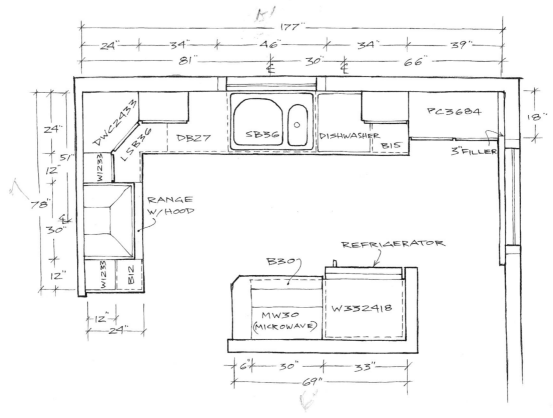

do this for you, based on decisions made in consultation with your designer.

If you are seeking bids for work that is not complicated, you can probably just tell prospective contractors what you want done and get bids that are fairly uniform. However, for full-scale kitchen remodelings, it is always better to provide everyone with the same set of written specifications for the work you want done. If you don't have identical specifications to provide to bidding contractors, how can you compare price quotes from

each? You can't. If a complete job description is not part of a job contract, how will you avoid misunderstandings? You won't.

Unfortunately homeowners rarely provide clear written specifications for contractor candidates to bid on. Most homeowners will call a few contractors, maybe hand them a cabinet layout, verbally explain what they want, and leave it up to the contractor to interpret and put into words what was discussed. As a result, the specifications drawn up by different contractors are never the

ELEVATION FOR THE SAME REMODEL

same and rarely complete. If you operate in this manner, you will never be comparing apples to apples.

Furthermore, by not writing a careful description of the work you want done, you open yourself up to lowball bidding, which is when a contractor gives a price that is lower than it should be. Often, lowball bidding is done just to get the job, but sometimes it is not; the contractor may honestly forget to include certain things. Or the contractor may think that cheaper construction methods and materials will be saving you money (and the contractor might, indeed, be doing you a favor, but it all needs to be made clear and understood). When the job starts, if short-

comings come to light, correcting them will become an additional cost. Either way, the incomplete or substandard lowball bid will end up costing you more money, or you will get a lower-quality job.

Most contractors expect you to solicit prices from other contractors. But many of the higher-quality craftsmen (the ones you should be looking to hire) will shy away from giving you a price if they sense you don't have a clear idea of what you want and they think that you are shopping among other contractors who have the reputation of being lowball bidders. Contractors like to know who they are competing against, and they will often ask (and you should be honest with them) because they know from experience that they are usually wasting their time by competing against a contractor who has lower standards.

However, it's a completely different situation if you make an active and intelligent effort to draw up "specs" for your job. Then you're taking charge, and this will set you apart from most other remodeling homeowners. Any reputable contractor will respect this and want to work for you. And the more thorough the work description, the more comfortable the contractor will feel giving you a competitive price for the work.

Some kitchen designers will draw up job specifications for you, as will most architects. It's also possible to hire a contractor to draw up specifications for bidding purposes (along with an itemized estimate of the labor and materials costs for the job). Some contractors might balk at this sort of thing, but I suspect that most would be receptive, especially if you paid them. If you approached me with the offer, I'd take you up on it. If you had a fairly clear idea of your specifications (which you should after getting a design, going on shopping expeditions, and reading this book), I'd figure six to eight hours of labor to give you a final document. The cost would be less if I merely reviewed a document you had prepared. Having your specs reviewed by some sort of building and remodeling professional is a prudent idea.

Putting a job description down on paper forces you to make all of the important remodeling decisions in the design and planning stages of the project, and that is a good thing, since procrastination and indecision are stumbling blocks to progress, and they often lead to increased costs down the road.

Putting together a written job description

Start with the new plan that you and your designer have created; just about everything else will relate to that. From there, you can model your job description on the sample in pp. 27-29. When you're done, look at what you've written with an eye toward misinterpretations (this is where a professional review can prove most helpful) and clarify any wording that could be misconstrued.

Keep in mind that too much information is always better than too little, but don't make your specifications ridiculously detailed. If an approximate measurement will suffice, then say "about" in the specs because it's easier (and cheaper) to achieve; if you want something exact, make that clear too.

Every remodeling project will, of course, be different, but the written job description needs to answer the same basic questions:

■ WHO? Who is responsible for doing what tasks? Who will supply various materials?

■ WHAT? What will be done? What specific materials will be used (brands, model numbers, sizes, colors, etc.)?

■ WHERE? A kitchen plan will answer most questions of placement, but not all. For example, if the backsplash tile will also cover the wall behind the refrigerator, say so.

■ WHEN? If it's important that certain parts of the job be done before others (e.g., vinyl floor down before baseboard) then say so.

■ HOW? For the most part, you don't need to tell contractors how to do their job, but if you want something done a certain way, spell it out in the specs.

On the pages that follow, you will find an example of how written job specifications might be worded and some of the things they might include. The example we're going to look at is a fairly typical major kitchen remodeling at the home of a hypothetical couple, Jim and Joan Smith. Keep in mind as you read through the specs that they aren't meant to recommend one course of action over others, and they aren't even necessarily complete. This is just a sample to use as a guideline, whether you prepare your own specifications or have someone else do it for you.

When you submit your own written specs for bidding, you should include with your description a copy of your new kitchen's plan along with a list of cabinets, accessories and moldings that will be used. This list will be provided by your designer, or you can compile it yourself.

HOMEOWNERS: Jim and Joan Smith, 12 Forest Hill Drive, Anytown, NY; phone (123) 456-7890.
CONTRACTOR COPY TO: Bob Bestway, Bestway Construction, Anytown, NY; phone (123) 456-0987
PREPARED BY: Jim Smith

This is a job description for kitchen remodeling to be done on my home at the address above. All work, including electrical and plumbing, will be done to code specifications. Contractor will supply labor and materials for all of the work described here unless otherwise specified.

Feel free to refine these specifications with additional description in your bid. However, please do this to clarify, not to change the specifications substantially. Don't hesitate to call if you have any questions regarding this job description.

Thank you,
Jim Smith

DEMOLITION

Existing kitchen will be torn out down to wall and ceiling framing. Plywood floor underlayment with old linoleum will be removed. Garbage disposer, sink, and faucet will be saved.

FRAMING

Walls will be shimmed straight and plumb. New ceiling will be framed below existing one using light-gauge steel joists. Finished ceiling height will be about 8 ft. No corrective work will be done to floor.

DOORS

Existing entrance door into kitchen will be replaced with a new door. Size: 3' by 6'8". Brand: Stanley. Style: #1234. Options: magnetic weather-strip and adjustable oak sill.

(continued on p. 28)

Opening: In against wall. Primed brickmold casing on exterior. Homeowner will supply handle/lockset and deadbolt lock for contractor to install. Homeowner will paint door and exterior trim after installation.

WINDOWS

Window over sink will be replaced with new Andersen #CR135-3 casement window (rough opening: 4'3¾" by 3'5⅜") with standard insulated glazing and sandstone colored exterior vinyl. Options: Andersen screens and interior window grilles with sandstone finish on the grilles. Exterior of window will be trimmed with ¾-in. cedar boards to match siding. Homeowner will apply protective finish to wood after installation.

ELECTRICAL

Install 10 recessed canister lights in ceiling. Install 8 "puck" style under-cabinet lights. Install surface-mounted fluorescent fixture behind valance. Homeowner will supply all fixtures and bulbs and miscellaneous components for under-cabinet lights. Ceiling lights will be operated by 3 different switches (one of which will be a slide-style dimmer); other lights will be controlled by single switches.

All circuits in kitchen will be rewired back to the main panel. There will be 10 duplex electrical receptacles and 1 wall phone jack. Exact placement of receptacles, switches, and jack will be determined by homeowner and contractor after demolition. Refrigerator, microwave oven, and dishwasher will be on dedicated electrical circuits.

Switch to outside light by door will be replaced with a new one. All switches and receptacles will be white with white plastic cover plates.

HEATING

Heating system will remain unchanged except for the two heat registers that are in the floor, where cabinets will be going. These will need to be ducted out the cabinet toe kicks.

PLUMBING

Existing galvanized drain line from kitchen will be removed back to 4-in. cast-iron main drain in basement. New drain lines will be PVC plastic. Sink drain will be vented. Plumbing connections from sink to drain line will be made with PVC plastic tubular parts.

Existing water-supply lines will be removed all the way back to the water heater and replaced with ½-in. type-L copper pipe. Supply lines in basement will be insulated with foam-insulation pipe wrap.

Ball-valve shut-offs will be installed on the hot- and cold-water lines inside sink base cabinet, and on the hot line going to dishwasher.

WALLS AND CEILING

Walls will be insulated with unfaced fiberglass. A 6-mil plastic vapor barrier will go on over insulation. On walls and ceiling, ½-in. drywall will be installed. Drywall will be finished ready for paint. Two coats of drywall primer will be applied to all drywall, followed by one finish coat.

Ceiling will be finish painted with one coat of latex flat white. Contractor will supply good-quality primer; homeowner will supply paint for finish coat.

CABINETS

Install cabinets with molding and accessories as per kitchen plan by PMB Designs dated 1/12/97 (copy attached to this). Homeowner will supply all cabinets and cabinet-related components.

APPLIANCES

Install built-in microwave over stove, and duct to outside through roof. Duct pipe will be insulated in attic. Homeowner will supply microwave. Contractor will supply all components needed for hookup and ducting.

Homeowner will supply new freestanding range. Contractor will supply power cord and electrical hookup.

Homeowner will supply new refrigerator. Contractor will provide materials and labor to hook up ice maker.

Homeowner will supply new dishwasher. Contractor will provide material and labor to install.

Contractor will install new double-bowl stainless-steel sink, faucet, and sink basket as supplied by homeowner. Old garbage disposal will be reinstalled in new sink.

COUNTERTOP

Plastic-laminate countertop will be custom made square-edge style (horizontal-grade Pionite #000-00) with a matching self edge. There will be one surface seam in top through sink. Overhang at front of cabinets will be about 2 in.

Countertop backsplash will be basic 4-in.-sq. white ceramic tile on entire wall between countertop and upper cabinets. Tile will also cover wall behind refrigerator all the way to floor. Grout color will be white. Contractor will submit tile sample to homeowner for approval.

FLOOR

Homeowner will arrange (and pay) to have vinyl floor installed by The Floor Store. Contractor will coordinate with The Floor Store to have them install ¼-in. plywood underlayment and vinyl near end of remodeling, but before contractor installs baseboard moldings.

TRIM

Window and door casing will be "colonial" style stock molding as carried at Miller's Lumber. Baseboard will be matching colonial style. Wood will be clear pine (not finger jointed), stained to match cabinets and finished with two coats of water-based polyurethane. Contractor will submit molding and stain sample to homeowner for approval before using. Contractor will install 1¾-in. cove molding around ceiling and paint to match ceiling.

MISCELLANEOUS

Contractor will dispose of all work-related refuse. Contractor will take care of all permits and inspections.

CHAPTER 3

FINDING A REPUTABLE CONTRACTOR

It's been said that the home-improvement industry generates a disproportionately large number of the complaints that come in to consumer-protection agencies. After 20 years in the remodeling business, I don't doubt that is true. The tales of woe are familiar: contractors who start a project, tear the house up, and then leave the partially done job to languish while they turn their attention to other work; contractors who never show up; and contractors who just plain do bad work. Homeowners have plenty of grievances, and the common refrain, heard across the land, is, "Where do you find a good contractor these days?" This chapter will answer that very question.

Despite the statistics, let me assure you that there are plenty of contractors who care deeply about their work and their reputation and who can deliver excellent service along with quality workmanship. What's more, although hiring a contractor to do your re-modeling work is an extremely important decision for you to make, I don't think it has to be a terribly complicated one. If you have hired the services of a skilled residential con-

tractor in the past, and you were satisfied with the work, and the contractor is an experienced kitchen remodeler, there is no need to look any further. Count your blessings, and skip to the next chapter. Otherwise, let me explain how you can find some promising candidates and choose a good one. Then I'll tell you some things you can do to make sure the business relationship with your contractor is a smooth one.

If you go with the cheapest bid without regard for other factors, you will probably get what you pay for.

The subject of money, as it relates to hiring contractors, will be conspicuously absent from this discussion; that's because it's covered in Chapter 4. Don't let money be the most important issue in your search for a reputable contractor to work on your home. I think most people would agree with that statement—at least in theory. If you go with the cheapest bid without regard for other factors, you will probably get what you pay for. Don't expect professionalism, don't expect quality workmanship, don't expect the job to get done on schedule, or, for that matter, to get done at all. Keep in mind, though, that while looking for the cheapest job is practically an invitation for disaster, spending a lot of money is not in itself a guarantee of remodeling success. Money has a way of complicating the question at hand, which is, if you will recall, finding a reputable contractor.

What exactly is a contractor?

A contractor in the building trades is any person with whom you have a contract (an agreement) to do a specific job. If this person is self-employed and makes his or her living as a builder or remodeler, that person is referred to as a professional contractor.

Many small contractors are highly skilled and capable craftsmen who have low overhead and can give you excellent value for your money.

Professional contractors carry out their responsibilities in one of two ways: as a general contractor or a subcontractor. A general contractor is a person (or company) who does a variety of different types of construction work and whom you can hire to do extensive projects, such as kitchen remodeling, that may require the skills of several trades. A subcontractor is any contractor who is hired to perform all or part of a general contractor's contract. Subcontractors work for general contractors. Although a subcontractor might be another general contractor, more often, subcontractors will be people who specialize in one aspect of building, such as plumbing or electrical work or drywall finishing.

General contractors come in "sizes" that refer not to their physique but to the scope and structure of their business organization.

Small contractors

Most residential contractors in this country run small operations. Sometimes also referred to as "independent contractors," these people perform almost all aspects of the job themselves. For example, a small general contractor who does kitchen remodeling will not only be the person you call to discuss the details of the job, who figures the prices, and who signs the contract, but also the person who shows up when the job starts and works on it every day until it's done. Small contractors can do their own demolition, framing, electrical wiring, plumbing, drywall, trim, cabinet installation, and just about anything else. Work will be subcontracted only if local codes or licensing requirements stipulate it, as is often the case with plumbing and electrical work, or if the job to be done is highly specialized, such as countertop fabrication or wallpapering. Small contractors typically operate as one- or two-person operations. A small contractor usually has a home office, which might be the kitchen table.

"Smallness" does not imply that the person's abilities are substandard or insufficient. On the contrary, many small contractors are highly skilled and capable craftsmen who have low overhead and can give you excellent value for your money. When the person you hire is the person who actually does the work, misunderstandings and communication glitches are less likely to occur. What's more, the quality of workmanship will always be up to the contractor's personal standards. However, small-scale contractors can only handle so much work in a year, and you may have to wait a while longer for them than you would a bigger contractor. Also, a small contractor may not be able to (or want to) deal with really major kitchen remodeling on a tight deadline.

Bigger contractors

Small contractors who do a good job often have more work coming in than a small-business structure can accommodate. This leaves two options: stay small and do only what can be handled in that capacity, or expand to take on bigger jobs or more than one job at a time. The contractor who takes the second route enters the realm of the bigger contractor.

To handle the increased workload effectively, bigger contractors hire more workers and/or subcontract out a lot of the work they previously would have done themselves. They may have a real office with some secretarial help. Some bigger contractors have salesmen, estimators, and designers on their staff. If your remodeling is "high end" or exceptionally extensive or complicated, or you want it done soon and as quickly as possible, your best move is probably to hire a bigger contractor.

How do I find a contractor?

Contractors are always looking for their next job. Lining up work, fitting it all into a schedule, and keeping the ball rolling is one of the greatest challenges of being a contractor. The universal fear is that the economy will slow down, the phone won't ring, and work will dry up. It rarely gets quite that bad, especially for a reputable contractor, but the specter of no work is always there. So contractors rely on different ways to get new customers. Direct marketing, general advertising, home shows and word of mouth are the four ways remodeling contractors get their work, and they are also the ways you can find likely contractor candidates.

Be wary of companies that solicit your business through a telemarketing campaign or mass-market direct mail. These companies may well do a great job for you, but they will likely send a well-trained salesman out to "reel you in," and they often charge exorbitant prices. Also, companies that market on a large scale cover a large territory and may not be local, which, as I'll explain shortly, isn't necessarily good.

Look more kindly on a selected mailing that comes to you because you live in a neighborhood where the contractor often works or is currently working. Or perhaps your name was suggested to a contractor by someone who knows you are considering work. More than once, I've sent an introductory letter and information about my services to homeowners I heard were thinking about remodeling their kitchen.

Advertising

Local contractors often advertise in the local newspaper, but keep in mind that such ads are no guarantee of a good reputation. Ads in the Yellow Pages are considered by many to be inherently more credible than newspaper ads. They indicate a measure of business stability because the contractor must have a separate (more expensive) business phone line and pay a monthly advertising fee to the directory company. However, telephone directories do not vouch for the credibility of their customers, and many reputable small contractors don't bother with them.

Home shows

Home shows are another way to find contractors. The great thing about home shows is that you get to see several contractors at once. You can ask them questions, collect any literature they have, and evaluate some of your possibilities (get those important first impressions) without going to the trouble of scheduling appointments and having them all visit your home.

Word of mouth

What's the best way to find a contractor? Word of mouth. Everyone knows that already, but it's so true that it needs to be repeated. Word of mouth is the reputable contractor's best friend (and the incompetent contractor's worst enemy—horror stories spread even faster than success stories). You can learn a lot just by asking around. Start by chatting with your friends and neighbors about contractors, and also check with your designer or architect. Let the word get out that you are planning to have some work done, and see if the same name or names come up in conversation.

Another excellent place to inquire about reputable contractors is at the places they buy their materials. The managers of long-established lumberyards and home centers are usually keenly aware of the reputations of their regular customers. They've seen contractors come and go. They're tapped into the contractor grapevine. They know who pays the bills and who doesn't, and who the best craftsmen with stable businesses are. If you want an honest opinion, don't make your inquiry in a crowded store where contractors or one of their employees may overhear the conversation, because this could put the manager in an awkward position. Take the manager aside, and ask who he would hire to work on his own house. If you get one or two recommendations, they will probably be very good referrals.

What's the best way to find a contractor? Word of mouth.

Word of mouth, however, should be taken with a grain of salt because it reflects the limited experiences and very often biased opinions of the people you talk to. For example, if your hair stylist raves about her brother-in-law contractor's remodeling abilities, her view may not be entirely objective (but if she warns you not to hire him, it might be). Word of mouth is not a way to choose a contractor, it is a way to find a contractor.

Narrowing the field

Now that you've got what may be a sizable list of prospective candidates, you need to narrow the possibilities before you call them up and start the interview process. Here are four approaches you can take:

Hire local contractors

Start paring down your list by considering only established local companies. The reason for this is that local contractors have a local reputation (based on word of mouth) that is worth protecting and cultivating. A local contractor has more at stake when working for you than an out-of-town contractor would.

What do I mean by "local?" Within a half-hour drive would probably apply to most situations. I often get calls about doing work more than an hour's drive away, and I tell the people they should find someone nearer to their home. A contractor who works close to home has an easier time of lining up materials, and if problems develop on the job, they are more easily attended to. Most reputable remodelers want the benefit of local exposure and can find plenty of work near their homes.

Hire established contractors

I'm astonished that homeowners will hire contractors who are not established in their community. When a new contractor moves into town, some people will actually get it in their mind that the contractor is somehow a better craftsman simply by virtue of the fact that he or she used to work "out West" or "down South." The assumption seems to be that contractors who worked elsewhere are intrinsically more talented than contractors who work locally.

Yes, newcomers may indeed be better at their craft, but 9 out of 10 times they're not. Contractors who worked "elsewhere" may even have left town in the middle of the night with jobs partially done and bills unpaid. You won't have a way of seeing examples of their work or checking their references. Undependable contractors who come and go and leave bad experiences in their wake are typically friendly, likable folks who generate trust, but lack the self-discipline and integrity to run a business properly. Limit your candidates to established local contractors, and you are unlikely to be disappointed.

Hire experienced contractors

If you were in need of heart bypass surgery, and you had the choice of being operated on by an experienced heart surgeon, a wet-behind-the-ears intern, or a truck driver who does heart surgery on the side, which would you choose? The answer is self evident: In any line of work, experience counts for a lot.

How much is enough experience? Well, no one ever reaches total wisdom and ability in any craft or business. But in the building trades, it takes at least 5 years of full-time work for a craftsman to develop a decent level of professional skills and judgment. If I were hiring a kitchen remodeler, I'd look for someone with at least 8 to 10 years of experience.

Do a little sleuthing

If you've taken my suggestions thus far, it's likely you have a short list of prospective candidates. A half-dozen names would be fine, but if you have two or three and you feel they are top candidates, that's fine too. Now you need to see if these contractors have any unresolved complaints on record. Do this by calling your local Better Business Bureau—the phone number can be found in the White Pages of your phone book. It's clearly a worthwhile service. You can also check on a contractor's background with your local building inspector, if you didn't already ask this person for referrals.

I've read one kitchen remodeling book where the author recommends that you have your attorney find out whether a contractor you are about to hire has any liens or judgments against him. The author goes on to suggest that you have a banker check out the contractor's credit history. You may want to do those things—and I wouldn't fault you if you did—but they aren't typical procedures.

Setting up an appointment

Now it's time to call each finalist to set up a meeting. At the same time, you want to continue the qualifying process. Start by telling the contractor where you live. Give a brief description of the work you want done (minor, major, or really major kitchen remodeling), and mention any important completion deadline. Then ask if the contractor has any interest in the project. Don't assume, as many people do, that every contractor they call is itching to do work for anyone who

calls them. That isn't the case. The person you're talking to may not work in your area, may not feel comfortable with the scope of the job, or may foresee a problem with your deadline. By asking, you provide an opportunity for the contractor to decline your job, saving you both the time and trouble of scheduling an unnecessary appointment. More than likely, though, the contractor will ask some questions of you. When a contractor shows an interest and starts to ask questions on the first phone call, that's a good sign. The contractor wants to understand your remodeling plans and may want to qualify your project.

Reputable contractors keep their word and make it to scheduled appointments. Promptness indicates a consideration for others and a well-organized approach.

I always ask people how they heard about me. If it was a referral, my interest is piqued, because my best jobs come from word of mouth and it shows that the homeowner has done a little homework. A contractor may ask you if you have a design worked out, as well as more details about your plans. Some contractors will ask how much money you have budgeted for the project. If this happens, don't be shocked or suspicious—the question is appropriate. Its purpose is to find out if your plans are realistic from a financial point of view. If your tastes are champagne and your budget can only afford beer, the contractor doesn't want to waste time with you. Can you blame anyone for that?

If the call goes well, set up an appointment to meet at your home. Ask the contractor to bring some customer references. Make certain that everyone who will be involved in decision-making will be present. It is unfair, for example, when just the wife meets with the contractor unless only she will be making all the decisions and writing out all the checks—and that's not likely.

It often happens that contractors make appointments but don't show up. It may be common, but it's extremely rude. Take it as a sign, and go on to the next person on your list. Reputable contractors keep their word and make it to scheduled appointments. Promptness indicates a consideration for others and a well-organized approach. Lateness is understandable (within reason), but standing someone up is inexcusable.

Meeting with contractors

When you meet with your contractor candidates (one at a time, please), you will be showing them your layout drawing and job specifications (see pp. 22-29), and you'll be discussing the project. At this point all of the details of the job should be pretty well figured out. Use this meeting to find out more about the contractor's business and what you can expect if you close the deal. Here are some questions to get you started:

- Who will be doing the work? The contractor? Employees of the contractor? Will portions of the work be subcontracted out?
- Will the subcontractors be local? How experienced are they? How often have these subcontractors been used in the past?

- How many people will be working on the job at one time?
- Who will be in charge of the work? If the contractor is not there every day, how will good quality and communication be assured? Will a lead carpenter or foreman be in charge? If so, who will that person be? How long has that person worked for the contractor? Will that person be there at all times until the job is done? If the contractor will not be there every day, make it clear that you want one foreman or lead carpenter to start the job and see it through to completion.
- What are the contractor's normal work hours? Does the work day start and end on a set schedule or do people show up sometime before noon and work until midnight? Do they work on weekends? If you are living in the house, these things will be important to you.
- Once the project is started, will it continue uninterrupted until completed, or will the contractor be leaving to work on other projects? Make it clear that you expect the job to proceed without delays.
- Does the contractor have insurance coverage? If not, and somebody is hurt or damage is done, you may be left holding the bag. Check with your own insurance carrier and see the sidebar on p. 38.
- Who will take care of getting any permits? You should probably have the contractor take care of this (see the sidebar on p. 41).
- Who will take care of refuse disposal? Again, the contractor should probably be responsible.
- If you were to hire the contractor, when could the project start?

Every professional contractor should have liability insurance. A contractor who has employees or uses subcontractors with employees should also carry worker's compensation insurance. I know a contractor who has neither, but when customers ask if he has insurance, he says that he does. He "rationalizes" that he isn't really lying—he has car insurance, home insurance, and life insurance. How should the homeowner deal with weasels like this? Ask the contractor to supply you with a current certificate of insurance. It's a legitimate request. All the contractor has to do is call his insurance carrier, and a certificate will be mailed right out to you. Tell the contractor you will need insurance certificates for subcontractors too. Make sure to have the certificate before you get to the contract-signing stage.

When you get the certificate, check it carefully. If you have doubts about the adequacy of the coverage, have your insurance broker review it too. Also check the dates of coverage. If the certificate indicates that coverage will lapse when your job is being done, make it clear that you will want an updated certificate at that time.

No detail is too minor to discuss if it's something that concerns you. Will the electricity and water be shut off? If so, for how long? What about bathroom use? If you don't want the workers to use yours, make this clear to the contractor, who can rent a toilet and plunk it in your yard. What about music? I once worked for a guy who wouldn't let his employees play a radio on the job. They didn't care for that rule, but I think the customers appreciated it. See how receptive the contractor is to your questions and concerns.

I'll spare you my opinions about first impressions and how to "read" a contractor on the first meeting (hint: don't assume the one with the newest and nicest pickup truck is the best). Suffice it to say that you should trust your instincts. Was there a meeting of the minds? Good rapport? Did your personalities "click" or clash? The bottom line is whether you liked the person. If you did, move on to the next step: talking to people the contractor has worked for in the past.

Checking references

References are invaluable in evaluating a contractor's integrity. Contractors who can provide you with a prepared list of customer names are telling you that they value their reputation. The more references the contractor lists, the better. Three names would be a minimum, but three pages of names would be even better.

Don't just read the list of references. Call people who have had work done that is similar to what you want done. A list of many garages and decks but few kitchen remodels should give you reason to pause. Skill at building garages and decks doesn't imply skill at remodeling kitchens. You should be looking for an experienced kitchen remodeler.

You may think to yourself that there is no sense in calling contractor-supplied references because the contractor has, no doubt, stacked the list with satisfied clients. That's probably a correct assumption, but it doesn't mean the people on the list are going to lie to you. More than likely, they will give you a very honest assessment—and some important insights—into the contractor's workmanship and business habits, especially if you poke around a bit. Here are some questions to ask:

- What kind of work did the contractor do for you?
- Were you satisfied with the quality of the craftsmanship?
- Did the contractor make an effort to keep the job site neat and clean?
- Did the workers seem like decent people? Were they considerate of your property?
- Did you find the contractor easy to work with and responsive to your concerns?
- Did the job get done on schedule?
- Were there problems with inspectors or code violations?
- If the contractor uses a crew foreman or lead carpenter, who was that person? (If he or she gets a glowing review from a couple of references, you may want to stipulate that the person work on your job.)
- Did the job come in on budget? Were there any surprise costs at the end?
- Were there unresolved problems?
- Would you hire this contractor again?
- Is there anything you would do differently if you were to do the job again?

Inspecting a contractor's work

If you locate a contractor by word of mouth, it's very likely that you will have already seen an example of the person's work by viewing a friend's kitchen. If not, I'm going to differ with other advice-givers on the subject and tell you that you don't need to ask a contractor to show you past jobs as part of the qualifying process. If the contractor is an established and reputable craftsman with good references, that is sufficient. If you can get some photos to look at, that would be a plus.

The problem with viewing finished jobs is that it can be an imposition to ask past customers to let strangers into their homes. They feel they have to prepare for the inspection by putting extra effort into cleaning and making it look really good. Nevertheless, if you feel strongly that you should inspect a prospective contractor's work, ask to see one example of a completed kitchen. Most contractors have a few choice customers who they know won't mind—once in a while. When checking references, you may even talk to people who offer to show you their kitchen, and you could then take them up on the offer.

Being a good customer

Just as there are good and bad contractors, there are also good and bad customers. Being a good customer is in your own best interest—it's the best customers who get the best service and and the finest workmanship. Here are some ways you can endear yourself to your contractor. Doing your part will improve the business relationship and ultimately help you get the most for your money.

- Start off on the right foot by submitting a kitchen design and job specifications to the contractor. This makes bidding easy (see pp. 44-47) and also shows that you are an exceptionally well-organized customer who fully expects professionalism.
- Allow enough time for the remodel. Unrealistic expectations are stressful to the contractor, and projects that are rushed seldom go as smoothly as they should.
- Trust the contractor you select. Skepticism and suspicion are counterproductive to a good working relationship.
- If you take it upon yourself to supply some of the components (such as a sink, faucets, or cabinets), make sure these materials are on site before they are needed.
- When work starts, get out of the way. Don't help. Don't hover. Don't hang around and shoot the breeze. The workers are trying to make progress, and nonessential talk is not the best use of their time. Save the friendly conversation for lunch break and after work.
- Keep an eye on the progress (inspect it every night) and make a list of questions as they come to mind. If something isn't being done according to plan, bring it up immediately. For example, if you don't see the electrical receptacle you expected on a wall, mention it before the area is drywalled and tiled. Your concern may be unwarranted because you misinterpreted something, but that's okay. Do not hesitate to call attention to such details. The contractor will appreciate it—especially if the workers really did forget to do something.

- Don't make major changes to the plan after work starts, and keep minor changes to a minimum.
- Be available. If possible, leave your work phone number or other number where you can be reached. Talk with the contractor or job foreman every morning, or in the evenings after you've had a chance to look over the day's work. Leave a note if you won't be there in the mornings to comment on the job.
- Acknowledge and be friendly to all the workers.
- Keep pets and children out of the work area while work is in progress.
- When you're happy with the way something turns out, praise the contractor and crew. Reputable contractors take great pride in their work and want to be recognized for a job well done. Praise from a satisfied customer is a great incentive to please.
- Pay promptly when payment is due. When the conditions of the work agreement have been met, there is no excuse for holding up payment. The contractor shouldn't have to suffer if your CD doesn't come due until next week; that's your problem. Have your finances in order before you hire someone to work for you.

You'll notice that I haven't said anything about supplying food or beverages. That's because these things are not necessary, and they can be a hindrance. If the workers are coffee drinkers, they will have had their morning cup by the time they get to the job. However, if you want to be a gracious host, leave some soft drinks or iced tea for the workers—it will be greatly appreciated.

Chances are that you will need a permit to remodel your kitchen. A permit is written permission from your local municipality allowing you to do the work. You get the permit by filling out a form and paying a fee. Most people chafe at having to pay for permission to do work on their own home, but that's the way the system works, and I advise you to follow the rules. Inspectors are supposed to make sure that the work being done meets minimum safety standards and accepted building practices. In theory, the inspector's function is to make sure you get a good job, and that's good.

If you're doing your own remodeling, you should check into the requirements, legalities, and fees by inquiring at your city hall, town hall, or village office. Ask specifically what the procedure is, whom you see, and in what order. You will also want to find out the cost for the permit and if there will be any additional inspection fees. The prices and procedures can vary greatly from town to town.

The contractor you hire should have a pretty good understanding of local permit requirements and can also take care of getting the permit for you. More than that, a professional remodeler will be familiar with building-code requirements and required inspection schedules. If the building inspector is familiar with your contractor's work, the inspections may be merely perfunctory.

In some areas, notably bigger cities, you must hire only people licensed by the city to do plumbing and electrical work. In many parts of the country, contractors are also licensed.

After you get your permit, one or more inspectors will become involved in the project. The inspection process varies from town to town, so you should check your local regulations. If your remodeling is minor, a building inspector may just look the work over when it's completed. If your remodeling is major or really major, a separate inspector for electrical, plumbing, and HVAC (heating, ventilation,

and air conditioning) may also enter the picture. With mechanical systems, a rough inspection is usually done before the walls are insulated and drywalled, and a final inspection is done when the job is completed.

There are other legal restrictions that could come into play with your project. Some towns have zoning statutes that dictate the height of new structures and the distance they must be built from neighboring property lines. These issues would be a concern if your project called for an addition on the house. If your home has historical significance, there might be state or federal restrictions that apply to the remodeling. Answers to these questions can also be found at the town hall.

Does all this sound confusing? It can be, but that's the nature of the bureaucratic beast. Usually, though, for a kitchen remodel the process is not complicated and will go smoothly. Just find out the rules that apply and follow them, or have your contractor take care of everything.

CHAPTER 4

MONEY AND CONTRACTS

The problem with money is that it comes hard, goes easy, and there never seems to be enough. How much is enough? A little bit more. Nevertheless, the challenge when remodeling is to be smart with the money you have and not spend more than you should. To do this, you must establish a budget. You also need to evaluate the different price quotes you get from contractors. And in the end, you need to have a good written contract with your contractor. This chapter will examine each of these money-related issues.

Establishing a budget

The budget is a predetermined amount of money you allocate to your kitchen remodeling project. If you don't impose a limit on yourself, you will probably end up spending more money than you can afford—or at least more than you ever expected.

Your budget will depend on what your particular financial situation allows and what your better judgment dictates. Turn back to p. 6 for the current average price of a minor and major kitchen remodeling project. In most instances, these figures alone should be enough to establish a preliminary budget. Later, in the design and planning stages, when you get some ballpark prices, you can use those to verify your budget or make minor adjustments, and then confirm the final budget amount.

There are two ways to work within a budget. You can set the amount and proceed with the thought in mind that you won't spend a penny more than you have to on everything and hope to have some money left over. Or you can operate under the assumption that you will probably spend all of that money, and concern yourself with getting the most value for the full budget amount. The difference between these approaches is subtle but profound; the second option implies a completely different attitude about spending money, and I hope you see it.

Whatever your budget is, it's a good idea to build in a contingency amount of 15% to 20% for possible cost overruns. That might seem like a lot, but it isn't. Some kitchen remodeling advisors actually recommend as much as 30% to 40% to cover unexpected cost overruns. But if you take an active role in your kitchen remodeling plans, as I suggest in this book, you shouldn't incur too many unexpected costs. In theory, if you do your planning properly, there shouldn't be any cost overruns at all. But in reality, it's likely that you will forget some details or add some extra work. Holding some cash in reserve is only prudent.

Whatever your budget is, it's a good idea to build in a contingency amount of 15% to 20% for possible cost overruns.

Should you reveal your exact budget amount to bidding contractors? You don't have to, but you should be prepared to supply them with a realistic ballpark figure (less the contingency). Of course, you should also make it clear that you're looking for the best price within that budget amount. Reputable contractors will have a higher regard for you when you are up front about your budget and your expectations.

Getting price quotes

Chapter 2 discusses the importance of preparing a good job description for bidding purposes. Chapter 3 tells you how to locate reputable contractors to bid on your specifications. Now let's take a closer look at the bids and how to evaluate them.

Fixed price vs. time and materials

Contractors bill for their work in one of two ways: by sizing up the job and quoting a fixed price for everything or by billing the customer for materials and charging an hourly rate for labor for as much time as the job takes to complete. Each system has its advantages and disadvantages. A fixed price allows you to compare prices easily when you are selecting a contractor (provided, of course, that everyone bid on the same specifications). And if you know exactly what the remodel will cost, you can budget accordingly. But more than that, having a fixed price is less risky for you. What if the cost of materials goes up? What if the job requires more time and labor to complete than the contractor figured on? What if the contractor overlooked something in the bidding calculations? With a fixed price, the contractor assumes responsibility for the price and you aren't left guessing (or worrying) about the final cost of the project. Most contractors prefer to work on a fixed-price basis.

The alternative to working with a fixed price is to hire a contractor on a time-and-materials basis. The trouble with this approach is that you never know exactly how much your remodel will cost until it's done. You might save some money by hiring a contractor to work by the hour, but it's clearly a gamble on your part. The contractor may want to work on a time-and-materials basis if the homeowners don't have clearly stated specifications for the work they want done or if there are other substantial unknown factors involved in the job. But these instances are rare (and they shouldn't be the case with your job). I strongly recommend you not hire a contractor by the hour when doing a job as big and complex as kitchen remodeling. Figure out exactly what work you want done, and get fixed-price quotes on the job.

Single price vs. itemized

There are two ways that contractors can supply their quotes: single price and itemized. A single price is just that—one total amount for the work specified. An itemized quote shows you the price breakdown for materials, subcontractors, labor, refuse disposal, permits, etc. The advantage to an itemized quote is that you can see exactly where your money is going, compare costs among contractors, and make better-informed decisions. However, contractors rarely go to the trouble of putting together an itemized price quote. Such a document takes considerable time to prepare, especially for a prospective job that may never materialize. I don't think you need an itemized quote from a contractor, but if you feel it's important, make that clear to your bidders. If they are accustomed to itemizing their quotes, there won't be any problem. If they aren't used to itemized bidding, you'll probably never get a price from them.

QUOTES VS. ESTIMATES

Quotes and estimates are not the same thing. Many people mistakenly use the term "estimate" when they mean a bid or quote, and I don't want you to do that. A bid or quote (the terms are used interchangeably) is a clearly stated price to do a specified job. An estimate is by definition an approximation, nothing firm. Estimates are useful when you are trying to determine the job budget. But when you are trying to choose a contractor, quotes are what you need—comparing approximations won't be very helpful.

Evaluating price quotes

You would think that if you got three price quotes from three reputable contractors, they would all be relatively close (give or take a few hundred dollars), and they might be. If so, then your job of is going to be easy; choose the contractor you like the best.

But it's also possible that the quotes will differ considerably. Since you are comparing quotes on uniform job specs from established local professionals with proven track records, you can theoretically go with the lowest bid and get a satisfactory job. However, if "a little bird" says otherwise, listen to your intuition. Let's say that a higher price comes in from the contractor that your research indicates is most talented and experienced contractor of the bunch, and you had the best rapport with that contractor. When that's the case, I believe you should consider paying more for that contractor's services. How much more? Probably not much more than 10%.

Paying a bit more for a well-qualified person is money well spent. However, don't assume that a high bid indicates a high-quality job. That is often not the case. The contractor might have higher overhead expenses or might add in a higher percentage of profit, or might have workers who are slow. The contractor may not even care about getting the job and just be tossing out an inflated price.

DON'T HAGGLE

Some people like to negotiate with a contractor to get a reduction in price. You haggle over the cost and get the contractor to throw in some extra things for free, or something like that. Every contractor I know is offended by this practice. Dickering over a price implies that the contractor is trying to rip you off or that you are trying to rip off the contractor. It isn't a very good way to start a working relationship that should be built on mutual trust. That isn't to say you shouldn't ask honest questions about how you and the contractor can work together to trim down a quoted price. That's a reasonable—and non-adversarial—response, especially if the price comes in high and you sincerely want to hire the contractor.

What to do if bids come in over budget

If you've established a realistic budget based on the advice of a designer and/or contractor, your bids should not be over budget. If they are, then something may have been amiss with the preliminary estimating. Or, as often happens, you might have changed your mind about some things along the way, and the new specifications had more of a price impact than you anticipated. If you are just a little over budget, you can absorb the cost with some (but not all) of your contingency budget (see pp. 43-44). Otherwise, you must now go back to the drawing board, figuratively if not literally. Here are three ways to cut your costs. But whatever you do, don't settle for less than the best craftsmanship.

Simplify the design

If you have to cut costs, ask the contractor for suggestions about where prices can be cut without sacrificing quality. It could be that some elements of your design will be particularly time-consuming to execute; simplifying them will save on labor.

Use less costly materials

If you don't find the price reduction you need by simplifying elements of the design, take a hard look at the materials in your specifications and consider less costly items (consult with your designer or suppliers). There are plenty of ways to do this. Custom cabinets could be changed to stock cabinets. Solid-surface countertops could be changed to plastic laminate. Or you could do without a cold-water dispenser in the refrigerator door.

Supply the materials yourself

When it comes to getting prices from contractors, you can have the contractor supply all materials or you can supply some of them. If you do the latter, you could save some money on materials.

Many people think that contractors can buy remodeling materials for a discount and that they pass the discount on to the homeowners they work for. In fact, however, that rarely happens. Most of the time contractors do indeed get a discount from their suppliers, but they rarely pass the savings on to you. Contractors typically charge the customer more than they pay for their materials, and they do this because they are in business to make a profit, not just a living wage. This might not sound right to you, but I guarantee that if you were a self-employed remodeling contractor, you would have a different perspective. The extra charge also offsets the time contractors have to spend ordering, receiving, and handling these items. In any event, what this means is that if you shop around, you can sometimes buy items for less than the contractors would charge you in their price quotes.

The "materials" I'm talking about here are the big-ticket or specialty items—cabinets, sink and faucets, appliances, and lighting—not miscellaneous building materials such as lumber, insulation, and plumbing. Always let the contractor take care of these major and minor construction-related materials; doing otherwise would be unreasonable and probably even counterproductive. Things like tile for a backsplash and wood flooring, which involve figuring and ordering specific pieces and quantities, are also best left to the contractor to supply.

There are some risks you incur by agreeing to supply materials. If you buy the cabinets yourself and some come in damaged, then you absorb the cost of rectifying the situation, and that's clearly a disadvantage. If the contractor provides an item and there is a problem with it, it's the contractor's responsibility to correct the situation. That's another reason that contractors mark up the cost of supplying the materials.

If you want to supply some items as a way of reducing the cost of the job, I suggest that you shop for what you want and make a note of the best price you find. Then note in your specifications that you intend to provide the items. Then, after you've selected a contractor to do the work, find out if the contractor can supply those items for less than what you can get them for (tell your price). Chances are, the contractor will offer to provide them for the same price if not a bit less, but the cost would probably be several dollars less than if the item were buried in a price quote. If the contractor's prices come in higher, then you can decide if it's worth your while to supply the items or not. If you do supply the items, you should also be responsible for seeing that they get to the job site.

Drawing up a contract

Some contractors and homeowners do business based on a verbal agreement and nothing else. Others may seal the deal with a handshake. Such arrangements are admittedly easy and they can work, but they are an invitation to misinterpretation and conflict, particularly if you're doing an involved job for a fixed price. Having a contract, a written agreement outlining the terms and details of the work to be done, is the only wise course of action when you hire a contractor's services. I further suggest that you let the contractor go to the trouble of drawing it up.

Three types of contracts that contractors typically use are the standard proposal form, the AIA form, and the custom contract. Whichever one you use, make sure you clearly understand what you are signing. If you have any doubts, questions, or suspicions about anything in the contract, consult an attorney. It will cost you, but if it puts your mind at ease or forestalls future legal problems, your money will be well spent. All contracts should comply with any federal, state, and local laws that govern contracts. You can find out about laws that pertain to home-improvement contracts by contacting your state's Attorney General's office.

A treatise on contracts is beyond the scope of this book. Here I intend to touch on the high points, the ones that you need to know about before you put your signature on a contract to remodel your kitchen. If you'd like more detailed information, turn to Resources on pp. 194-197 for a couple of books that should prove helpful, as well as sources for contract forms and an inexpensive contract review.

The standard proposal form

Many, if not most, remodeling contractors submit their bids on a standard proposal form, with their name and other company data imprinted on the top. The contractor then fills in the appropriate spaces with pertinent information and job specifications (or attaches pages with the specs), the price, and the payment schedule, then signs it and hands it off to you. You sign at the bottom of the form where it says "Acceptance of Proposal," and the agreement is made.

Standard proposal forms usually have a small section of obligatory "fine print" on the front. Occasionally, there will be a list of terms and stipulations on the back side. No one likes to wade through this sort of thing, but before you sign, make the effort; don't take any wording for granted. If you don't understand something, get an interpretation. If you don't like something, have it crossed out or changed.

The beauty of a standard proposal form is its simplicity. There is little legal jargon to complicate and intimidate, but the virtues of the form can, at the same time, be its shortcomings. Some attorneys argue that a basic proposal document is not good enough because there isn't enough legal detail to cover certain contingencies.

That may be, and I'm certainly not qualified to second-guess their legal opinions, but I will say this: If I were a customer and an established and reputable local contractor handed me a proposal agreement, I would not fret over every jot and tittle of legalese. I would concentrate instead on the heart of the document—the details of the work to be done and the clear delineation of responsibilities for both parties involved. More about these elements shortly.

The AIA form

Contractors may elect to use a more legally detailed contract form than the standard proposal form (and you may very well want this too). One popular version is put out by the American Institute of Architects (AIA). The "Abbreviated Form of Agreement Between Owner and Contractor for Construction Projects of Limited Scope Where the Basis of Payment is a Stipulated Sum," also known as Form A107, is quite detailed, considered fair to all parties involved, and—as you might guess from its title—carefully worded. Copies can be obtained for a small cost from the AIA (see Resources on pp. 194-197).

Custom contracts

A few contractors hire an attorney to draw up a contract form tailored to their particular needs. They usually do this for one of two reasons: They've done work for an attorney who told them they should, or they had some sort of contract problem in the past and don't want it to happen again.

The elements of a good contract

The first standard proposal form I ever filled out was for a kitchen remodeling project I designed, sold, and installed as an employee for another contractor. I filled out the details, my boss signed his name in the appropriate place, and I met with the customers to get their signature. However, the half-page of space allotted for job specifications was not nearly enough for me, and I ended up using four pages. When I asked my boss if I needed to fill in the customer's name, address, and other such information again on every page after the first, he told me he didn't know—he had never used more than one page. I was dumbfounded. My boss was one of the finest contractors I have ever known. He had been in business for years. He had done some very big projects. And he had never used more than one page!

Different contractors approach contracts in different ways, and a lack of detail in a contract is not necessarily an indication of a poor contractor. My former boss had a great reputation, and his customers trusted him—the contract was just a formality. But clearly, a detailed contract is preferable to one that is not; it is in everybody's best interest and you should expect it.

For some jobs, a one-page contract is sufficient. But for a typical kitchen remodeling project, there should be several pages. My typical kitchen remodeling contract consists of a cover page, where both parties sign, with several attached pages of specifications and drawings.

The work to be done and materials to be used

The single most important element of any work agreement is a clear description of the work to be done and the materials to be used. If you take an active part in your remodeling project and draw up job specifications as suggested on p. 26, you will lay the groundwork for a good contract. You will probably modify your original specifications somewhat as you go along, but the changes can be easily noted on a separate page or be incorporated into a revised set of specifications before you sign the contract.

The vast majority of misunderstandings between homeowners and contractors can be traced to an inadequate (or nonexisting) written description of the work to be done and the materials that will be used to do that work. In the event that you don't draw up specifications, do make sure that the contractor you hire spells out the details in the contract. The sample job description on pp. 27-29 will prove helpful.

The vast majority of misunderstandings between homeowners and home-improvement contractors can be traced to an inadequate (or nonexisting) written description of the work to be done and the materials that will be used.

Assigning responsibility

The contract needs to spell out who is responsible for various aspects of the job. Who obtains the permits? Who pays the inspection fees? Who supplies what materials? Who takes care of refuse disposal? These and similar issues may already be dealt with in your specifications, but if not, they should be mentioned in your contract.

Insurance

The contract or attached specifications should make it clear that the contractor and any subcontractors hired by the contractor will carry proper insurance. You should have a certificate of insurance for all parties involved (refer back to the sidebar on p. 38).

Protection from mechanic's liens

This may come as a surprise to you, but in many states, if your contractor buys materials for your project and never pays for them, you are legally obligated to pay the bill, even if you've already paid the contractor. If you don't pay, the materials supplier can have a "mechanic's lien" put on your home. (A lien is a security interest on your property, similar to that which a mortgage holder has on your home.)

The intention of the mechanic's lien law is to give a contractor relatively easy recourse if a customer refuses to pay a final draw. Unfortunately for the customer, the "recourse" also extends to material suppliers and even to subcontractors the general contractor doesn't pay. But instead of the lien being against the contractor, it's against you. Crazy, eh? This is all the more reason to deal only with reputable contractors who have a good track record.

To protect yourself against mechanic's liens, your contract could stipulate that the contractor must prove that bills relating to your job are paid before you pay the contractor, or at least before you pay for the whole job.

Start and completion dates

You may want to make start and completion dates an integral part of your contract, but many contractors are reluctant to commit to a specific time schedule in writing because they consider it too much of a burden. Unless you must have the job done by a very precise date, agreeing on approximate start and completion dates is more amicable.

Some contracts stipulate that the contractor has to pay you a set amount for every day the job goes past the agreed completion date, and that's a stipulation many contractors will also balk at. However, if you feel you must have a penalty for late completion, in the spirit of fair play you should also have a reward for each day the job is completed ahead of schedule.

Third-party arbitration

The purpose of a contract is to prevent misunderstandings and ensure a business relationship that is trouble free. With a decent written agreement, it usually is. But sometimes things go wrong. If you and the contractor cannot resolve the problem between yourselves, what do you do? You can always go to court, but who wants to do that?

The better (less expensive and faster) solution is to agree ahead of time to have another person (a "third party") act as an arbitrator. That person will listen to both sides of the dispute and decide how it should be resolved. If you and the contractor agree to do this, and agree that the arbitrator's decision will be final, and you make this a part of the contract, you are doing a wise thing. See Resources on pp. 194-197 for information about arbitration services.

Change orders

In a perfect world, no changes or additions would be made to the specifications after the contract is signed. It's best to make all your remodeling decisions before the contract is signed and then stick with your choices. In reality though, it's not always possible to hold perfectly to the plan; inevitably there are afterthoughts.

Many contracts stipulate that changes to the contract specifications require the contractor to draw up a change order describing the change and how it will affect the contract price. The customer acknowledges the change by signing the change-order document.

However, you might find that many contractors do not use change orders. They sound good in theory, but in actual practice it's a bother for the contractor to fill out a form and get approval from you for every little change. In my own work, I bill customers for minor extra work on a time-and-materials basis (as indicated in my contract), so I don't feel it is necessary to draw up a separate little contract addendum for each change. Different contractors handle changes and additions differently. The most important thing is that the contract make it clear how changes to the contract's job specifications will be handled, and that everyone is comfortable with the arrangement.

Whatever the change-order procedure, do be sure you find out the exact cost of the changes, or at least have a very good idea. Have the contractor keep a running tally of additional charges, and supply you with the information on a weekly basis, if not more frequently.

If you do make changes, additions, and substitutions to a job after the contract is signed, be aware that you are almost certainly going to pay more, and sometimes a lot more. In addition, you could well be delaying the completion of the job. What may seem like a minor change to you may not be a minor change to the contractor. For example, something as "trivial" as moving a light switch could take a few hours and hold up other work. Replacing a window specified in the contract with one that is a little wider can really cost you if that window has been special ordered, and if the larger size requires reframing the opening. You could be looking at an additional bill of hundreds of dollars— just for a couple of inches.

If you do make changes to a job after the contract is signed, you are almost certainly going to pay more, and sometimes a lot more.

Payment schedule

The total cost of the work to be done and the payment schedule are an integral part of any contract. But it's hard to say exactly what a normal payment schedule is because every contractor does things a little differently.

One large contractor in my area doesn't require any payment for a job until it's done and the customer is completely satisfied with the work. That's a very rare arrangement. In my work, if I'm supplying most of the materials for a kitchen remodeling job, I get 50% down payment with the signed contract and the balance upon completion of the work. If materials costs are not large (for example, the homeowner is supplying the cabinets), I ask for 25% or less at the start and get the rest when I'm done, But I don't have employees to pay or a lot of overhead.

Some remodeling consultants suggest spreading payments out on a percentage basis over the course of the job. For example, there might be a small down payment when the contract is signed, a little more when the job starts, another draw after the old kitchen is demolished and electrical and plumbing are roughed in and inspected, another draw when the walls are drywalled and finished, and so on. The payment percentage would correspond roughly to the percentage of that job that's completed.

Whatever approach you and your contractor decide on, make sure you are comfortable with the schedule. Obviously you shouldn't hand over all the money at the beginning, and you should be sure to hold on to at least 10% for the final payment. You pay up when you're completely satisfied that the work as specified in the contract has been completed. Not surprisingly, some contractors and homeowners differ on the definition of the word "completed." Therefore, the requirements for final payment should be discussed ahead of time and clearly understood by both parties.

CHAPTER 5

CONSTRUCTION BASICS

This part of the book deals with the products and procedures involved in kitchen remodeling, starting with the demolition and the preparation work that a carpenter would typically do on a major kitchen remodeling job before installing cabinets and other such components. I'm not trying to tell you how to remodel your own kitchen, but to educate you about some of the things that are involved in the process. After you've read these pages, you will be better prepared to discuss your remodeling plans with a designer or contractor and make intelligent choices and decisions. If you will be putting together job specifications for the work (as described on p. 26), this and subsequent chapters will prove very helpful.

Because no two kitchen remodeling jobs are alike, I won't be able to anticipate every contingency that might arise in each and every project. By necessity, this discussion will be somewhat general, and will cover common situations and materials. You may want to delve deeper into a subject, especially if you are doing your own remodeling.

In Resources on pp. 194-197 you'll find books that will help you in your research. Your contractor should also be able to advise you as choices arise.

Demolition

When a room is remodeled, the first order of business is stripping down the existing cabinetry and wall surfaces so work can begin on the new design. Two professionals can usually rip out an old kitchen and pack it in a dumpster in four or five hours, which is just in time for lunch. By then, your old kitchen will only be a memory (be sure to take "before" photos). The demolished room will be a dark shell of wall studs and ceiling joists, with dangling electrical wires and plumbing pipe stubs.

Demolition is dirty and hard work, yet it can also be satisfying because it goes fast. Sometimes you discover hidden "treasures." Old baseball cards, letters, and coins fall behind cabinets over the years. In wall cavities you may find rodent nests and old yellowed newspapers that are fun to read. Once I found a diamond ring, and a friend of mine found an old gun. And one remodeling homeowner in my town hit the mother lode—a hidden cavity packed with gold coins. Kind of makes you want do a little demolition work of your own, doesn't it?

Before any demolition starts in the kitchen, you will want to remove all pictures, knickknack shelves and other stuff on the back side of kitchen walls. Those walls will be shaking a bit as old drywall or plaster is

IS IT WORTH SAVING?

Saving a component of your old kitchen usually means that considerably more care must be taken to remove it. The demolition process will take longer (and consequently cost more). For example, if you want to save a stainless-steel sink, it could take half an hour to unclip it and break a stubborn caulk seal, whereas it would take only a couple of minutes to pull it up with the countertop and toss the whole business in the garbage. It doesn't pay to save things unless you really have plans to reuse them. Not everything can be saved, anyway; if your old cabinets were built in place, there is no way they will come out as a unit—you will have a pile of pieces.

ripped off. It's a good idea to remove glass globes on wall or ceiling lights along pathways into the house where lumber, cabinets, or large appliances will be carried through. Workers usually try not to damage walls, ceilings, and doorways, but don't always notice lights that hang down or stick out.

Some components of your old kitchen may be perfectly functional, and you may want to sell them or reuse them in the remodel. There are drawbacks, however, to saving things just for the sake of saving them (see the sidebar below left). If you do decide that you want to save certain components of your old kitchen, make that perfectly clear to your contractor in the job specifications.

A word about insulation

During demolition work, insulation should be stripped out of the walls and replaced—insulation is cheap enough. Most remodelers still use fiberglass, but there are plenty of other options, ranging from cellulose to cotton and sprayed-on foams. My feeling is that all of them are suitable if installed properly. Fiberglass, however, is commonly available and does the job, so it's what I almost always use.

Walls

Everyone knows what walls are, but not everyone knows what's inside them. For a little lesson, see the drawing on the facing page. For the sake of simplicity, let's assume that your home is like most—a modern, wood-framed structure. If that's the case, your walls consist of upright pieces of wood

THE WALL REVEALED

A typical stud wall

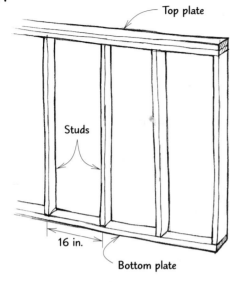

Top plate

Studs

16 in.

Bottom plate

Interior vs. exterior walls

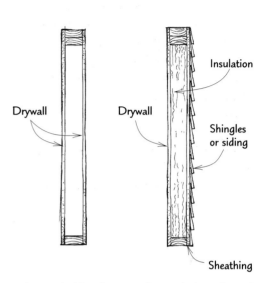

Drywall

Drywall

Insulation

Shingles or siding

Sheathing

In a typical interior wall, both sides are covered with drywall.

In a typical exterior wall the stud cavities are packed with insulation.

called studs that are nailed between horizontal top and bottom plates, also of wood. Studs are spaced apart at regular intervals, usually 16 in., and their width determines the thickness of the wall. Interior walls, which are built with 2x4 studs, are usually 3½ in. thick; exterior walls will be 3½ in. thick if they are built with 2x4s or 5½ in. thick if they are built with 2x6s.

Typically, there are two kinds of walls—load-bearing walls and partition walls. Load-bearing walls carry the weight of the upper floors and the roof. Load-bearing walls almost always run parallel to the length of the building and perpendicular to the joists

(the long boards on edge that support a floor) in the ceiling above. Exterior walls that hold up the end of roof rafters or trusses are also load-bearing. Partition walls are not structurally important to the building; they merely separate one space from another. Walls running parallel to the joists are generally partition walls.

How do you know for certain if a wall you want to remove is load-bearing? If it isn't obvious, in the planning stages of your project get the professional opinion of a qualified contractor or architect before deciding to have a wall removed.

Drywall, a man-made sheet of wallboard that consists of a gypsum core with a paper facing on the front and back, comes in 4-ft.-wide by 8-ft.-long (or longer) sheets that are screwed or nailed to the wall studs (preferably screwed). For walls and ceilings, ½-in.-thick sheets are best. Drywall is relatively inexpensive, goes up fast, and takes paint nicely. The biggest drawback to the material is that if the seams between sheets and recessed fastener heads are not finished properly, the surface will look mediocre at best.

To finish drywall, at least three coats of joint compound are applied. Each coat must dry before the next is put on. The final step is to finish-sand the surface, which makes for a lot of dust. Occasionally I hear of someone using a sponge to finish the seams (without making any dust), but I have yet to see a professional drywall finisher who does a premium job and uses a sponge. Some finishers now have sanders that are connected with a hose to a vacuum cleaner, which reduces the volume of dust quite a bit.

Finishing drywall is not a skill that can be mastered quickly, so if you elect to do your own kitchen remodeling I strongly urge you to sub out this part of the job. I can always spot a novice remodeling job by looking at the drywall, especially on the ceiling. You want a perfectly smooth, professional-quality finish on your drywall surfaces whether you are painting or wallpapering, and, in the case of a ceiling, even if you are applying a textured finish. Anything less than the best finish will show through.

In the event that you do minor remodeling and don't tear out the old drywall, you should know that a proficient drywall finisher can patch cut-out holes, recoat bad seams, and fix just about anything else by spackling and skim-coating the surfaces. You will end up with a smooth, paintable finish just as if you had opted for new drywall.

Most major kitchen remodeling work involves tearing off the interior wall surface and sometimes rewiring; exterior walls are often insulated or re-insulated, and new drywall is often put up. In a really major remodel, walls may even be moved or removed. Drywall is the most popular wall and ceiling finish material used in remodeling and new construction. For more on this material, see the sidebar above.

Removing a wall

Removing a wall may or may not be a simple job. Partition walls can be cut right out without any qualms, but load-bearing walls require more care and attention because the load they carry must then be supported in some other way.

Some homeowners think it will be prohibitively expensive to have a load-bearing wall removed, but that's usually not the case. Load-bearing walls can almost always be eliminated, and though it does involve more money, the cost might well be less than you expect. When a load-bearing wall is removed, the studs are taken out and a beam is installed in their place. The beam supports the load the studs once carried, and distributes it to its ends, where solid posts support it (see the drawing below). A beam is usually positioned underneath the joists because that's the easiest way to do the job. But if you don't want a beam hanging down into the room it's also possible to inset the beam into the ceiling, with the joists attached to either side with joist hangers.

REMOVING A LOAD-BEARING WALL

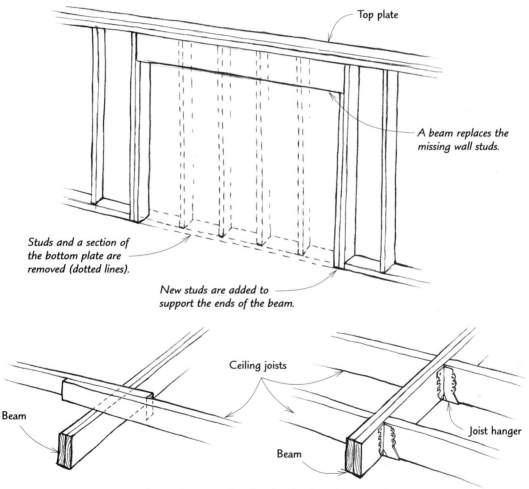

Top plate

A beam replaces the missing wall studs.

Studs and a section of the bottom plate are removed (dotted lines).

New studs are added to support the ends of the beam.

Ceiling joists

Beam

Beam

Joist hanger

The new beam may be placed under the ceiling joists (left), or set into them with the aid of joist hangers (right).

The introduction of lightweight engineered lumber has made it much simpler to support loads than it used to be. Laminated veneer lumber (known as LVL in the trades) is made primarily for support beams. It is composed of thick (1¾-in.) plywood-like boards that come in widths from 9¼ in. up to 18 in. and lengths from 6 ft. to 60 ft.. LVLs are very strong, straight, and true and they are sized (and can be grouped together) to handle virtually any residential load with ease.

Naturally, the size of the beam must be engineered for the particular application. Manufacturers provide span and load tables, but every time I've used LVL, I've given the specifications (size of house, placement of beam, etc.) to the salespeople at the lumberyard. They, in turn, have had the proper size beam figured out for me by the LVL supplier. LVL should be available by order from any lumberyard.

Fixing out-of-kilter walls

Few walls in a house are perfectly plumb, straight, and flat, and that is to be expected. Most carpenters can work with minor discrepancies so they don't become obvious in the finished product. That is part of the challenge of being a professional remodeler. But sometimes—old farmhouses come to mind—the framing is really out of whack and the walls should be "fixed," especially if you are going to hang cabinets on them.

Walls can be straightened by shimming or reframing. Over the years, I've become adept at shimming walls with pine furring strips applied horizontally over the studs. But rebuilding an interior partition or restudding a wall alongside the old studs is sometimes faster. It's also a good idea to make sure that inside corners where cabinets will hang do in fact meet at 90°.

If the walls in a kitchen are really out of kilter, I prefer to shim, reframe and square them all. Once this is done, the entire job, from hanging cabinets to laying a floor, will go together so much better. However, correcting all the framing can be take a lot of time and drive up the cost of the job. If you don't mind a little crookedness (that's the beauty of an old house, right?), then you can cut costs by limiting the amount of wall-frame preparation.

In a typical remodel, after the demolition and framing work, the plumbing, electrical, and other mechanical systems are roughed in. I'll discuss those things in Chapter 6. For now though, let's continue with the carpentry-related work.

Window and door framing

When your plan calls for new exterior windows and doors, you will want them installed shortly after demolition. Interior doors are put in later, after the drywall is on and finished, but the openings need to be framed when all the other framing is being done. Window and door choices are discussed in Chapter 7, but we'll take a look at the rough-framing needs for these items here.

When an opening is cut in an exterior wall or a load-bearing wall for a new window or door (see the drawing on the facing page),

TYPICAL FRAMING AROUND OPENINGS

Door

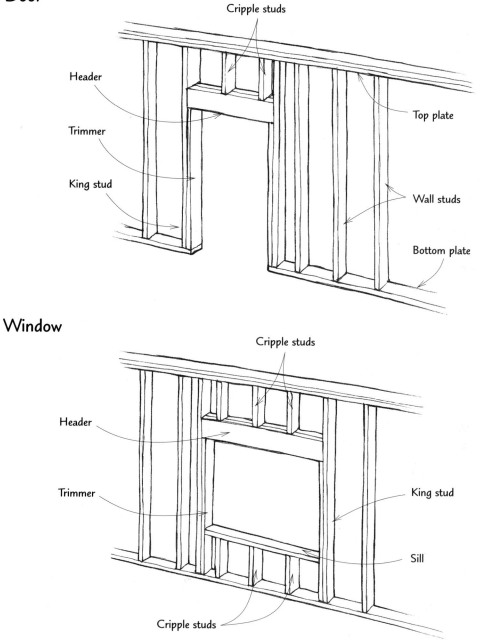

Cripple studs

Header

Trimmer

King stud

Top plate

Wall studs

Bottom plate

Window

Cripple studs

Header

Trimmer

King stud

Sill

Cripple studs

some of the supporting studs in the wall are cut out. To carry the load of those missing studs, a small beam, called a header, must be framed over the opening.

When you want to replace an existing window or door with a wider one, the old header will have to be removed and a new, longer header installed. That isn't necessarily a hard thing to do, but it is more involved than fitting a new window or door into an already framed opening.

Also keep in mind that moving or replacing windows and doors affects the exterior siding of the house. If your remodeling plans include new siding in the near future, there's no problem. Otherwise, you will have to patch and piece in the siding. With wood and shingle siding, this can be accomplished very successfully, but sidings like stucco and aluminum, not to mention brick, can be a real pain in the neck. When something is a pain in the neck, it will be more expensive, so keep that in mind if you are remodeling on a tight budget.

Floors

Your kitchen floor might or might not require any special attention. If it's level and structurally sound, the type of preparation it will need will depend on the type of flooring you decide to install (see Chapter 13 for details). Any rough preparation, such as tearing up old layers of plywood underlayment and putting down new plywood) should be done at the demolition stage of the job.

If your old floor has a lot of bounce, it is probably due to insufficient framing underneath or framing weakened by rot or insect damage. In my part of the country, many of the old farmhouses have small-diameter logs spaced a couple of feet apart for floor joists and, although the arrangement has held together for a long time, it doesn't make for a solid or a flat floor. (When I hear the old-timers' lament, "They don't make houses like they used to," I can't help but think it's a good thing, at least in some instances.)

If your floor is in bad shape, now, before the kitchen goes in, is the time to address the problem. One way to stiffen a weak floor is to sister some solid 2x10 or 2x12 floor joists along the existing ones. But if the floor is really bad, the best remedy is not repair but replacement. Cutting out the old floor and framing in a new floor sounds like a daunting task, but to an experienced carpenter it's pretty much a walk in the park. There are always exceptions, but in a couple of days, the old floor can be ripped out and the new subfloor (a flat, level, and solid frame with ¾-in. plywood decking) can be in place.

Ceilings

If a kitchen ceiling has an attic above it and it's loaded with insulation, I recommend leaving the drywall or plaster alone; just have holes cut as needed for installing lights or running wires, and have a new layer of ½-in. drywall installed over the old ceiling using long drywall screws. When the old ceiling is uneven or out of level, it can be straightened out with furring strips (applied perpendicular to the ceiling framing), and then the new drywall can be installed.

Some older houses have extra-high ceilings. When that's the case, you may want to consider framing in a drop ceiling below the old one. By framing a ceiling down, you have less room to heat. It is also much easier to install lights and any necessary ductwork in a new framework.

An excellent way to frame down a ceiling is with light-gauge steel joists. Steel has many advantages over wood when it comes to non-load-bearing applications. Unlike wood, steel studs and joists are light in weight and straight. And they are dimension-ally stable, which means that once they are installed, they won't twist or warp or shrink, and the fasteners that are used to attach the drywall won't end up "popping" (showing through the drywall finish a few months down the road) as is common with wood framing. Light-gauge steel costs about the same as wood and sometimes even less.

Soffits

The space between your wall cabinets and the ceiling is called a soffit. The soffit space can be left open or closed in, depending on the design you want. A closed soffit gives the

DEALING WITH DUST

Construction of any sort is a dusty business, and for any remodeling job, the work area should be sealed off from the rest of your house. If it isn't, demolition dust, as well as the various construction dusts to follow, will waft through your living space and settle on every exposed surface. Nobody likes a dusty house, but some people find it particularly horrifying. Besides being a nuisance, construction dust can also be a bother to people with allergies. Demolition dust in particular can harbor some nasty spores and molds.

Hanging a dropcloth over doorways is not sufficient dust control. The area needs to be as airtight as practical. Make it clear to your contractor that you want special measures taken to keep dust from filtering throughout your home. Heavy plastic sheeting should be duct-taped or otherwise secured over doorways. If you have a forced-air heating system, the registers should be sealed off. If the kitchen is open to the rest of the house, then a temporary plastic-covered wall can be built with furring-strip studs.

However, even with the best precautions in the world, a hermetically sealed kitchen is virtually impossible. Some dust will inevitably get through, and that should be expected.

SOFFITS

Open soffit

Wall cabinets

Countertop

Flush soffit

Extended soffit

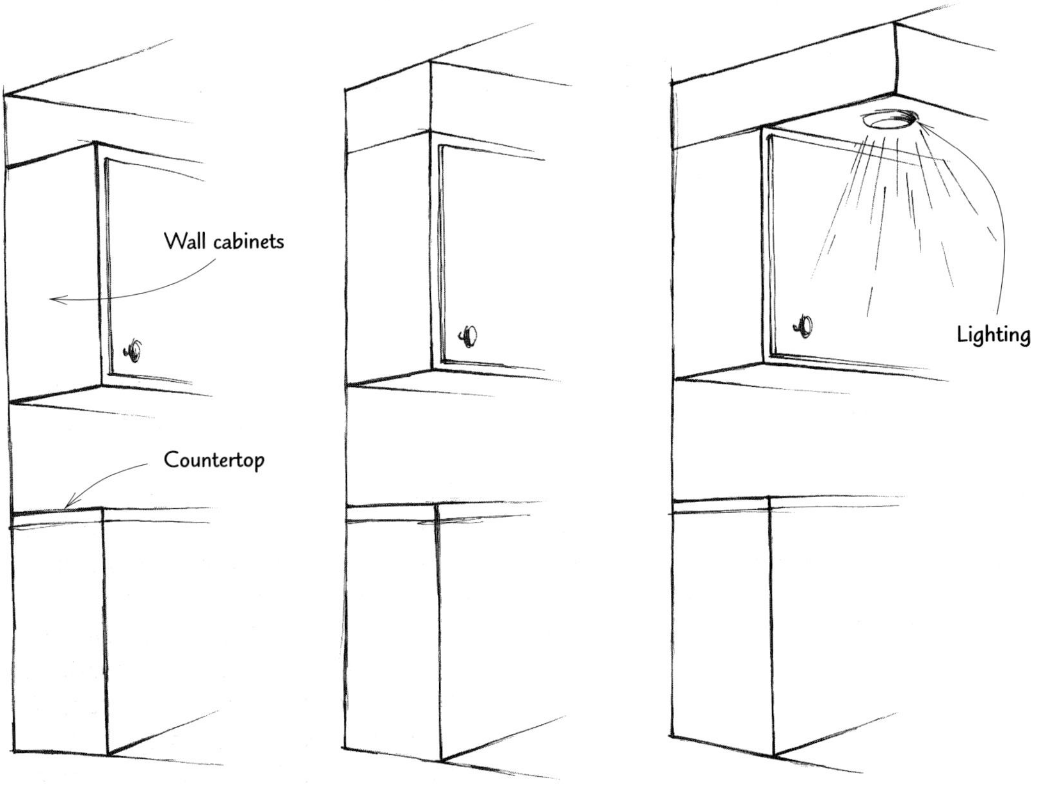

Lighting

The soffit is the space between the wall cabinets and the ceiling. It may be left open, or it can be closed in flush with the cabinets.

An extended soffit can accommodate lighting fixtures.

kitchen a more built-in, or custom, look. It also serves as a convenient place to install lighting and route ductwork through for an exhaust fan.

Closed soffits can be flush with the cabinet faces, overhang just a bit, or extend out 1 ft. or so and house some lighting (see the drawing above). Extended soffits typically get framed up after the ceiling and walls are dry-walled. This is another excellent place to use light-gauge steel framing. Having an enclosed soffit will drive up the price of remodeling. But a flush soffit will cost you considerably less to install than an extended soffit.

CHAPTER 6

MECHANICAL SYSTEMS

To accommodate your new kitchen plan, modifications may need to be made in the plumbing, electrical, heating, and other utility-related systems. Builders refer to these systems as mechanical systems. Mechanical rough-in work is done after demolition and framing, but before the insulation and drywall are installed. The fewer the changes that need to be made, the better, at least in terms of costs. Plumbing modifications in particular can run up the bill, especially if rerouting pipes means circumventing existing physical obstructions; it's something to keep an eye on in the design phase of the project. But in most instances, pipes, wires, and ductwork can be rearranged as needed without any big problems.

All mechanical systems have a lifespan and eventually fall into disrepair, and at the demolition stage you have the opportunity to rejuvenate or upgrade these systems. Putting money into the improvement of utility infrastructures that are out of sight in the basement and behind walls is not quite as satisfying as buying new tile and cabinets and appliances, but it is, nonetheless,

very important. It will probably never be cheaper or easier to do than when you do your remodeling.

At the mechanical rough-in is when subcontractors typically enter the picture. And due to the nature of the work being done, progress will not be as obvious as it was when things were getting torn out and re-framed. When the the plumbers, electricians, and any other subcontractors are done, the work will probably need to pass inspection before the walls are closed up. The general contractors should arrange for the necessary inspections as soon as the work is done, so the remodeling schedule won't be delayed.

Your kitchen plan, showing the exact position of all appliances (see p. 24), will answer most of the big questions of where the wiring and plumbing lines will need to go. If you are supplying any appliances or plumbing fixtures for the job, they should be on site by this time so the contractor can know the exact placement of things like electrical wires and plugs, gas outlets, and ductwork. If these appliances aren't available, you should at least provide the installation manuals. There

TYPICAL KITCHEN PLUMBING

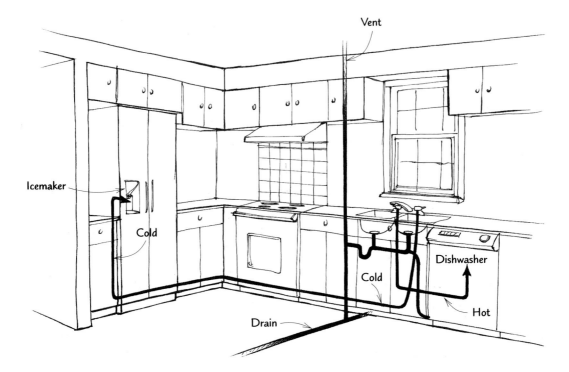

is a fax and Internet site that can furnish current size specification sheets for almost all kitchen appliances (see Resources on pp. 194-197).

When a mechanical plan has been drawn up in addition to the regular kitchen plan, that will answer almost all the other questions regarding the location of "little" things such as lights, switches, receptacles, and phone jacks. If there is no mechanical drawing, you will need to explain in your job specifications what you want done and then be around at the right time to make it clear exactly where you want various things to be. If your directions are vague ("I need a light switch by the entrance door and another one

somewhere over on the opposite wall"), the exact placement will be left to the contractor's judgment, which is usually fine. But contractors are not mind readers, so if you are persnickety about such things, discuss and decide on the exact placement of these elements with the contractor ahead of time.

This chapter will provide you with some general information about utility requirements and specifications. The information and recommendations I give here are contingent on building codes in your area. The codes are, by and large, uniform throughout the country, but with plumbing in particular, different municipalities adopt slightly different standards. To confuse the issue even more, individual building inspectors have their own interpretations and opinions regarding plumbing materials and practices. Your contractors will be familiar with the local rules—and with the inspector—so you should defer to their professional advice.

Plumbing

Plumbing in the average kitchen is fairly straightforward (see the drawing on the facing page). Hot- and cold-water pipes are run into the sink base cabinet to supply the sink faucet, and the hot-water line branches off to the dishwasher. If your refrigerator has an icemaker or water dispenser, it will require a cold-water line. Extra sinks or other water-related appliances, such as a hot-water dispenser or a water-purification system, don't usually complicate things too much, especially if they are part of your original planning. Waste water from the sink, garbage disposer, and dishwasher are typically routed out through the sink drain. Drain pipes must be vented, as discussed in the sidebar on pp. 68-69. Gas lines for a gas cooktop or oven also are considered plumbing.

In plumbing lingo, any appliance that uses water is called a fixture; the most common kitchen fixtures are a sink and a dishwasher. Pipes that bring water to fixtures form the water-supply system; pipes that carry water and wastes out of the house are part of the drain, waste, and vent (DWV) system.

Water-supply lines

With water-supply lines, the major issue is the choice of materials. Water-supply pipes can be either galvanized steel, plastic, or copper.

Galvanized steel Galvanized steel, once universally used in water-supply systems, is now virtually obsolete. It is heavy and awkward to work with because fittings have to be threaded and screwed together, which makes it quite tedious and expensive to install. Galvanized pipe typically clogs with minerals over time and corrodes on the inside. If your old plumbing is galvanized steel, it's usually a good idea to upgrade to a more modern material.

Plastic The most common plastic pipes for water supply are CPVC (chlorinated polyvinyl chloride) and PEX (cross-linked polyethylene). Polybutylene (PB), a gray or cream-colored flexible tubing used extensively in some areas of the country only a few years ago, is no longer being made due to lawsuits that arose when defective fittings leaked.

CPVC is a cream-colored rigid plastic that is joined with glue, or "solvent welded," using various plastic fittings. It is probably the most common plastic pipe used for supply lines. However, CPVC is not allowed by code in my area. Even so, the local hardware store stocks it and sells a lot of it to homeowners who do their own plumbing renovations, and who disregard codes and bypass inspections. The major attraction of CPVC is that it's cheap and very simple to put together. However, the material is not very durable and does not meet professional standards of quality. My advice is not to use it.

PEX is a stiff, yet flexible, tubing that is sold in long rolls. That's a real advantage, because you don't often need connectors when changing direction; the pipe is simply snaked wherever it needs to go. Where connections are needed, they are made either with bulky plastic compression fittings or barbed brass fittings to which the tubing is crimped on using a special tool. PEX will take a considerable freeze without bursting, unlike other kinds of piping. However, there are some disadvantages to using PEX. The rolls are unwieldy, and connections to fixtures are not as solid as with other piping (e.g., copper); occasionally they will leak. From an aesthetic standpoint, flexible pipe just doesn't look as nice as a carefully plumbed rigid pipe system. Though the situation may well change in the future, PEX is still considered unconventional, and unless you have big problems with pipes freezing, I don't recommend PEX for water supply in a home.

WATER SUPPLY FOR THE REFRIGERATOR

I f you are upgrading your refrigerator and the new model has an icemaker or a water dispenser, it will need a cold-water supply line run to the back of it. This can be done in two ways (see the drawing at right).

One way is to have it spliced in, using a saddle valve that fits over ½-in. copper pipe and pierces the line when it's tightened on. The saddle valve has its own shutoff valve built into it and a connection for ¼-in. vinyl or soft copper tubing (copper is the better choice because the fittings are less likely to leak). Another option (and probably the better one) is to have an angle-stop valve installed on the copper pipe. The valve can go under the kitchen sink or in the basement, or it can be recessed into the wall behind the refrigerator. Later on, ¼-in. soft copper tubing can be run to the appliance.

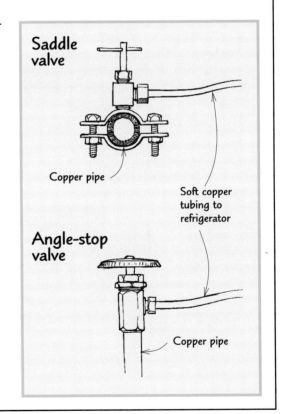

Saddle valve

Copper pipe

Soft copper tubing to refrigerator

Angle-stop valve

Copper pipe

Copper If you live in an old house that has undergone several plumbing modifications over the years, the water lines in your basement may be a mishmash of several different kinds of pipe, with an assortment of misplaced shut-offs and capped ends, all running to and fro with no apparent order. If that's the way your basement looks and the pipes are all easily accessible, consider having the whole mess cut out now and replumbing a simple, organized water supply system of all copper. It will probably cost less than you might think.

Copper comes in two forms: rigid lengths and soft rolls. The rigid costs less than the soft and is what should be used primarily, but the soft pipe is handy for making certain connections. Copper pipe is connected with copper fittings that are soldered, or "sweated," together using a torch.

It's a good idea to insulate copper pipes in the basement. The insulation will prevent condensation from forming on the cold-water line when the air is humid, and it will help prevent heat loss on the hot-water line. If pipe freezing is a possibility in the climate you live in, the insulation will obviously help prevent that, but a better insurance is to invest in a good-quality heat tape, which is an electric heating wire that is wrapped around the pipe. Pipe insulation can be fiberglass strips that are wrapped around the pipe or foam tubes that slip over the water pipe. The foam tubes insulate better but are more difficult to fit around pipes that make a lot of turns.

The importance of shutoff valves

Every fixture should have a shutoff valve on the water lines going to it. Without one, water to the whole house would have to be shut off just to change a faucet washer or repair the dishwasher. Shutoffs for the sink, dishwasher, and refrigerator (for refrigerators with icemakers and water dispensers) are usually installed right in the sink base cabinet, where they are readily accessible (see the drawing on p. 70). You can also have the shutoff valve located in the basement on the water line going off to the kitchen "zone." For shutoffs installed in a straight section of pipe, have the plumber use brass ball valves. They are easier to turn off and on and will hold up better over the years than many other valves. If the supply pipe enters the sink cabinet through the wall, a 90° angle-stop valve will have to be used.

DWV plumbing

A home's DWV plumbing system consists of pipes that drain away waste water and pipes that vent the plumbing system. Vent pipes are actually extensions of drain pipes. The need for proper venting in the DWV plumbing system of a house is something many people don't understand. In fact, I often encounter kitchen drains that are not vented. For an explanation of this essential topic, see the sidebar on pp. 68-69.

Just as with the supply system, you have material choices to make for DWV plumbing. These include cast iron, galvanized steel, PVC pipe, ABS pipe, and copper.

Venting is an important thing for you as a homeowner to understand, so I'm going to give you a little lesson: If you fill a plastic drinking straw with water and hold it upright with your finger over the top end, you have an unvented pipe, and the water stays in place. However, if you remove your finger from the end, the water flows right out because you vented the pipe.

Water in a pipe needs relatively equal air pressure on either side of it to drain effectively, and vent pipes allow air into the drain system. If your home's plumbing system isn't adequately vented, water will drain sluggishly and the pipes will be prone to clogging.

Look at the roof of your house and you will probably see one or more open-ended vent pipes sticking out (see the drawing on p. 64). But just because your roof has a vent pipe doesn't mean your kitchen is properly vented—the vent you see could be the one for the bathroom. Venting was often neglected in older kitchens set apart from bathrooms because the original plumber either didn't understand the need for venting or didn't consider it important enough to run another vent pipe just for the sink. If your current kitchen drain is not properly vented, you really should rectify the situation when remodeling. This is something to discuss with your contractor.

If it is logistically difficult to fit a conventional pipe vent in an existing kitchen, the simple answer to the problem might be a mechanical vent valve, also known as a mechanical vent or a "cheater vent." It typically goes on pipes under the sink (see the drawing on the facing page), which is a whole lot easier than running pipes up through the attic and roof. The mechanical vents that have been around for years have a thin rubber diaphragm with a spring behind it. The vent opens and closes automatically to allow air into the system as water goes through the pipes, and it also seals out sewer gas from escaping into the house.

Cast iron and galvanized steel Cast iron and galvanized steel drain pipes are found on many old plumbing systems, usually with the smaller-diameter galvanized lines running into a large-diameter cast-iron pipe. Most of the time, the cast-iron pipe will be in good shape on the inside and can stay, but the inside of the galvanized pipe will probably be corroded and half clogged and should be replaced.

PVC and ABS For new drains, I recommend PVC or ABS rigid plastic. PVC is white or cream-colored, and ABS is black. There are no differences in quality or performance between the two pipes that I'm aware of, but whatever you use, stick to one or the other. They shouldn't be mixed because each kind of pipe

Unfortunately, most plumbing codes and inspectors do not look favorably on mechanical vents because they feel that such vents will eventually fail. Vents with a spring-backed rubber diaphragm are almost universally frowned upon (even though they are widely available in home centers). But the good news is that there are now advanced mechanical vent designs on the market and they are gaining more widespread acceptance by codes. In Resources on pp. 194-197, I list a brand of vent that is highly regarded. In any event, do make sure that any mechanical vent you use is approved by local plumbing code.

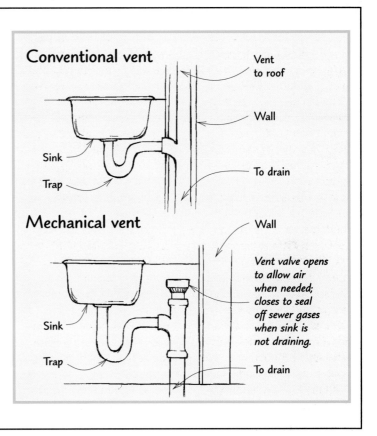

requires a specific glue that is not compatible with the other. Both kinds of pipe are joined by solvent welding using fittings made of the same plastic material as the pipes. Plastic drain pipe is relatively cheap and easier to work with than any of the other drain pipes.

Copper Once in a while I run into a house that has been plumbed with copper drain pipes. When I do, I match up any new drain work with the copper. Otherwise, I don't use copper for drain lines. Unlike copper supply pipe, the drain pipe is quite expensive and rarely used these days.

SHUTOFF VALVES UNDER THE SINK

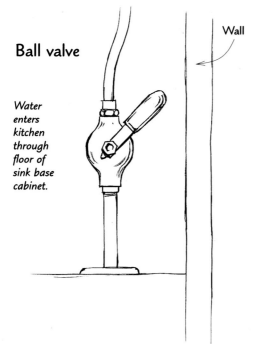

Ball valve

Water
enters
kitchen
through
floor of
sink base
cabinet.

Wall

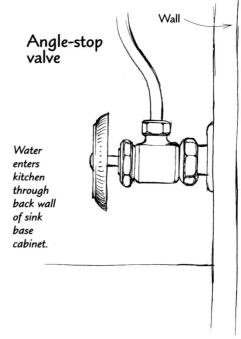

**Angle-stop
valve**

Wall

Water
enters
kitchen
through
back wall
of sink
base
cabinet.

Gas lines

If your remodeling plans include moving or installing a gas line for a gas cooktop or oven, don't even consider doing the work yourself—call a professional, usually a plumber. Natural gas is typically run in black steel pipes that are threaded together, and there is an accessible shutoff valve close to the appliance. LP gas is often run in flexible copper pipe. For both types of gas, the piping materials and installation procedures are specified and regulated by code for your protection.

Electrical

The electrical system in your home is, in some respects, similar to the plumbing. Wires are indeed little "pipes" that carry current instead of water. However, while water is relatively benign, electricity is not. This point is driven home to me every time I inadvertently cut into a "hot" wire with electrical pliers. After the blinding flash, I look at the hole I just blasted through the cutting blades and thank God for insulated handles. Rule number one is, when working with electricity, make doubly sure the power is off before you start.

Electricity typically enters a home through a weatherhead mounted outside the house (or sometimes through underground pipes called conduit). From there it passes through a meter, then travels to a main panel box. Inside the box, the power is distributed into electrical circuits that go throughout the house. Each circuit is protected by a fuse or circuit breaker, which automatically shuts down the circuit in the event of an overload or a short on the line (either condition could could lead to a fire). There is also a main power switch that can shut off electricity to the entire house.

Electrical requirements for kitchen circuits

Kitchens are heavy users of electricity and require several circuits to comply with code requirements and to ensure safety. For example, the electrical code typically requires that a kitchen have two separate circuits over the countertop to supply small appliances. Microwaves and dishwashers usually require their own separate circuits. Lighting must be on a circuit separate from the two small-appliance circuits. An exhaust fan, trash compactor, garbage disposer, and other "hard-wired" electrical appliances may or may not need a dedicated circuit; it depends on their electrical requirements and on the code in your area. Electric ranges will, of course, require a separate circuit. Refrigerators usually don't have to be on a separate circuit, but they can't be on the small-appliance circuit. That is only a brief overview of your kitchen's electrical requirements; the electrical code is much more specific. However, the finer points of electrical code are also sometimes vague, open to interpretation, subject to change, and hotly debated by electricians.

Electrical rough-in

When new circuits are required, new fuses or breakers will have to be added to your main panel. If the main panel is full and there is no room for new circuits, you will need a new sub-panel, which is a smaller circuit distribution box that is fed off the main panel. If your electrical panel is old and inadequately powered for the modern electrical demands of

SHOULD YOU DO YOUR OWN WIRING?

Most building codes that require electrical work be done by licensed electricians make an exception for property owners who wish to do the wiring of their own homes. This could be good news if you are doing your own remodeling, but my experience has been that many electrically handy homeowners who think they know what they are doing really don't. Every electrician can tell you stories about foolish and unsafe things they've discovered in homes where homeowners have done their own wiring.

I'm not telling you that you shouldn't do your own wiring. But if you do, take the matter very seriously. Before playing the part of an electrician, make absolutely certain that you know what you are doing. The electrical how-to books cited in Resources on pp. 194-197 are a good place to start. If you have any questions at all about how to proceed with an electrical project, it's wise to consult an electrician or your local electrical inspector.

your home, you may have to upgrade your service by installing a new panel with a higher amperage rating. Some old service panels are rated at 60 amps (a measure of how much power is available), which is puny when you consider that most new homes have 200-amp services to power modern appliances. In any event, your general contractor or, preferably, a licensed electrician will be able to advise you in your particular situation.

Electrical rough-in should also include wiring for phone jacks, television cable, smoke alarms, security systems, sound systems, intercoms, and thermostats. If you are doing minor remodeling, new wires can be "fished" under floors, over ceilings, and into walls to get them where they need to go. Some holes may need to be cut in the drywall to do this, but this is not a problem—the holes can be repaired like new (see the sidebar on p. 56). When I do a minor remodel, I almost always replace existing receptacles and switches with new ones. The old ones eventually wear out, and besides, new ones look better.

When you are doing major remodeling, the exposed framing makes the job of wiring a whole lot easier, and it allows an electrician to assess the condition of old wires and wiring practices. You can also take advantage of the exposed framing to run some extra lengths of wire (or a pull string) from the basement up through the walls to the floor above if you anticipate doing any future

wiring in rooms above your kitchen. This is much easier to do while the walls are open, rather than after the remodeling is complete.

Heating

If your remodel isn't changing the size of an existing kitchen or significantly altering the cabinet layout, your heating system probably won't need any modifications or upgrading. However, a substantial reworking of the room's layout, not to mention a kitchen addition on the house, will call for some changes.

Most homes in this country have a forced-air heating system, and the ductwork can usually be extended or modified to relocate registers and cold-air returns as needed. With a kitchen addition, you will want to make sure your furnace can effectively handle the extra heating demand. The same goes for hydronic (hot-water) heat. If you have an old steam-heating system and want to keep it, try to work around the existing radiators because such systems are complicated to alter.

If your remodeling plan calls for adding a lot of new windows or a patio door, the heating demands of the room will increase. Even if the glass is energy efficient, it won't prevent heat loss as well as an insulated wall. Conversely, the load on your heating system may decrease if you are adding insulation to the room or replacing old leaky windows with energy-efficient windows. I'm talking

The typical radiant-floor heating system is hydronic: Hot water circulates through pipes under the floor. When this is done, the entire floor becomes the heating panel. The result is more even, more comfortable, and more efficient heating than any system of little individual heaters can provide. There are no awkward registers or baseboard heating units to take up wall space and design around. And there are no hot-air ducts to harbor dust and allergens such as mold spores and circulate them into the house.

Radiant-floor heat has been popular in Europe for many years and is increasing in popularity in the United States, but it has been slow to catch on because of its higher installation cost. But the quality of the heat and the long-term savings make it a premium heating system. Every person I know with radiant-floor heating raves about how well the system works.

Besides installation cost, the disadvantage to radiant-floor heat is that it can't serve the dual purpose of cooling or humidifying the air the way a furnace with ductwork can. Damage to pipes and wires rarely occurs, but if it does and the floor is tile or concrete, it can be a real chore—and a major expense—to repair.

Because of its relative newness (it's actually an old technology that has become popular again), not every heating contractor is mentally geared for radiant-floor work, so you will need to choose one who is.

Besides hydronic radiant heat, there are also electric radiant systems that are designed primarily to go under ceramic-tile floors, thereby solving a major complaint with tile—that it is cold underfoot. However, radiant electric systems are seldom as economical to operate as hydronic systems. Manufacturers caution that they are more suited for "comfort heating" of small floors (as in a bathroom) than space heating of large rooms.

about heat here, but the same considerations also apply if you have central air conditioning. In any event, a qualified HVAC (Heating, Ventilation, and Air Conditioning) contractor can give you the professional counsel you need.

One of the growing trends in home heating is radiant-floor heat (see the sidebar above). Radiant-floor heat is considered vastly superior to forced air, both in comfort and efficiency. If you are looking to improve the heating system in your kitchen, you really should look into this option.

CHAPTER 7

WINDOWS AND EXTERIOR DOORS

Virtually all kitchens have windows, and many have exterior entrance doors as well. You may be perfectly satisfied with their existing arrangement and just want to spruce up their look or do a little repair. Or you may want to upgrade your old units as part of the remodel for aesthetic or functional reasons. As part of a major remodel, you may even want to add new windows to bring more light into the room or move existing windows and doors to make a more pleasing layout.

Homeowners in the market for windows and doors are often surprised by how many options they have in terms of sizes, styles, colors, glass types, frame materials, and warranties. This chapter should go a long way toward helping you sort through the possibilities and narrow your choices.

Windows

Windows that open are made up of sash and a frame. The sash consists of the glass and the framework that holds the glass. The window frame is what holds the sash.

The most common window styles found in a kitchen are double hung and casement (see the drawing on the facing page). Double-hung windows have two sashes, or frames (one above the other), that move up and down in the opening. Casement windows are hinged on the side and swing out like a door. Double-hungs cost less than casements, but casement windows have a convenient crank handle on the bottom. When a casement window is over a countertop, the handle makes it easier to open than a double-hung window. Casement windows also seal tighter than double-hung windows when closed and locked.

Other styles, such as bay and garden windows, can be put to good use over the sink or elsewhere in the kitchen. These cost considerably more, but add a custom touch.

Existing windows

In the event that your new kitchen design does not call for adding or removing window space, you might want to keep the windows you have, especially if they are serviceable. Unless the frame of the window is rotted, the

COMMON WINDOW STYLES

Double-hung

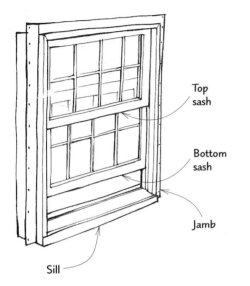

Top sash

Bottom sash

Jamb

Sill

A double-hung window is opened by sliding the sashes up or down against the jambs.

Casement

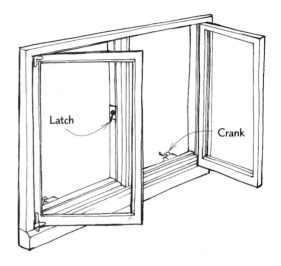

Latch

Crank

A casement window is opened by turning a crank. The window pivots outward on hinges, like a door.

existing window can probably be renovated by replacing some of its components. This usually makes better economic sense than replacing the entire window, provided the windows are of good quality to begin with.

In my own kitchen, the wood-framed double casement window over the sink is about 35 years old, but my house is only 15 years old. The window is an Andersen brand unit that I salvaged from a remodeling project. Andersen windows have been the top-selling window in this country for many years, and it's quite likely your existing windows are Andersens. If so, it might interest you to know that every part on that window, from locks and hardware to weatherstripping and sashes, is still readily available. At one

time or another, on various remodeling projects, I've replaced all of those components. You can tell an Andersen window by looking closely on the bottom corner of a pane of glass—the Andersen name and logo will be printed in white. Any home center that sells Andersen windows can get you the parts. For other brands of windows, if you can't get parts from the original manufacturer, you should be able to find hardware parts from a company listed in Resources on pp. 194-197.

Replacement windows

If you just don't want to bother with renovating the old sash and hardware, consider installing a replacement window unit in the existing window frame. Replacement windows are easier to install than a whole new unit—and therefore more economical—because you don't have to tear out the old window frame and deal with piecing in exterior siding or replacing interior trim (though you will probably want to replace the interior trim anyway).

Several manufacturers now make a wood replacement window kit for double-hung windows that consists of two new sashes and an insulated vinyl jamb liner, which is attached to the sides of the frame with metal clips (see the drawing below). You can buy these kits in stock sizes or custom sized for special requirements. You can also buy replacement windows that consist of new sashes mounted in their own frame, and the whole unit fits inside the old window frame. In my experience, a replacement window with its own frame is easier to install and seals and opens better than new sashes with jamb liners will—particularly if the old

REPLACEMENT-WINDOW OPTIONS

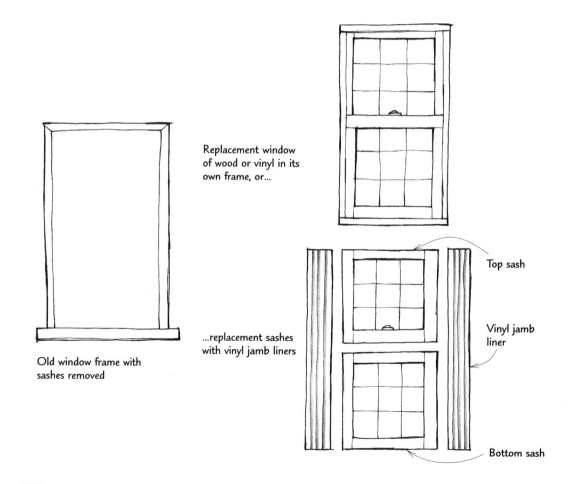

Old window frame with sashes removed

Replacement window of wood or vinyl in its own frame, or...

...replacement sashes with vinyl jamb liners

Top sash

Vinyl jamb liner

Bottom sash

window opening is a little out of square. Framed replacement windows are usually made with solid-vinyl frames, but some companies offer wood-framed replacement units. Although solid-vinyl-framed windows are available in just about any style (i.e., double-hung, casement, and others), wood replacement windows come only as double-hungs.

The average functional lifespan of a solid-vinyl-framed window is only 8 to 12 years; a good-quality wood-frame window should last 20 to 30 years.

Solid-vinyl windows have become very popular in recent years (not only as replacement windows, but also as original units in new construction) because they are relatively inexpensive and the vinyl will never rot or need painting. Nevertheless, as popular as vinyl has become, I want to make it perfectly clear that vinyl is not final, as some people are led to believe. The average functional lifespan of a solid-vinyl-framed window is only 8 to 12 years; a good-quality wood-frame window should last 20 to 30 years. Vinyl is not a time-proven material when used in exterior applications. In accelerated testing, the product doesn't rot, but it does discolor, become brittle, and crack. If exposed to extreme heat, vinyl extrusions will "relax" and deform. Although many people in the home-improvement industry have hailed vinyl as the be-all and end-all of window technology, I think it's telling that the three largest window manufacturers in the country (Andersen, Pella, and Marvin) have refused to make a solid-vinyl window. They know it won't hold up over the long haul.

Am I suggesting that you should avoid solid-vinyl windows? No. What I'm saying is that if you do use them, don't expect them to last as long as good-quality wood windows.

Be that as it may, over the past several years I have put in a fair amount of vinyl replacement windows, and almost all of my customers have been satisfied with them. The only complaint I've heard (so far) is that the relatively thick vinyl window frames and sash frames reduce the amount of daylight that gets through the window. If you put a vinyl replacement unit in an already small window frame, the difference is especially noticeable. Wood, because it is inherently stronger than vinyl, can be used in smaller dimensions to make frames and therefore won't block as much light.

If you do opt for vinyl replacement windows, the absolute best selection you can make is a window from an established name-brand manufacturer who offers a good warranty. Don't judge by warranty alone though, because any company can put a great warranty on its product. You want a manufacturer that has been around, and therefore is more likely to continue to be around in the future to honor the warranty. And by the way, a local contractor can usually put in top-quality vinyl replacement windows for you at a fraction of the cost of out-of-town replacement window companies with big advertising budgets and well-trained salespeople.

New windows

If you are considering installing entire new window units, you'll be subjected to a lot of hype from the various window manufacturers regarding the "superior" energy efficiency of their windows. You'll hear talk of fenestration ratings and thermal performance data, but there's no good reason to get mired in that sort of comparison. Instead, look only to long-established name-brand window manufacturers with a reputation for good window engineering and an excellent product warranty. (I recommend four such sources in Resources on pp. 194-197.) If you take my advice, you can shop for style, features, and price knowing that you will get a good-quality window. The major choices you will make have to do with the type of glass (glazing) and the frame materials.

Glazing You can buy windows with single-pane or double-pane glass in them (see the drawing below). Double-pane insulated glass is pretty much standard issue these days. The two pieces of glass are separated by a spacer around the edge, which is sealed with silicone

GLAZING OPTIONS

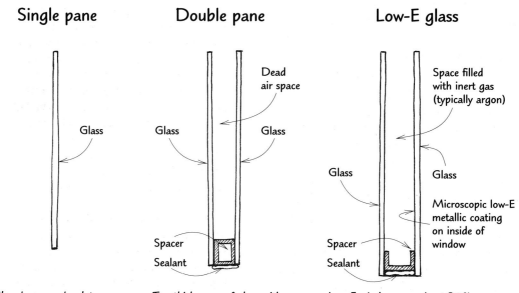

Single pane

Glass

Glass is a poor insulator, and single-glazed windows will suffer from extreme condensation and frosting in cold climates unless a storm window is used.

Double pane

Dead air space

Glass

Glass

Spacer

Sealant

Two thicknesses of glass with a sealed air space between them insulate better than a single pane. With double-pane glass, storm windows aren't needed.

Low-E glass

Space filled with inert gas (typically argon)

Glass

Glass

Microscopic low-E metallic coating on inside of window

Spacer

Sealant

Low-E windows are about 30% more energy efficient than standard insulated glass.

caulk (or something similar). The dead air space is a relatively good form of insulation—though it is nowhere near as good as an insulated stud wall.

Insulated glass with a low-E (the "E" stands for emissivity) metallic coating is a step up in glass quality and if you opt for insulated glass, I do recommend low-E. Without getting carried away with scientific explanation (you can read about it in most window manufacturers' literature), let me just say that the coating reduces heating and cooling costs in your home. In addition, low-E glass blocks much of the ultraviolet (UV) rays coming through the window. Ultraviolet radiation is what fades curtains and upholstery. Some manufacturers inject an inert gas (typically argon) into the space between panes of glass for even better insulation value. In most instances you can't distinguish low-E glazing from regular insulated glass just by looking at it, but the energy savings will certainly make a difference on your heating bill.

One thing you should know about insulated glass is that manufacturers warranty their glass seal for different time spans (20 years is tops). This isn't to say that the seal will fail as soon as the warranty is up, it's just that the quality of the seal and construction do vary. When the seal does fail, the window may fog up between the panes and be impossible to clean. If that happens, the glazing will have to be replaced.

If you live in a cold climate, double-pane glass will go a long way toward reducing window condensation and icing in the winter, but it may not always eliminate the problem. Some homeowners are led to believe that a window with insulated glass will never have any moisture buildup, and that might well be the case. But if environmental conditions are right, some condensation may still occur, particularly around the edges of the glass.

Frame materials Materials commonly used for window and sash frames include solid vinyl, painted wood, and wood with an aluminum or vinyl cladding on the exterior; these options

SKYLIGHTS

Skylights are windows in the roof, and they can be a nice touch. Almost any kitchen can use the increased natural lighting (see the sidebar on p. 96) and, if you get a skylight that opens, the extra ventilation is also a good thing. However, a cheaply made, poorly designed, or improperly installed skylight will leak and be more trouble than it's worth. The best advice I can offer you on this subject is to use skylights made by a reputable manufacturer (see Resources on pp. 194-197 for a recommendation).

To open ventilating skylights, you turn a long aluminum pole that hooks into a mechanical turn-knob on the window. For more convenient operation there are electric controls that work with the push of a switch. The motorized feature also extends to different kinds of window treatments, such as shades and blinds. It's even possible to get a skylight with a rain sensor that will signal the motorized closer to do its thing automatically.

Windows and exterior doors **79**

MATERIALS FOR WINDOW AND SASH FRAMES

Natural wood

Solid vinyl

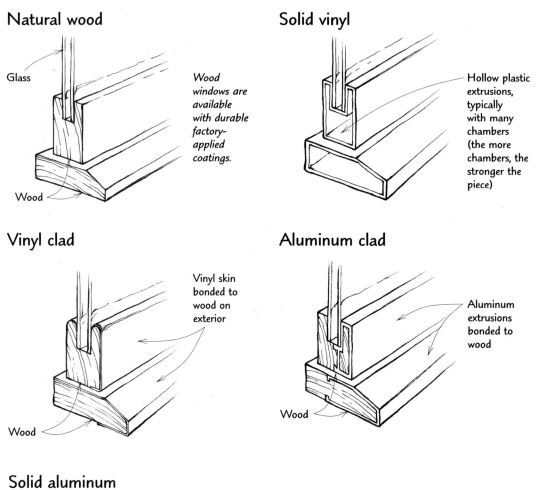

Glass

Wood windows are available with durable factory-applied coatings.

Wood

Hollow plastic extrusions, typically with many chambers (the more chambers, the stronger the piece)

Vinyl clad

Vinyl skin bonded to wood on exterior

Wood

Aluminum clad

Aluminum extrusions bonded to wood

Wood

Solid aluminum

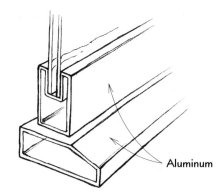

Aluminum

are shown in the drawing on the facing page. The vinyl- and aluminum-clad frames offer two big advantages: a maintenance-free exterior and a nice-looking natural wood interior. Unlike solid-vinyl frames, the vinyl on clad window frames is not a structural element of the window, and it has been used successfully for many years. I think aluminum-clad windows are a better choice because the cladding is more durable, but they are also more expensive.

Don't confuse aluminum-clad windows with solid-aluminum frames, which have almost no insulating value. Don't even consider solid-aluminum frames unless you live in a warm climate. If you get a window without an exterior cladding, check out the durable factory-applied paint-type coatings that some manufacturers offer. Such coatings will typically last for many more years than any layer of paint you would be able to apply, and the coatings are a good value.

Relatively new to the marketplace are window frames made of fiberglass or a composite formulation of wood fibers and vinyl. Both materials look promising but are, as of yet, largely unproven.

Exterior doors

Entrance doors into a kitchen usually come from the garage or the side or back yard. Aesthetics aren't the primary issue here, so you won't have to hand over big bucks for a fancy door with transoms and side lites. You want a service door that will stand up to a lot of everyday use, and yes, of course, you still want it to look nice. If your present kitchen door has seen better days or is a

MATERIALS FOR EXTERIOR DOORS

Steel clad

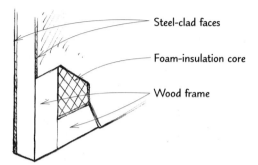

Steel-clad faces

Foam-insulation core

Wood frame

Fiberglass clad

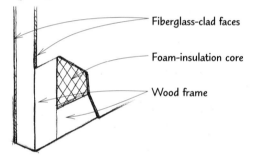

Fiberglass-clad faces

Foam-insulation core

Wood frame

Solid wood

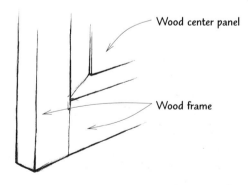

Wood center panel

Wood frame

source of air leaks, it's probably not worth trying to fix it unless it has some old-house historical value. In most instances, you will get a better job by installing a whole new door unit prehung in a jamb with attached weatherstripping and threshold. There are countless door styles to choose from in three materials: wood, fiberglass, and steel.

Wood

Wood doors have the aesthetic edge—real wood is just plain beautiful with a natural finish. But exterior-grade wood doors are also expensive, and they don't offer the insulative value of other doors. In addition, they sometimes warp and crack. The finish on a wood door won't hold up very well if the door is directly exposed to sun and rain. It's better to shelter the door under a roof. If the door is directly exposed to the elements, a storm door is a necessity, and paint, will protect a door much better and longer than any clear finish. When painting a wood door that will get a lot of sun, keep in mind that dark colors will absorb heat and can lead to warping and cracking of the unit.

Another thing you should know about wood doors is that they don't make them like they used to. Instead of being constructed of solid wood of the same species throughout, wood doors nowadays are typically made with wood veneer. The relatively thin skin is applied over a core of lesser-grade wood pieces glued together (sometimes referred to as stave core) or exterior-grade particleboard. Of these two, the stave core is the better choice in terms of durability.

Fiberglass

Fiberglass doors are actually molded fiberglass panels applied over a wood frame that is filled with a high-density foam insulation. The insulation makes for an energy-efficient door, and the fiberglass is more durable than either wood or steel because it won't chip or dent if banged into. The nice thing about a fiberglass panel door is that it has a wood-grain pattern that can be stained to look remarkably like wood. However, just as on wood, stains and clear finishes on fiberglass don't stand up very well to the elements. Furthermore, fiberglass doors have a thin coating over their surface that is engineered to take a stain, but if that coating is damaged (scratched) it is difficult ever again to stain the spot to match the rest of the door surface. Fiberglass door units cost more than steel but less than wood.

Steel

Steel doors are similar to fiberglass doors except that the flat or molded panels on each side are made of steel, not fiberglass. Insulated steel doors are by far the most common service doors because they are relatively inexpensive, energy efficient, and durable—they don't crack or warp, and the painted metal will withstand weathering quite well. On the down side, steel doors dent easily and sometimes even rust, especially if you don't paint them (steel doors come with an applied primer that doesn't look half bad by itself, but is only a primer).

If you buy a steel door and you live in a cold climate, get one with exposed wood edges instead of steel joined with a folded lock seam. The wood insulates better than steel and makes a better "thermal break" (see the drawing below). Some steel doors are made with steel edges and have a small piece of vinyl plastic as a thermal break, but I'm not convinced it is as effective as wood. There are also steel-edged doors that have no thermal break engineered into their construction.

The thickness of the steel cladding on doors can vary. Don't get a door that has less than 24-gauge steel for the skin; 22-gauge steel is noticeably thicker (the lower the number, the thicker the metal) and therefore more resistant to denting. Most steel doors are embossed with an indented pattern that resembles a wood door. But for a bit more money, you can also buy steel doors molded with profiles that project a bit from the face of the door, creating deeper shadow lines and giving the door more visual appeal.

STEEL-CLAD DOORS FOR COLD CLIMATES

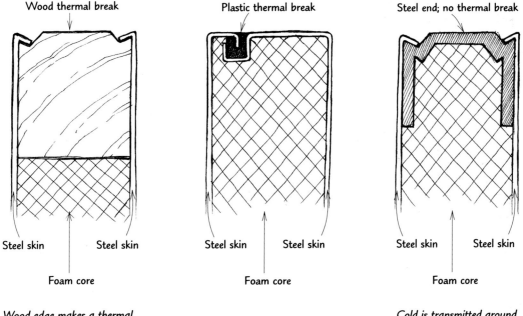

Wood thermal break

Plastic thermal break

Steel end; no thermal break

Steel skin   Steel skin

Foam core

Steel skin   Steel skin

Foam core

Steel skin   Steel skin

Foam core

Wood edge makes a thermal break between steel skins, interrupting the flow of cold from exterior to interior.

Cold is transmitted around edge of door.

CHAPTER 8

LIGHTING

Everyone knows that good lighting makes a kitchen attractive, comfortable, and productive to work in, but you don't have to look far to find kitchens that are afflicted with poor lighting. In fact, it's a good bet that the kitchen you want to remodel has insufficient, misplaced, or inappropriate illumination. Most folks are completely in the dark when it comes to proper lighting design. However, after reading this chapter, you will no longer be one of those people.

Most folks are completely in the dark when it comes to proper lighting design.

Everyone loves natural light, and if your kitchen has limited exposure you will certainly want to bring in more (see the sidebar on p. 86). However, natural light has its limitations (it's only there for part of the day), so every kitchen needs a carefully planned artificial lighting scheme as well.

Contrary to the conventional wisdom of a generation ago, good kitchen lighting is not achieved with a single light fixture in the center of the ceiling. Nor does good lighting simply mean having a lot of light. And it certainly goes way beyond just having pretty light fixtures. Over the years, advances in lighting technology, as well as our understanding of the dynamics of lighting in a kitchen, have made the subject of lighting considerably more complicated than it used to be. And to make the issue even more complex, lighting is as much an art as it is a science; there are different schools of thought about how best to light a kitchen. This chapter aims to cut the subject down to manageable size by taking a look at some "fundamental truths" and popular lighting options and to introduce you to a versatile lighting plan that will accommodate the lighting needs of different people, different kitchens, and different kitchen activities.

Getting help with lighting design

You should know that there are people who specialize in lighting design, and I do suggest you consult with one of them. Some kitchen designers can be a great help with lighting advice, but you can also get professional lighting direction from many stores that specialize in the sale of lighting fixtures. Such stores often have a salesperson who has training in lighting design.

One way to find a qualified lighting designer is to call the American Lighting Association (ALA), listed in Resources on pp. 194-197, and ask for the names of ALA-qualified lighting showrooms in your area. The ALA is an organization that offers professional training and certification. ALA students first work their way through a residential lighting training manual and take a test. If they pass, they become ALA Lighting Specialists. After considerably more training and experience, they can earn the higher designation of ALA Certified Lighting Consultant.

You should stop by a lighting store after you have a basic kitchen layout but before the final plan is drawn, because you might want to make minor changes in the plan to accommodate your lighting. Discuss your needs with a lighting pro, ask to see the many possible options, decide on the fixtures and bulbs to use, and then have the store quote you a price (with specifications) for all of it. You definitely want a price for budgeting purposes because light fixtures and bulbs will be costly. You may wish to supply the lighting fixtures, but before you buy them, I

recommend you check with your contractor, who can review the plan for possible problems with installation. Any fixtures you get should be UL (Underwriter's Laboratories) rated, and they should be installed in accordance with the manufacturer's guidelines.

A quick lighting lesson

You don't need a doctorate in physics to figure out how to upgrade the lighting in your kitchen, but you do need to know a few things about light to be able to weigh your options and make good decisions. So here's some basic information to get you started.

Ambient, task, and accent lighting

Designers consider the lighting needs of a room in terms of function. Ambient lighting, or general lighting, refers to the level of light in the room; you need a comfortable level just to find your way around. Task lighting is more intense and directed at a particular area; for example, you need task lighting where you will be reading a recipe and preparing food, or writing a letter. Accent lighting, which is directed at a painting, a special piece of furniture, or a sculpture, is more decorative than practical.

Direct vs. reflected light

One important thing you need to understand about light is that it's visible two ways: at the source and when it's reflected off objects. Since it isn't very useful (or comfortable) to look directly at a light bulb, we depend on

Natural light from the sun is the standard by which all artificial lighting is measured. It is the ideal, and a properly designed kitchen will provide for plenty of daylight. If your current kitchen space is starved for natural light, you should look for ways to design more daylight into your plan.

WINDOWS

The most obvious way to bring in more natural light is to increase the size of existing windows or add new ones (see pp. 74-79). Although new windows cost more than light fixtures, the quality of natural light and the positive effect it has on a room (and the people in it) usually make them a worthwhile investment. One guideline for natural lighting is that the window area of the room should equal at least 10% of the floor space. Thus, a 200-sq.-ft. kitchen would need at least 20 sq. ft. of windows.

SKYLIGHTS

When the circumstances allow it, you might consider adding one or more skylights to your remodel plan. These windows on the roof bring in an astounding amount of daylight and can really add character to a room. A north- or east-facing skylight is considered ideal because it will let in plenty of good quality light throughout the day. South-facing skylights will also let in a lot of solar heat, which is sometimes good and sometimes not so good. In any event, a window covering would be in order. West-facing skylights are the least desirable because the setting sun casts a harsh glare, and heat gain in summer can be considerable.

OTHER OPTIONS

Another way to get natural light into a room is through the top window of an entrance door that opens to the outside. Glass patio doors off the kitchen are yet another lighting possibility; they are essentially big windows. And if your dark kitchen adjoins a room with an abundance of natural light, it might work to remove the separating wall to let some of the light in.

reflected light for virtually all of our lighting needs. However, not all the light that strikes a given surface is reflected; some of it is absorbed into the color of the surface it strikes, and dark colors absorb more light than light colors. White will reflect about 80% of the light that hits it, but light brown will reflect back less than half of that. So the amount of light your kitchen needs depends a lot on the predominant colors of the room.

Age and vision

Another thing to keep in mind is the effect of age on human vision. To see well, a 55-year-old needs twice as much light as a 20-year-old. If you are getting on in years, I don't have to tell you that. But even people of the same age will have a different interpretation of comfortable lighting. So one of the key elements of good lighting design is to have a variety of different light sources and controls that allow you to vary the intensity of light to suit individual requirements, as well as the collective lighting demands of different group activities.

Task lighting

The single most important kind of light in a kitchen is task lighting (see the drawing below). Some task lighting is built into kitchen appliances. When you open your refrigerator, a task light goes on, and there is usually a task light inside exhaust-fan hoods that are mounted over a stove. Other areas

you need to be concerned with are over the sink and work-surface countertops, as well as eat-at counters, kitchen tables, and dining nooks.

Task lighting is not served very well by the old-fashioned approach of a light fixture in the middle of the room, because a person standing at a countertop will block the light, leaving the work surface in shadow (see the drawing below). Center fixtures can be an excellent source of general lighting, but not task lighting.

How do you provide adequate task lighting? The answer is with lights mounted directly over the task areas. Task lights are bright lights that shine directly down on work

GOOD TASK LIGHTING MAKES A BIG DIFFERENCE

Lighting in center of room

Lighting directly above work surface

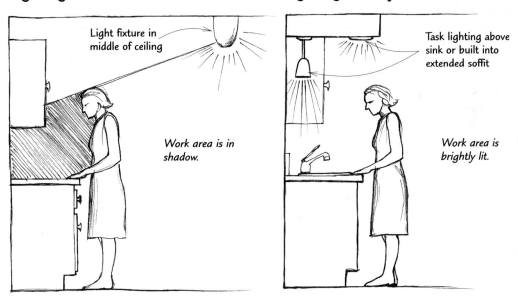

Light fixture in middle of ceiling

Work area is in shadow.

Task lighting above sink or built into extended soffit

Work area is brightly lit.

Recessed canister lights are without a doubt the most versatile lighting fixture for illuminating a kitchen. Several manufacturers make them in sizes ranging from about 3 in. to 7 in. in diameter, with 6-in.-dia. units the most common.

When you buy a recessed fixture, you will need to select three different parts: a housing, a finish trim, and a bulb (see the drawing below left). The components are purchased separately to fulfill different lighting requirements. Most lighting companies make an economy line of housings. These lesser-priced units accept a limited selection of trims and bulbs (or, more specifically, bulb wattage ratings).

Here we'll take a closer look at housings and finish trims; bulbs are discussed on pp. 97-99 in the main text.

HOUSINGS

Housings are the part of the fixture that you don't see. They fit into the ceiling, hold the bulb and trim, and have a junction box on them for making electrical connections. The kind of housing you buy will depend on the installation.

Housings designed for new construction, or remodeling where the ceiling is open, have a framework and are fastened into ceiling joists before the ceiling is drywalled (see the drawing below right). Housings

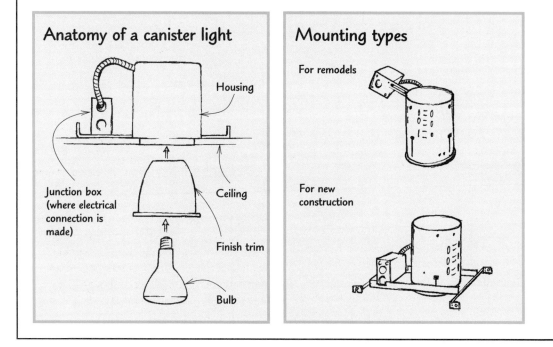

Anatomy of a canister light

Housing

Junction box (where electrical connection is made)

Ceiling

Finish trim

Bulb

Mounting types

For remodels

For new construction

designed specifically for remodeling (when the ceiling will not be removed) come without a metal hanging frame; they slip up through a hole cut from inside the room and are clipped onto the ceiling. Remodeling canisters cost more than canisters for new housing.

Housings are also classified by their insulation rating as IC or TC (see the drawing at right). IC units can come in direct contact with thermal insulation (i.e., fiberglass) and can even be covered with it. But TC fixtures (also known as non-IC) cannot be installed near insulation; it must be kept back at least 3 in. from the fixture to avoid overheating. Although IC housings are more expensive, they will save you money on heating and cooling costs because insulation can be packed against them. Better-quality IC housings are completely sealed and have an air gasket to reduce heat transfer where the ceiling and housing join.

When you are shopping for housings, you have to take into account the available depth of space in the ceiling. Some housings require as much as 9 in., but about 7 in. is typical for a 6-in.-dia. fixture. You can also get shallow housings that are about 5½ in. high.

FINISH TRIMS

Finish trims fit into housings, surround the bulb, and have a flanged bottom that rests against the ceiling and finishes off the installation. They are installed after the ceiling is finished. Besides being decorative, they serve the very important function of provid-

Housing types

The TC housing must be at least 3 in. from insulation.

The IC housing can be covered with insulation.

ing lighting effect. Some lighting manufacturers offer more than two dozen different trims. There are various interior surfaces (i.e., white, silver, and black) and also different internal shapes—each kind of trim does something different with the light. The most common and least expensive trims have black baffles, which help to reduce glare. You can also get trims that look like small surface-mounted fixtures, and eyeball trims that allow light to be aimed at an angle, instead of straight down.

surfaces. You will want task lights over a sink and over the countertop. With an island or peninsula countertop, task lighting sometimes takes the form of one or more lights that hang from the ceiling. A hanging light used for task purposes should have a shade that directs most of the light downward.

Light fixtures

Light fixtures that hang down or are otherwise obvious are known as decorative fixtures. Your choice of decorative fixtures can make a style statement as well as light the area. However, not every light you use needs to be a decorative fixture, and most designers agree that decorative fixtures should be used sparingly. Most of the fixtures in a kitchen should be inconspicuous.

Fixtures for task lighting

One popular approach to kitchen lighting design, particularly for task lighting, is to utilize recessed canister fixtures (see the sidebar on pp. 88-89). These lights that are mounted in the ceiling or in an enclosed soffit built over the cabinets (see p. 62). When recessed "cans" are installed 20 in. to 25 in. (to center

of light) out from the wall, they do an excellent job of directing light down to the task surface. Over islands, peninsulas and eating surfaces, the cans would be positioned along the centerline. How far apart you space cans will depend on the height of the ceiling and the bulbs you use (your lighting consultant can help you with this).

Task lights must never be positioned behind a person standing at the counter, or the person's body will block the light. Task lights positioned in front of wall cabinets will illuminate the front part of the countertop and the contents of the cabinets when doors are opened. The light does not, however, reach all the way under the cabinets, and to eliminate a dark shadow, you'll also need under-cabinet lights (see the sidebar on pp. 92-93).

Fixtures for general lighting

In some kitchens, especially small ones, ceiling- or soffit-mounted canister task lighting will reflect into the rest of the kitchen and suffice for general lighting. But in most instances, it's a good idea also to have one or more centrally located ceiling fixtures for general lighting. That way, when all you need is low-level general light, you depend on the

CEILING FIXTURES

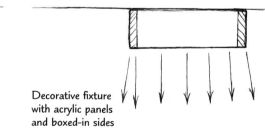

Surface-mounted
fixture with acrylic
diffuser

Decorative fixture
with acrylic panels
and boxed-in sides

reflected task lighting, but when you want a lot of general lighting, you turn on the general light fixture(s).

The trouble with relying on canister lights for general lighting is that they cast their light down and leave a darkened ceiling. A fixture that puts a little light across the ceiling is preferable. For good general lighting in a kitchen, it's hard to beat a surface-mounted fixture with a white acrylic globe (see the drawing on the facing page). Although the fixture, which takes one or more fluorescent bulbs, does hang down a bit, it blends in well with the ceiling. These fixtures are available in many sizes and shapes, and are inconspicuous. Don't confuse these fixtures (which are not considered decorative) with box-type decorative fixtures that have wood or metal sides and an acrylic panel on the bottom. Such fixtures do not diffuse light as well as a globe. They will do a decent job of sending light down, but they won't illuminate the ceiling.

Another fixture that you could use for general lighting is a large hanging light with a globe that diffuses light all around. You can also get a light like this on the bottom of a ceiling fan. (If you do install a ceiling fan, don't make the mistake of putting canister lights above or near the fan blades; when the fan is on, the lights will flicker, and it will be very annoying.)

If your wall cabinets have an open soffit, you might want to install fluorescent or incandescent low-voltage halogen fixtures out of sight on the top of the wall cabinets, where they will reflect onto and across the

INDIRECT GENERAL LIGHTING

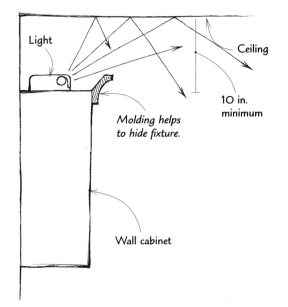

ceiling (see the drawing above). It's an indirect general-lighting approach that gives the room a nice ambience. However, don't use this method of soffit lighting unless there is at least 10 in. of open space above your cabinets.

Another neat idea is to install light strips up under the toe kick of base cabinets. When the lights are turned on in a dark room, the floor is illuminated and the cabinets almost appear to be floating. This arrangement makes a great night light. It could be considered accent lighting, but it would also serve double duty (as all lighting does) by creating low-level general lighting.

Countertop work surfaces that have wall cabinets over them are at a lighting disadvantage because the cabinets block ceiling light and cast a shadow on some of the countertop. Under-cabinet lights can solve the problem by putting excellent task lighting directly where it's needed—on the countertop. For the absolute best countertop task lighting, you will want to use under-cabinet lighting in conjunction with canister task lights over the counter. That may seem like a lot of lights, and it is, but it's better to err on the side of too much rather than too little light in a kitchen. If you want to save money on lighting, you can forgo the canister lights and just have the under-cabinet lights installed. If you do this, make sure you have a good source of ceiling general lighting in the room.

The two basic options are fluorescent fixtures and low-voltage halogen fixtures. Which is better? Opinions vary. My advice is to look into each system and compare costs and qualities. If you want a nice upscale touch and your budget will allow it, go with the low-voltage track system. Otherwise, fluorescents will be fine.

FLUORESCENT FIXTURES

Fluorescent fixtures have been used under wall cabinets for many years. Since the fixture is only about 18 in. off the countertop, the intensity of the light is more than sufficient. However, standard fluorescent fixtures, (about 1¾ in. thick and 4½ in. wide) can be a bit bulky (see the drawing below). For about twice the cost, you can get "slimline" fixtures that are about 1⅛ in. thick.

Fixture lengths range from 18 in. to 48 in. As a rule, the row of fixtures should be at least two-thirds as long as the wall cabinetry.

Most traditional-style cabinets with a face frame have a recessed bottom (typically 1¼ in. deep) that the fluorescent fixtures can fit into, but to shield the light and reduce glare there should also be some sort of molding around the bottom of the cabinets. Ideally, the molding should hang down 1 in. below the light fixture. If you're having trouble visualizing how this will look, your kitchen designer will be able to help you find a suitable style.

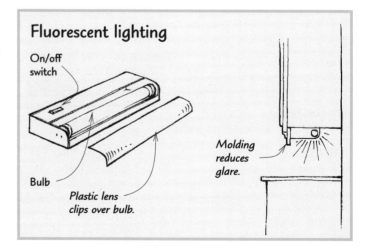

Fluorescent lighting

On/off switch

Bulb

Plastic lens clips over bulb.

Molding reduces glare.

Under-cabinet lights should be mounted behind the front edge of the cabinets, not against the wall (make this clear in your job specifications). When the light is toward the front, it is distributed to the countertop better and the fixtures are better concealed.

Although fluorescent fixtures usually have a switch on them, it's a good idea to have them all wired to one wall switch. That way you can turn them all on and off at once and not have to fumble around for individual switches.

LOW-VOLTAGE HALOGEN FIXTURES

Low-voltage halogen fixtures are relatively new for under-cabinet lighting, but they are well suited to the task. The concentrated white light has excellent color rendition and a bright, vibrant quality. And halogen fixtures can be dimmed more easily than fluorescents. Low-voltage fixtures are commonly installed on small linear tracks or as little circular fixtures, which are often referred to as puck lights because they look like hockey pucks (see the drawing at left).

Puck lights are about 1 in. thick and 2½ in. in diameter. Sometimes they can be recessed (in which case they project about ¼ in.), but that isn't usually practical in a wall cabinet. Puck lights are best installed behind a light molding and spaced about 18 in. apart.

Miniature halogen bulbs that clip on to a track are the other low-voltage option. On one such system, the track measures only ¾ in. by ¾ in. and can fit into very small places, yet the bulbs put out excellent light. To my mind, a linear system is better than pucks because you can distribute the lights along the track as you want).

Low-voltage lighting requires a transformer that is sized to meet the wattage requirements of the bulbs. The transformer needs to be accessible, yet out of sight, such as inside a cabinet or in the basement. One nice feature of low-voltage fixtures is that the wires are thin and can be easily routed inside cabinets and through small holes. With many light systems, hookup is simplified with snap-together connections. If you are so inclined, you can save some money by having your electrician install the transformer and you take it from there; low-voltage fixtures can usually go in when everything else is done, and the 12-volt wires are not dangerous to work with.

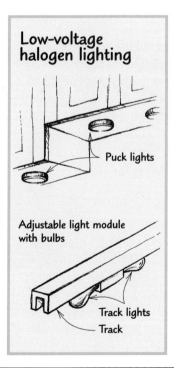

Low-voltage halogen lighting

Puck lights

Adjustable light module with bulbs

Track lights

Track

Lighting controls

Not every light fixture in your kitchen needs to be on its own switch, but most should. Put light fixtures and groups of fixtures (such as recessed canister lights in a soffit) on different switches so you can fine-tune your lighting design to meet the requirements of different activities. You can also use lighting controls to create a mood.

Give some serious thought to the type, grouping, and location of your light switches. This is something a lighting designer can help you with. The information presented here can serve as a starting point.

There are two types of lighting controls: switches and dimmers. Switches turn a light on and off. Dimmers do that too, but also allow you to control the intensity of light.

Switches

Basic switches are inexpensive and common, but there are plenty of other switch options that offer more convenience or a stylish look (see the drawing on the facing page), though they can be more costly. Here's a brief overview of your options:

- A single-pole switch controls a light, or group of lights.
- A three-way switch allows you to turn a light on and off from two different locations.
- A four-way switch allows you to turn a light on and off from three different locations. This is done by using a four-way switch in conjunction with two three-way switches. Single-pole, three-way, and four-way switches look the same once installed, but they are different on the inside and back side where they are wired.

- A pilot-light switch has a small light that glows when the switch is on. Pilot-light switches are commonly used when the switch operates a light that is not in the kitchen—for example, for basement and garage lights.
- A lighted switch has a small light inside it that glows when the switch is off. The light makes it easy to find the switch in a dark room.
- A sensing switch allows you to turn lights on and off like a regular switch, but if someone leaves the room without turning the lights off, a sensor will detect the absence of motion in the room and automatically switch lights off. You can adjust how quickly the sensor responds. Sensing switches are expensive but they can pay for themselves if you (or your kids) are forgetful about turning off lights.

Toggle switches are the standard switch style that has been used for many years now. A style that is gaining somewhat in popularity is the paddle switch, sometimes called "decorator style." There is no functional difference between the two switch styles, but the decorator versions cost about three times more than the common toggle switch.

Dimmers

Dimmers work by switching the power on and off to the bulb many times each second. When the dimmer is turned down, the current is off for a longer period of time than when the dimmer is turned up. Since the switching happens so rapidly, you don't see a flicker, you see the dimming effect. Dimmers

SWITCHES FOR KITCHEN LIGHTING

The standard choice

Single-pole, three-way and four-way switches all look the same on the outside.

Toggle vs. rocker styles

Toggle switches are the common style.

Switches with lights

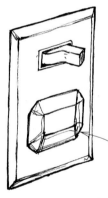

Light

A pilot-light switch has an indicator light that glows when power is on to the fixture the switch serves.

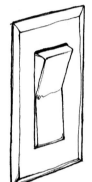

Rocker switches lend a more contemporary look.

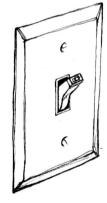

A lighted switch has a small light inside that glows when the switch is off.

Sensing switch

A sensing switch turns on the light when motion is detected and turns it off again automatically in a preset amount of time.

DIMMER SWITCHES

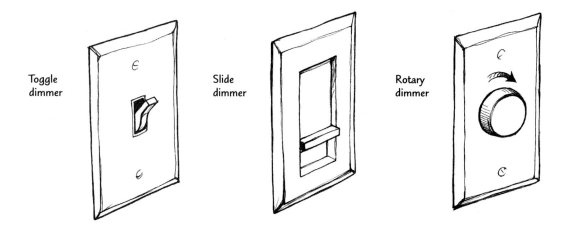

Toggle dimmer

Slide dimmer

Rotary dimmer

will most certainly cost more than a basic switch, especially if you opt for a high-tech system with programmable-memory features.

Dimmers have two advantages. First is their ability to change the level of light to suit the situation. Second, dimming saves energy and considerably extends the life of a bulb. An incandescent bulb dimmed 10% will use 5% less electricity, and the life of the bulb will be doubled. So if you have cathedral ceilings or other relatively inaccessible spots where light bulbs are installed, you could install a higher-wattage bulb than you might normally use, dim it, and greatly reduce the frequency of bulb changes. (Dimming a fluorescent bulb, however, does not extend its lifespan.)

Dimmers are most often used on incandescent lights that use regular household voltage (120 volts). Some low-voltage incandescent lights cannot be dimmed; others can but require a special low-voltage dimmer. Fluorescent lights can be dimmed but it is rarely done because it requires electrical

alterations that are relatively costly. What's more, fluorescent bulbs can only be dimmed down 10% to 20% of their total light output (which isn't much). Incandescent bulbs can be dimmed anywhere from full on to dark.

Dimmer switches come in various styles (see the drawing above) and are available in single-pole and three-way versions. Three-way dimmers are used in place of a regular three-way switch; however, only one dimmer can be used to control a light. In other words, if you have two or three different switch locations for a single light, only one of those switches can be the dimmer control. Some dimmers allow you to set the light level separately and then turn the switch on and off at that level. There are also elaborate dimmer systems with computerized memories that are designed to control all the lights in a room. With these systems, you can pre-program several lighting scenarios and change the lighting effect in the room at the touch of a single button.

Dimmers come with different wattage ratings, and these should not be exceeded. For example, if you buy a 300-watt dimmer, the combined wattage of bulbs controlled by that dimmer should not exceed 300.

Never use a dimmer to control an outlet where an electrical appliance might get plugged in because the automatic on/off cycling action of the dimmer will damage the appliance's motor. For the same reason, never use a light dimmer as a variable-speed control for a ceiling fan. A special fan-speed control (which resembles a light dimmer) should be used instead.

A common complaint with dimmers is that they put out radio-frequency interference, which often causes an annoying buzzing sound to come over your radio when the light is on. To reduce the chances of the noise, the lighting circuit should be separate from the one the radio is plugged into. Also, you can buy "quiet" dimmers that are designed to reduce the chances of radio-frequency interference. For more information about lighting controls, consult with your electrician or a lighting professional.

Light bulbs

Light bulbs have a tremendous bearing on the quality of light in a room. In the lighting business, light bulbs are referred to as "lamps," and what most people would call lamps are referred to as "portable fixtures." However, for our discussion here, I'm going to say light bulbs when I'm talking about light bulbs.

Light bulbs come in scores of shapes and sizes, not to mention technical specifications. Lighting designers toss around terms like lumens and foot-candles, beam spread and color temperature, when speaking of bulbs and their applications. All of those things are important, and if you want to learn more about them, the American Lighting Association (see Resources on pp. 194-197) is a good place to start. Here, we'll stick with the basics.

Which should you use? In the final analysis, there is no single "perfect" light bulb. Incandescent bulbs come close with their quality of light, but fall short on energy efficiency. Nonetheless, I think incandescent light is worth paying a bit more money for, especially since lighting accounts for only about $1\frac{1}{2}$% of the average home's electrical bill. However, fluorescent fixtures do have their place. Compact bulbs and warm white tubes can be an excellent source of diffused general light. The most important thing is to give your kitchen lighting the attention it deserves. Consult with a lighting professional early in your planning phase, and create an intelligent lighting plan for your kitchen.

The four kinds of kinds of bulbs commonly used in kitchens are incandescent bulbs, tubular fluorescents, compact fluorescents, and halogen bulbs (see the drawing on p. 98).

Incandescent bulbs

Incandescent bulbs glow when electricity flows through a tungsten filament and it heats up. Light is actually somewhat of a by-product with incandescent bulbs because about 90% of the energy they consume is given off as heat, which means incandescent bulbs are not very energy efficient. They also

BULBS FOR KITCHEN LIGHTING

Incandescent

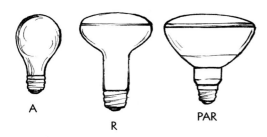

A

R

PAR

Fluorescent

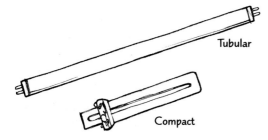

Tubular

Compact

Halogen

PAR20

Low-voltage wedge

have a short lifespan compared to other kinds of bulbs. However, incandescent bulbs are relatively inexpensive, and they put out light with excellent color rendition, which means that objects (and people) in the room look natural and pleasing when illuminated by incandescent light.

There are three basic incandescent bulbs: A, R, and PAR. A-style bulbs are your good old average light bulb. R (reflector) bulbs have a reflective coating on the inside and a clear face. They put out about twice the amount of light as an A-bulb of equivalent wattage. PAR (parabolic aluminized reflector) bulbs are similar to R bulbs but they put out about four times the light of an A bulb. All three bulbs are used in canister fixtures for different applications. The sharp, concentrated light from R and PAR bulbs is particularly well suited for task lighting. Again, your lighting consultant will be able to help you choose which ones to use in your kitchen.

Tubular fluorescents

Fluorescent bulbs give off light when high electrical current is directed into mercury vapor and a special coating on the inside of the bulb fluoresces. Traditional tubular fluorescent bulbs are straight, circular, or U-shaped. When it comes to energy efficiency, fluorescent bulbs are light years ahead of incandescents. They require substantially less energy than incandescents to put out the same amount of light, they don't burn hot, and they last at least ten times longer.

However, traditional-style fluorescent bulbs are not without flaws. People's faces look pale and sickly, food looks drab, and reality is distorted by the horrendously poor color rendition of the average fluorescent bulb. More expensive bulbs (usually described as warm white) help considerably with color rendition, but they rarely put out the light quality of an incandescent. Another drawback with tubular fluorescents is that they require a device called a ballast, which produces the high electrical current needed to make them operate. Some ballasts (particularly those that are not electronic) make an audible and annoying humming noise. Although a ballast can be removed to a remote location (basement or attic), that gets expensive. And you can't put a dimmer on fluorescent fixtures without going to special measures. Also, tubular fluorescents sometimes flicker. Even so, fluorescents have their place in kitchen lighting. With the warm white bulbs, they are well suited to under-cabinet lighting, and they are typically found in general lighting fixtures with acrylic diffusers.

When it comes to energy efficiency, fluorescent bulbs are light years ahead of incandescents.

Compact fluorescents

One of the newer developments in fluorescent lighting is compact fluorescent bulbs. They are smaller than the tubular versions, and they have the same energy-efficient qualities. Compact bulb ballasts don't hum, and they have excellent color rendition. Although they may flicker a few times when starting, it isn't anything that lasts. Compact fluorescents fit in fixtures designed specifically for them or, in some instances, they can be retrofitted into a fixture that's designed for an incandescent bulb (including some recessed canisters). Compact fluorescent bulbs are more expensive than incandescent or tubular fluorescent bulbs.

Halogen bulbs

Halogen bulbs are like incandescents but the filament is enclosed in halogen gas. The bulbs burn very hot and thus put out a more intense white light than any other incandescents, so halogens are in a league of their own. The light also has excellent color rendition and is much crisper and clearer than that of an incandescent. Dishes and glassware will sparkle under halogen light.

Many halogen bulbs use low voltage (12 volts) and require a transformer to cut the household line voltage (120 volts) down to size. Low-voltage bulbs can be used only in special fixtures that are somewhat expensive. However, low-voltage fixtures are typically smaller and less conspicuous, and therefore more versatile, than other incandescent fixtures. You would think that terms like low voltage and small size would mean low lighting capacity, but that's not necessarily the case because halogen bulbs really punch out the lumens.

Some halogen bulbs operate on household line voltage, and there are even some versions that will work in the standard A-bulb sockets found in the average canister lights. Such bulbs are comparatively expensive but not prohibitively so. They are best used for task and accent lighting.

CHAPTER 9

KITCHEN VENTILATION

Steam, grease, odors, heat, and smoke—you can't cook without them, but if they are allowed to escape into your kitchen, the result can be messy, unpleasant, and even unhealthy. Steam condensing on cabinet faces and the ceiling can disfigure or ruin the surfaces. Grease is just plain gross; I've torn out old kitchens where the slick on the bottom of the cabinet over the stove was so thick I could have scraped off enough to deep-fry a batch of chicken wings. Stale odors are a more subtle pollutant. The garlicky reek of last night's pasta sauce may not bother you (because your nose is accustomed to it) but when your friends walk into the kitchen, they'll be struck by the smell—and they won't find it savory. And the heat generated by burners and ovens can be oppressive, especially in summer. Beyond these issues are the possible health hazards of breathing air laden with contaminants, particularly with gas-fired appliances.

All of this makes a convincing case for kitchen ventilation. Yet for many homeowners who remodel, kitchen ventilation is almost an afterthought, and if a system is installed, it is often inadequate and ineffective. This chapter offers a fresh approach.

Don't expect building codes to guarantee a top-notch ventilation system. In most parts of the country, if your kitchen has a window that can be opened, that is considered enough ventilation to satisfy the codes. But it is hardly sufficient for practical purposes. To deal effectively with "the bad stuff" you need to get the foul air away from the stove before it has a chance to dissipate into the room. Opening a window won't do this. Opening two windows is better, but its still nowhere near as effective as mechanical ventilation.

Recirculation vs. exhaust ventilation

There are two types of mechanical ventilation: recirculation and exhaust. Recirculation ventilation is a ductless system that takes air from above the stove, passes it through a filter, and recirculates it back out into the room.

Exhaust ventilation systems have a fan with ductwork that channels objectionable air out of the house.

The typical ductless system comes in the form of a range hood that mounts under a cabinet above the stove. The hood has a fan in it that pulls air through filters and blows it back into the room (see the drawing at right). Most systems have a filter of some kind to catch grease. To take care of odors, you can get a charcoal filter, which must be replaced every six months or so. But filters are only moderately effective, and they don't do anything to mitigate heat and moisture.

Despite the obvious shortcomings, many people install unventilated hoods because they are less expensive than a "legitimate" exhaust system. Some ductless hoods can be purchased for less than $50, and not having to run ductwork could save several times that amount. Another reason is convenience: If your stove isn't located on an exterior wall, it may be difficult or even impossible to put in exhaust ductwork, and when that's the case, filtration is the next option. It's better than nothing, but in all honesty, it isn't all that much better. Of my past customers who didn't opt for a good ventilation system, many told me later that they wish they had.

The bottom line is, unvented hoods don't do a good job. If you seriously want to deal with the problem, you must figure exhaust ventilation into the kitchen equation during the design and planning stages of your project. You (and your contractor or designer) should be able to come up with a pleasing kitchen layout that will accommodate a run of ductwork (more about this shortly).

RECIRCULATION RANGE HOOD

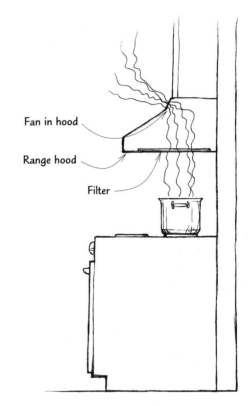

Fan in hood

Range hood

Filter

The dynamics of ventilation

Exhaust-ventilation systems vary considerably in their style and placement, and, more important (at least from a practical point of view), in their effectiveness. Let's take a look at some things you need to consider, and, in light of those factors, examine the different exhaust-ventilation options currently on the market. Then you can decide for yourself how to proceed in your kitchen.

When an exhaust fan sucks air off the cooktop, it is removing it from the house, and when air is removed from the house, new "fresh" air must move in to take its place. If replacement air can't get in, the air pressure in the house will drop. The structure won't implode, but what could happen can be just as bad.

If your home is energy efficient and relatively airtight (most homes built in the last 20 years would probably qualify), it's possible that there won't be enough cracks and gaps in the construction for adequate replacement air to flow in. When this is the case, the exhaust fan won't be able to draw properly, but more than that, the situation could create enough negative pressure in the house to reverse the natural flow of air up the chimney, pulling it back down into the house. This phenomenon is called backdrafting. If the chimney is used to vent a gas water heater or furnace or a woodstove, deadly carbon monoxide could be pulled back into your home.

Carbon monoxide is the leading cause of accidental poisoning in the United States. The gas is colorless and odorless, and can affect you gradually—people exposed to lower than lethal levels often exhibit flu-like symptoms. That's why it is important to have a carbon-monoxide detector in your home, if you don't have one already. (For obvious reasons, every kitchen should also have a fire extinguisher and a smoke detector.)

Backdrafting as a result of kitchen exhaust ventilation is a definite possibility, but there is some debate regarding its actual probability. Ventilation specialists disagree about the seriousness of the risk—of those I have spoken too, most feel that a 300-cfm exhaust fan shouldn't cause problems in the average home.

However, the best way to determine if your house is at risk for backdrafting is to have it tested. There are people who specialize in evaluating and solving indoor-air quality problems (it's a growing industry). Check in the Yellow Pages under Energy Management, or contact your local utility for qualified people. They can do a blower-door test that uses a big fan sealed in a doorway to put the interior of the house under negative pressure; then they determine the air exchange rate. If air doesn't come in fast enough on its own, they will recommend having an air-intake fan installed to bring air into the house as it's needed.

Your other option, a low-tech solution, is just to open the kitchen window when the vent is running. Even if backdrafting is not a problem, cracking the window will let in enough replacement air to ensure that the fan works at peak pulling power.

Updraft vs. downdraft ventilation

Hot air laden with moisture and grease rises up off the cooktop, so above the stove is the most effective location for an exhaust system. There are also downdrafting exhaust systems that attempt to suck the rising vapors back down and out a duct under the cooktop. Although downdraft systems do work to a degree (see pp. 107-108), they do not, as a rule, have the overall efficiency of up-draft ventilation.

Location of the cooktop

Your cooktop may be located against a wall, in a peninsula, or on an island. Regardless of the type of ventilation used, when a cooktop is out in the open, there is a greater likeli-hood that air crosscurrents in the room will interfere with efficient ventilation. Cooktops against walls, especially exterior walls, are the easiest to vent.

Capture

To range-hood ventilation specialists, "cap-ture" refers to how well a hood collects rising vapors and corrals them while the fan evacu-ates them as fast as it can. Because a hood has capture, it is considerably more effective than exhaust systems without a hood.

For the best capture, the hood should be at least as wide as the cooking surface, and 3 in. wider on each side is considered even better. In addition, hoods that extend farther out from the wall over the cooktop will be more effective than those with less depth—20 in. is considered a minimum depth. The height, or interior holding capacity, of the hood (referred to as the sump) is also a factor—hoods with more sump are able to hold more foul air. Finally, hoods against the wall should be 20 in. to 24 in. off the cooking surface, while 36 in. is standard for an island hood.

Rating of the exhaust fan

Exhaust fans are rated by how many cubic feet per minute (cfm) of air that they can move. Inexpensive "builder line" hoods may have a cfm rating as low as 150, which the Federal Housing Authority (FHA) recom-mends as a minimum. However, the National Kitchen and Bath Association (NKBA) recom-mends that wall hoods should have a mini-mum cfm rating of 300, and I strongly sug-gest you opt for the higher capacity. For hoods over an island or peninsula cooktop, the NKBA recommends a cfm rating of at least 600. To be most effective, downdraft ventilation systems should operate at 400 cfm to 500 cfm.

Configuration of the ductwork

The best exhaust-ventilation system in the world will be partially or completely useless if the ductwork is improperly installed. In fact, it's not at all unusual to find a duct that is too long, convoluted, or smaller in diameter than it should be. These conditions create air resistance that the fan cannot overcome, and the ventilation equipment simply is not able to do its job. Proper ducting is criti-cal. See the sidebar on pp. 104-105 for some guidelines.

Noise

The noise an exhaust system makes doesn't necessarily factor into how efficient it is, but fans do pull a large volume of air and can therefore be a bit loud. Hoods can be espe-

There is one basic rule for exhaust-fan ducting: Keep it short and simple. A brief run of pipe with few bends will expel air faster and be less noisy. The ideal situation is to install the stove and hood against an exterior wall have the duct run straight out the back (see the drawing on the facing page).

When there is a roof directly over the kitchen, another excellent option is to run the duct straight up through the roof. If you do this, make sure there will be a good-quality roof cap with a backdraft damper and bird screen. Most ventilation manufacturers sell caps to go with their fans. Even still, I have found, on some rare occasions, that even the best of caps will allow rain water in during a particularly nasty storm (such as when the rain is "falling" horizontally), so that's a possible drawback.

When remodeling old kitchens, I sometimes encounter ducts that vent straight into an unused attic space. This is a simple solution but not a very good one. Although I've not personally seen any serious damage, the excess moisture can lead to rotting of the roof sheathing. Worse, if a grease fire were to ignite in the duct, the open end would be a veritable flame thrower. Venting directly into the attic is not recommended.

Another option, when the possibility presents itself, is to duct up and then horizontally through an enclosed soffit or between floor joists and out the side of the house under the eaves.

The important thing when running ductwork is not to exceed the manufacturer's recommended "equivalent length" of duct for the fan. In most instances an equivalent length of 30 ft. (or less) is

best. Equivalent length is a rating given to elbows and transition fittings, which create turbulence and resistance in the duct, effectively adding to its length. For example a 90° elbow has an equivalent length of 5 ft., even though the actual length of the fitting is much less. If you need help on this obscure but necessary topic, contact the technical department where you bought the fan for guidance and advice.

OTHER THINGS TO KEEP IN MIND

■ The diameter of the duct can increase from the opening that exits the fan, but it should never be reduced.

■ Ductwork should be galvanized steel, not plastic, because of the slight risk of a grease fire.

■ Flexible metal duct should be avoided because the

cially bothersome because the fan (and the rush of air it creates) is closer to the ear than on a downdraft vent. But most of the noise problem can be attributed to the type of fan used and the qualities of its construction.

Inexpensive axial fans have propellers that resemble the propeller on a motorboat, and they are noisier than the better-quality, higher-capacity fans that use a centrifugal blower, or "squirrel-cage" fan. A high-

rough interior creates too much drag on the air flow.

■ Ductwork that passes through an unheated attic space should be insulated to reduce the likelihood of heavy grease condensation. You can wrap the pipe with 3½-in. fiberglass and then tape it completely with a "skin" of duct tape. It ain't pretty, but it does the job.

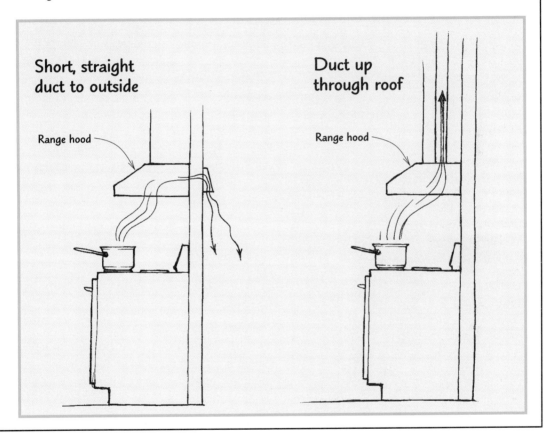

Short, straight duct to outside

Range hood

Duct up through roof

Range hood

capacity centrifugal fan can move a lot more air than an axial fan, and still run quieter.

The best way to compare the sound levels of mechanical vent systems is to check out their sone ratings. Sones are a measure of sound. The Home Ventilating Institute (HVI) tests fan units for the sound they put out and gives each a sone rating. You can compare the loudness of different fan units by looking up their HVI ratings in manufacturers'

REMOTE-MOUNTED FAN

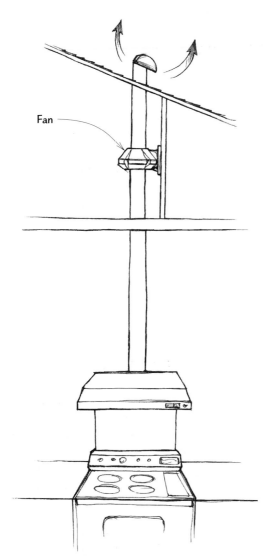

Fan

An exhaust system with an in-line fan mounted in the attic will be substantially quieter than a system with the fan mounted in the kitchen inside the hood.

catalogs. Fans with a lower sone number are quieter. For a good quality, high-capacity venting appliance, 5.5 sones is considered decent. And incidentally, a high-capacity fan rated at 5.5 sones will be substantially quieter on low speeds (fan speeds are variable), which you would use for general cooktop ventilation.

Another option for alleviating bothersome noise is to duct the range hood up through the roof (provided you don't have a second floor above) and mount an in-line fan in the ductwork in the attic (see the drawing at left), or on the rooftop underneath a cap. This set-up is referred to as a remote blower. Remote-mounted fans are currently not rated for noise levels by the HVI but the consensus is that they do run much quieter than other kitchen exhaust systems. See Resources on pp. 194-197 for a company that offers this type of system.

Exhaust-ventilation options

Now that you know something about kitchen ventilation, let's look at some popular exhaust-ventilation options. To learn more about what's on the market, you can contact manufacturers directly for information about their ventilation appliances (see Resources on pp. 194-197). Collect literature, compare appearances and specifications, and then call nearby dealers to consult with them and compare prices before you buy.

Downdraft systems

You can buy a range or cooktop that incorporates a downdraft exhaust system right in the appliance (see the drawing below). Jenn-Air pioneered the concept, but many other manufacturers now offer it too. In addition to standard stove burners, downdraft cooktops usually offer you the option of inserting different cooking surfaces (called modules) such as a grill or griddle.

Surface-level downdraft fans Surface-level downdraft systems do a fine job of whisking away smoke and odors from grill and griddle modules. They are also effective with pots and pans that are less than 3 in. high, but they don't have the pull to handle vapors from taller pots, or burners that aren't right next to the fan intake. Many people who have appliance downdraft systems say they are difficult to keep clean. They can also be more expensive than a range and conventional exhaust hood.

Pop-up downdraft fans Pop-up downdraft fans get my vote for niftiest ventilation option. When you push a button, a little "wall" rises up about 8 in. off the counter at the back of the cooktop. Along the top front of this wall is an air intake grill. Pop-up fans are separate from the cooktop, and because they have a blower motor underneath, they need a cabinet to fit into—which means these fans can be installed only with drop-in cooktops, not with ranges. As far as the fans' air-handling capability, the

DOWNDRAFT VENTILATION SYSTEMS

Surface-level downdraft fan

Surface-level downdraft fans work well on skillets and saucepans, but are not effective at handling vapors from taller pots.

Pop-up downdraft fan

Pop-up units rise 8 in. to 10 in. above counter at the touch of a button and retract when not in use. They don't work well with pots on front burners.

wall helps to block air crosscurrents, and the higher air intake works better at venting tall pots than a surface-level intake. But the system falls short of effectively handling pots and pans that are on the front burners.

Range hoods

A hood over the range is what most people are used to. Here, you have two options: conventional range hoods and low-profile slide-out hoods (see the drawing below).

Conventional range hoods Conventional range hoods are not sleek or inconspicuous, but they can still be quite stylish. More important, they work. If you are a serious cook and want the best ventilation possible, there is no question that you should get a hood. People on tight budgets can get a good-quality version of the common painted or stainless-steel fixtures that mount under a cabinet. The next step up would be a hood made of wood to blend in with adjoining cabinetry; in these the

OVER-THE-RANGE VENTILATION

Conventional range hood

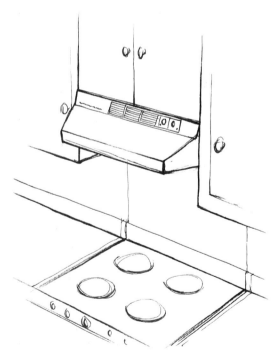

Positioned to capture cooking vapors, conventional range hoods work better than their alternatives.

Low-profile slide-out hood

Low-profile hoods look good, but don't have the holding capacity of conventional hoods.

ventilation equipment is designed to fit up inside. If your budget allows it, you could get a traditional wall or island canopy that hangs by itself. Some of the European canopies have real eye appeal.

Low-profile slide-out hoods If you don't like the look of a traditional hood, you can get an inconspicuous low-profile Euro-style unit that fits under the cabinet above the stovetop. Actually, the unit fits up inside the cabinet over the stove (and takes up most of it) but only a narrow strip shows along the front at the bottom of the cabinet. When you need the vent, you pull out on the strip. It has a tempered glass visor on it that extends out about 6 in. Pulling the visor out automatically turns on a light and the fan. For the light only, you can pull the visor out just a bit. The visor helps with capture and the units do a decent job, but they have very little sump, so the low-profile hood is not as effective as a conventional hood with a blower fan of comparable cfm. Another drawback is that grease collects on the glass visor, and it has to be cleaned regularly.

High-capacity range hoods In the event that your kitchen will have a commercial-style gas range or grill (these are becoming more popular in high-end residential kitchens), you will most certainly want to put in a high-capacity range hood (400 cfm to 600 cfm) because professional-level appliances generate a lot of heat. Most manufacturers of commercial-type stoves make an appropriate hood to go with their appliances. For more on cooking appliances, see pp. 176-187.

WHAT ABOUT HOODS ON BUILT-IN MICROWAVES?

Microwave ovens that are made to be installed above a cooktop against a wall have a ventilation fan in them (see the drawing below). You can modify the fan for ducted or ductless ventilation. We know that ductless filtration isn't of much use, but what about ducted microwave ventilation? Well, these units have a powerful squirrel-cage fan (typically 300 cfm), but no hood to collect air, and they extend over the cooktop only about 13 in. As you might guess, they are efficient only when cooking is done on the back burners of the stove.

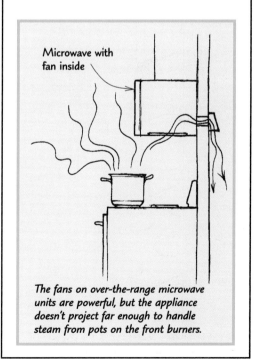

Microwave with fan inside

The fans on over-the-range microwave units are powerful, but the appliance doesn't project far enough to handle steam from pots on the front burners.

CHAPTER 10

CABINETS

Everything in the kitchen fits in and around the cabinets. They are the focal point of the room. They will also probably be the largest single expense in your remodeling project. The challenge in buying cabinetry is not usually in finding a style you like (that's the easy part), but in finding affordable cabinets that give you the best value for your money.

Go into any showroom, and you'll find a vast selection of cabinets. The features, quality, and price of low-end cabinets will be in stark contrast to the high-end offerings. But the overwhelming majority of cabinet lines fall between the high and low extremes, where questions of value and quality become muddled when you start to compare features and prices. To make some sense out of it all, you're going to need to know something about the materials, construction methods, and buying options that enter into this big decision you're faced with. That's what this chapter is all about.

Getting started

The best time to start your search for kitchen cabinets is in the preplanning stages of your project, as discussed in Chapter 2. Contact lots of cabinet manufacturers and request their product literature. One good way to collect literature is simply to call and request it from the many companies that advertise in kitchen idea magazines. Most of those magazines provide a postage-paid reply card that lets you request literature from several manufacturers at once by circling the appropriate numbers and then mailing back the card. Product information is usually free, but sometimes there is a small charge.

All the pretty pictures that arrive in your mailbox will be useful for design and planning purposes whether you are doing your own design or working with a professional. The literature you get also should include a description of how the cabinets are constructed. That is something you'll want to know more about (see the discussion that begins on p. 114). Cabinet manufacturers typically include the names of nearby stores that sell their products. Be aware that when you request information, you may get a follow-up call from those retailers, and that's good too. Just tell them you are in the preplanning stages of a future remodeling project and that you'll be in touch when you're ready.

A picture may be worth a thousand words, but seeing is believing. The important next step is to shop around and look at the different cabinets in several showrooms. See the sidebar at right for some hints on how to make the most of your visits.

Buying options

Besides building your own cabinets from scratch (a subject dealt with in many other books), there are a lot of different ways to get your cabinets. You can buy them ready made from a retail store, where you usually have a choice of stock, custom, and semi-custom lines. You can buy from a local cabinet shop that offers semi-custom and/or custom cabinets. Or you can buy ready-to-assemble (RTA) stock cabinets from a home center. Each choice carries with it questions of price, quality, and style. As is usually the case, so many options can be befuddling. So stick with me while I simplify the process.

Stock cabinets

Stock cabinets are just that—in stock. They are packaged and shelved in a warehouse, ready for delivery. Because of this, stock cabinets are available in a limited selection of sizes and styles. This isn't to say that there aren't many choices when it comes to stock

WHAT TO LOOK FOR AT THE SHOWROOM

Kitchen displays in showrooms are designed to present a line of cabinetry in its best light, but that doesn't mean they can fool you about quality—if you look closely. Don't just glance casually at a kitchen display. Give the cabinets a thorough inspection.

■ Open every door. Do they all open and close smoothly? What does the inside of the cabinet look like? Are the construction joints tight or are there gaps? Does the surface finish on the shelving feel durable?

■ Run your fingertips across the finish on the outside of the doors. Is it silky smooth? Sight across the surface of the doors. Are there drips and specks in the finish? Do you see sanding marks in the wood under the finish?

■ Look carefully at the quality of wood used in the doors. Is it matched for color? If there are glued-together boards in a door panel, are they matched for the best grain appearance?

■ Open every drawer. Do they all operate smoothly and quietly? Pull the drawer out halfway and wiggle it from side to side—is there a lot of slop, or is it relatively solid? Take a drawer out and see how well it's made.

cabinets because there are plenty. One company can have a multitude of different size cabinets and style choices, but those choices are, nevertheless, limited to what their catalogs specify.

As a rule, stock cabinet widths begin at 9 in. and increase in 3-in. increments up to 48 in. That's a pretty wide range of choices. But if you need a 20½-in.-wide cabinet to fill a space, you have to buy an 18-in. cabinet and put in a 2½-in. filler strip (see the drawing below).

Since stock cabinets are made only to predefined standards and specifications, they are manufactured efficiently and inexpen-sively in large quantities. The most inexpensive cabinets you will find are going to be stock cabinets. However, that doesn't mean that all stock cabinets are low quality. Some are, but many others are not, and those others can represent a decent value for your dollar. More about quality shortly.

Depending where you go, stock cabinets may be in stock at the store where you buy. If you have to place an order, the cabinets could take anywhere from a few days to a couple of weeks to come in.

FILLER STRIPS

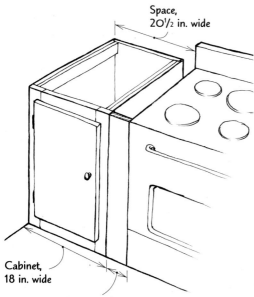

Space, 20½ in. wide

Cabinet, 18 in. wide

Filler strip, 2½ in. wide

If you have a stock cabinet that's too narrow to fill a space, filler strips must be used to take up the slack.

Custom cabinets

Custom cabinets are made to order especially for your kitchen; they have your name on them in the factory. You can have any door style, any finish, any size, any shape—anything! Naturally, custom cabinets are your most expensive cabinet option. And because you'll be spending a premium for them, it's usually safe to assume the quality of construction and materials used will be top-notch (though the quality of different custom lines may still vary).

Some manufacturers offer a line of custom cabinets in addition to their stock line, and you can mix the two in a kitchen. For example, that 20½-in. cabinet space that you see in the drawing at left could be fitted with a custom cabinet 20½ in. wide. It would cost you more than the stock cabinets around it, but you'd eliminate the need for a filler (and the labor to install it), and the resulting arrangement would look better and make more efficient use of storage space.

Custom-cabinet manufacturers market through retail kitchen stores, or you can probably find a small-scale local shop that makes cabinets in your community. If you do go to a local cabinetmaker, be sure to choose one based on the same criteria you'd use for selecting any other contractor (see Chapter 3). Make sure you take a close look at the materials and construction methods as well as inspecting a sample finished cabinet. You also need to consider the subject of warranties. Many large cabinet manufacturers offer lifetime or long-term product warranties; a local shop may or may not make similar offers.

If you go the custom route, it will take 6 to 10 weeks for your order to arrive.

Semi-custom cabinets

Some companies that offer stock and/or custom cabinets also offer a semi-custom line. Unfortunately, different companies interpret the term "semi-custom" in different ways, so it's hard to nail down a pat description, but I'll try.

Semi-custom cabinets offer many of the features of custom cabinets without custom-cabinet prices. Semi-custom cabinets are available in more sizes and styles than stock cabinets, and they typically have some higher-quality features than the average stock cabinet. For example, they may have better-made drawers and slides, or thicker shelving, or more accessory options. Semi-custom cabinets are priced somewhere in the middle, too. If you are looking for higher-quality cabinetry but don't want to pay a custom price, a semi-custom line will have what you're looking for. Lead times for semi-custom cabinets are a little less than for custom lines—about 4 to 6 weeks.

Your local cabinetmaker may offer a version of semi-custom cabinets. Many small cabinet operations buy ready-to-assemble-stock cabinets from a wholesale supplier and assemble them in their shop. If your plan requires a special size cabinet, they can make it from scratch. Cabinet shops that do this won't usually refer to their products as semi-custom; they will consider them to be custom cabinets. It doesn't really matter what they call them as long as you realize the difference and are fully aware of the quality and specifications of the cabinets you're buying. Many ready-to-assemble cabinets are of respectable quality, which brings us to the final cabinet option: buying your own RTA cabinets.

Ready-to-assemble stock cabinets

The first RTA cabinet I ever paid any attention to was one I bought for myself at a discount home center 14 years ago. It was a bathroom vanity cabinet and the price was right, but the thing was a piece of junk. Needless to say, I never bought another one. But the concept of RTA was good, and it was only a matter of time before some manufacturers started to offer RTA cabinets with better-quality features.

The hitch is that for RTA cabinets to be a really good deal, you have to put them together yourself. You wouldn't save much if you had to pay a contractor to do the assembly, because the work can be somewhat time-consuming. Assembling RTA cabinets is not hard (basic hand tools and maybe a drill are all you will need), but you should realize that it will be a Project (that's with a capital P). Each cabinet will come in a box; when you open it you'll find an astounding number of parts and pieces, and the instructions may not be clear without some study. You won't have a kitchenful of cabinets all assembled in an afternoon, but once you figure your way through a couple of cabinets, you'll realize they really are simple to put together. RTA kits are marketed to home-owners as a money-saving option, and you can indeed save money with RTA cabinets—sometimes a lot.

Keep in mind that RTA cabinets are available only in stock sizes, shapes, and styles. And, for the most part, RTA models available to homeowners are for sale only in frameless styles. That brings us to our next topic of discussion.

Face-frame vs. frameless cabinetry

Kitchen cabinets are really nothing more than boxes. They all have a bottom, a back, and two sides. Wall cabinets also have a top to them, while base cabinets usually don't

(the counter serves as the top). Those are the things that all cabinets have in common, but they part company where the doors and drawer fronts fit onto the unit (see the drawing below). Some cabinets have a face frame made of wood that's applied over the front of the box. Others have no face frame; the edges of the top, bottom, and sides serve as the front face. Face-frame cabinets are known as traditional-style cabinets, because that's the way they made them in the old days. Frameless cabinets are a more recent innovation.

Frameless cabinetry originated in Germany after World War II. Also called the 32mm system, it made efficient use of labor and materials, and resulted in a cabinet that was relatively inexpensive and durable—and didn't have a traditional face frame. The frameless cabinet (or Euro-style cabinet, as it's sometimes called) differs from face-frame cabinetry in many ways, but its chief distinguishing feature is full-overlay doors and

TWO BASIC TYPES

Face-frame cabinet

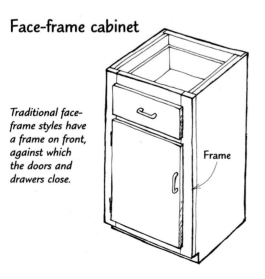

Traditional face-frame styles have a frame on front, against which the doors and drawers close.

Frame

Frameless cabinet

Frameless cabinets, also called Euro-style, have no frame, so drawers and slide-out shelves can be wider.

drawer fronts. The spaces between the doors and drawers, when closed, are typically very small—⅛ in. or less. With traditional-style cabinets, the spaces between doors are often 1 in. or more.

Euro-style cabinets were slow to catch on in the United States because the construction methods were so different that they required substantial (and expensive) retooling for American cabinetmaking shops. By the mid-1950s some brave U.S. shops had adapted, but it wasn't until the 1970s that Euro-style cabinets really gained a foothold here. Now, about one-third of all new cabinets sold in the United States are frameless. Although early Euro-style cabinets typically had flat, white, plastic-laminate-clad fronts with a strip of wood for a handle, today's frameless cabinetry can sport any type of door.

Whether you opt for Euro-style or traditional face-frame cabinets will depend a lot on which looks better to you, but there are some practical considerations, too. First, frameless cabinets usually cost less, especially if you decide to put together your own RTA units. Second, frameless cabinets allow better access to the interior of the cabinets. The average traditional face frame is about 1¾ in. wide and the frameless cabinet face is ¾ in. wide, so on each traditional cabinet, the opening is at least 2 in. narrower. You don't actually lose the space inside the cabinet, but you do lose the width on drawers and slide-out shelving.

A third consideration is door swing. Euro-style cabinet doors have cup hinges, and some cup-style hinges will allow the door to swing open only 95°, while others allow a 175° swing. I wouldn't recommend a door swing of less than 110°. Cup hinges are invisible when the cabinets are closed. Traditional leaf hinges are visible from the front of the cabinets, at least to some degree, and swing is not an issue. They open until something gets in their way.

Plywood vs. particleboard

Beyond the face frame (or lack of face frame) is the issue of materials. The big choice is between plywood (which in this context is called "solid wood") or wood-composite materials, such as particleboard and medium-density fiberboard (MDF). Plywood has clear advantages, but composite materials, with a couple of caveats, can function equally well for cabinet boxes.

There is a stigma attached to particleboard cabinets because for many years the most inexpensive traditional-style cabinets have been made of particleboard, and they have not performed well. The bad reputation is not entirely undeserved, but it so happens that some very good-quality cabinet lines have particleboard in their boxes.

This is something of a confusing dichotomy, until you know a little bit more about particleboard and cabinet construction.

Particleboard has great dimensional stability, so the cabinets go together square and true and stay that way for many years. Particleboard also costs less than plywood. However, particleboard is not as strong as plywood (see the sidebar on p. 116), and if it gets water on it, it swells up and rots away faster than any other wood product I know of. The problem usually manifests itself in sink bases when plumbing connections start to drip (as they invariably do) or on shelves, when glasses and dishes are put away before they are completely dry. Inexpensive particleboard cabinets have a very thin paper-like covering (often with a wood-grain pattern) that scratches easily and does almost nothing to protect the wood from water. Better cabinets have a vinyl covering; 2-mil vinyl is considered skimpy, a 4-mil covering is much better.

Another possibility is a melamine coating. Melamine is a plastic with superior water and abrasion resistance. It is similar in durability to the plastic laminate used to make countertops. Euro-style cabinets are usually constructed with melamine-coated particleboard. Plywood cabinets can have vinyl, melamine, or a sprayed-on polyurethane finish, which is a decent finish too.

Overall construction standards for Euro-style cabinet boxes are similar, so the biggest spread in box quality is found in traditional face-frame cabinets. I don't want to bury you under the minutiae of cabinet construction, so I'll just offer a few suggestions.

If you want traditional face-frame cabinets, go for plywood construction if you can afford it. For a given thickness and method of

THE CABINET THAT FELL APART

I once installed a kitchenful of cabinets that had nice-looking hardwood doors and face frames, but the cabinets were made of particleboard. A few days after the installation, the homeowner called and said one of the cabinets (a 12-in. wall unit) had fallen apart. "What exactly do you mean?," I asked. "The cabinet is broken," she said. "You mean the door has a crack in it?" "No," she said, "the door is fine but the cabinet fell apart."

I assumed we had a communication problem—new cabinets don't just fall apart. But when I got there and looked at it, I found that every joint in the box was broken and the unit was very close to falling off the wall. How did such a thing happen? The homeowner had packed it solid with canned food, and the weight was more than the cabinet could bear. That's the sort of disaster that has given particleboard a bad name.

However, that cabinet didn't fall apart just because it was made of particleboard. It fell apart because it was constructed with ⅜-in. particleboard that was held together with hot-melt glue and staples. Had the cabinet instead been made of ⅝-in. or ¾-in. particleboard (as most frameless cabinets are), and had the pieces been joined with dowels or special particleboard joint connectors (standard in frameless construction), there is little doubt that the cabinet would have been able to handle the load. In frameless or in traditional cabinets, thicker particleboard and stronger construction methods make all the difference in the world.

construction, plywood will always be stronger and inherently more resistant to water. The general consensus is that plywood is better than wood composites. If you intend to sell your house, plywood cabinets are considered something of a selling point.

If you can't afford plywood construction, don't worry about it. Particleboard cabinets should hold up well; they won't fall apart on you unless, maybe, you stuff a grocery cart full of canned food into one 12-in.-wide wall unit. Get the thickest particleboard you can afford (⅝ in. is good, ¾ in. is better). Get a 4-mil vinyl coating on the interior. Make sure the shelves are adjustable and at least ⅝ in. thick. Look for well-made drawers, good hardware, and a good finish on the doors (I'll have more to say about these last three things shortly).

In addition, if you can find particleboard cabinets with wood hanging rails (where you put screws through to attach cabinets to the wall), that's better than particleboard rails. And gusset blocks (placed in the top corners of base cabinets to give stability) of wood or metal are preferable to blocks of plastic or particleboard. These two things are not major buying considerations, but it is better to have a little "real" wood strategically placed in a particleboard cabinet.

One final suggestion: If the exposed side of a particleboard cabinet has an imitation wood-grain paper or a vinyl covering, buy a plywood panel to cover it (side panels are sold as cabinet accessories). The whole thing will look much better.

Drawers

Drawers get a lot of use, and if you have children, drawers can get a lot of abuse. Because of this, they tend to be one of the first things that fail on a cabinet. That's why you should opt for cabinets with the best drawers you can afford. If you buy a semi-custom or custom cabinet line, you're virtually assured of getting good-quality drawers and drawer slides, but with stock cabinets, that's not necessarily the case.

With all of that in mind, my first recommendation is to avoid drawers made with particleboard. If you can't afford anything else, make sure the sides are at least ⅝ in. thick. Otherwise, solid wood—either plywood or regular lumber—is best because the material is more durable and the joints used to connect the four sides of the drawer box will be stronger. When drawers are made of lumber, a hardwood like maple or birch is stronger and more desirable than a softwood like pine. The thickness of solid-wood drawer sides should not be less than ½ in.; ⅝ in. or ¾ in. is better.

Steer clear of drawer boxes with only three sides and a front that serves double duty as the front of the drawer box (see the drawing on p. 118). They don't hold up as well as a drawer with four sides, to which the front is then fastened on with screws from the back.

Drawer bottoms should be at least ¼-in.-thick plywood. If the plywood has a durable melamine layer on it, that's a nice feature; 4-mil vinyl or a varnish is decent too. Drawers that are wider that 30 in. should have thicker bottoms or an extra support piece under the center.

DRAWER CONSTRUCTION

Fronts

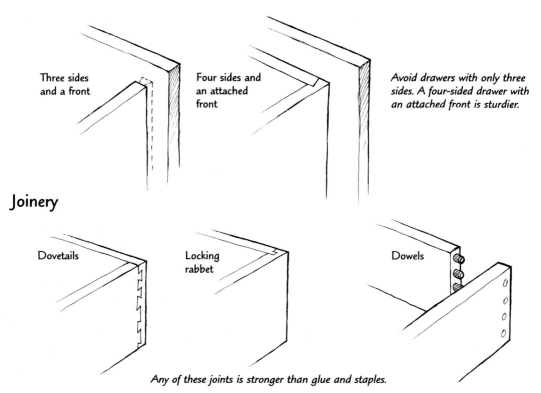

Three sides and a front

Four sides and an attached front

Avoid drawers with only three sides. A four-sided drawer with an attached front is sturdier.

Joinery

Dovetails

Locking rabbet

Dowels

Any of these joints is stronger than glue and staples.

It's best if the joint used at the corners of the drawers has some sort of interlocking feature, like dovetails, a locking rabbet, or even dowels. All these joints hold a drawer together equally well, even though the market perception is that dovetails are superior. Avoid drawers joined with glue and staples.

Drawer slides

Drawer slides are as important as drawer-box construction when it comes to the function and longevity of the drawer. If you do opt for

particleboard drawers, at least get them with good slides. Fortunately, most cabinet manufacturers now use Euro-style slides that fit along each side of the drawer and roll smoothly on roller bearings (see the drawing on the facing page). Another respectable slide that's becoming popular is the Euro-style undermount. It uses two slides that are similar in construction and operation to conventional side-mounted Euro-style slides, but they attach completely out of sight under the drawer. When you compare specifications, you'll see that all slides are rated for a certain load, and the drawers you buy should have slides rated for at least 75 lb.

The top-of-the-line Euro-style option is the metal drawer system. The sides of the drawers are durable aluminum or epoxy-coated steel and have part of the slide integrated into them. Make it a point to check them out when you're in a kitchen showroom. Metabox is the brand name used by one popular manufacturer, Julius Blum.

Most drawers that are outfitted with Euro-style slides are of the three-quarter-extension type. You won't be able to pull the drawers all

the way out, but three-quarters of the way is usually enough. Full-extension slides are nice, but a kitchen full of them can be expensive, so you might want to put them on only a few drawers (this would be an option with semi-custom and custom lines). Speaking of extension, take note of how long the drawers themselves are from back to front. Some cabinet lines cheat a bit and don't make their drawers as long as they could be.

DRAWER-SLIDE OPTIONS

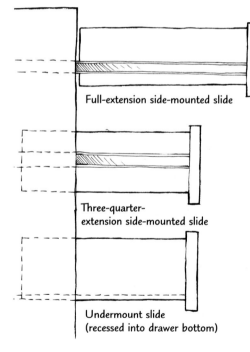

Full-extension side-mounted slide

Three-quarter-extension side-mounted slide

Undermount slide (recessed into drawer bottom)

Full-extension slides allow the greatest accessibility to the contents of the drawer.

Shelving

Cabinet shelves are usually made of particleboard, and their thickness varies among cabinet lines. Thicker shelving is better, especially in a wide cabinet, because it won't sag the way a thinner shelf would. The minimum shelf thickness you should consider is 5/8 in.; 3/4 in. is, of course, preferable. Plywood shelves are considerably stiffer than particleboard shelves of the same thickness. Adjustable shelving is more desirable than fixed shelving. In the standard base cabinet, it's common to have a single shelf that's only half as deep as the cabinet, but some cabinet lines give you the option of a full-depth shelf. Better yet are slide-out shelves, which are discussed on p. 124.

Doors

Much of the cost of manufacturing cabinets is in the doors, and when you go to a kitchen showroom it's usually the doors that catch your eye. You'll be treated to a range of designs, from plain to ornate. When it comes to style, there isn't much I can say—just choose something that appeals to you. So here we'll focus on the pros and cons of the various materials—plastic laminate, vinyl, and wood—and the various construction methods. These practical considerations will help you make a wise decision, whatever style door you want.

Plastic laminate

Plastic-laminate doors are made of the same sheet material used on countertops, but because doors don't get the wear action that a countertop gets, the laminate is thinner. Plastic laminate is used on flat door styles, such as the classic Euro-style mentioned on p. 115. The material is glued to both sides of a wood-composite coreboard, and the edges are banded with a matching vinyl strip.

The beauty of plastic laminate as a door material is that it is durable and easy to clean. The disadvantage is that if the vinyl edge banding is abused, it can chip off. Edge banding can be replaced, but chips and other damage to the laminate itself can not be repaired.

Some doors that look like plastic-laminate doors really aren't. What you get is not true laminate, but a thin layer of paper with a coating of clear melamine, similar to the melamine coating on the inside of some cabinets. Although melamine on the inside of a cabinet is just fine, it doesn't have anywhere near the durability of true plastic laminate (see p. 127). Don't buy doors that are faced with melamine.

Vinyl-clad

Vinyl-clad doors, also known as RTF (rigid thermal foil) doors, have become popular in recent years. The vinyl is a sheet of PVC plastic that is heated up and formed around a door blank of MDF. RTF doors usually look like raised-panel wood doors; the design is cut into the door blank using expensive computer-operated routing machines. When the vinyl is applied, it conforms to the shape and wraps around the edges; the final product closely resembles a painted door. The vinyl is considerably more durable than paint, and the doors cost less than genuine painted wood doors. The backs of RTF doors are always flat and have a melamine coating.

Wood

As popular as laminate and vinyl doors are in some markets, most people still want wood doors in their kitchen. People like the "warmth" of wood, and people like the idea of using a natural material. Yet because it is a natural material, it is never perfectly uniform in appearance. Random grain patterns and mineral discoloration are to be expected, especially if the wood doors you select have a clear finish on them. It's not uncommon for customers to complain that they don't like the way the grain pattern or color looks on a certain door in their kitchen. Unfortunately, no cabinet manufacturer will guarantee you that you'll be pleased with the way the grain looks on every door. It's the nature of the material to be quirky.

Nevertheless, on better-quality wood doors, the natural grain color and patterns will be more carefully matched up. If you don't want a lot of grain to show, you can opt for a darker stain, which helps to obscure natural color variations in the wood.

If you think you might like cabinets with painted doors, keep in mind that a frame-and-panel door that is painted will develop a hairline crack where the rails and stiles of the door frame meet. These cracks are the result of opposing dimensional movement in the pieces of wood (wood is always expanding and contracting a little in response to changes in temperature and humidity). It's not a structural problem—but it may well be an aesthetic one. I once had a customer who was miffed that her white painted doors developed paint cracks at the joints. I had warned her to expect cracking if she chose painted doors, and reminded her of it when the little cracks showed up. "But my friend has painted doors and they never cracked," she said. It turned out her friend's doors were vinyl clad.

The dimensional instability of natural wood (as opposed to wood-composite panels, which are inherently more stable) can also lead to warping. If this happens, one corner of the door will touch the cabinet when it closes and the other won't. A little bit of warp (usually up to ¼ in.) is considered normal and acceptable, and the contractor can usually make some adjustments with the cabinet hinges to ease the problem. If a door warps much more than that (which is rare), the cabinet manufacturer should replace the door for you.

Wood doors are relatively durable, depending on the type of wood. The three most popular door woods are oak, maple, and cherry—all three are harder than pine, which is downright soft in comparison.

Finishes You want to be discriminating when it comes to the finish used on the fronts and exterior surfaces of wood cabinets, because the quality of finish has a lot to do with how good the doors look and how long they will continue to look that way. Whatever kind of

VENEERED SOLID-WOOD DOORS?

Some wood doors appear to be constructed of solid wood but actually are made by gluing wood veneer over a wood-composite core. This is not only done with flat "slab" door styles, but also very convincingly with raised-panel doors. You can tell if a door is veneer over a wood-composite material by looking at the grain pattern on the front and back of the door. If the doors are "genuine" solid wood, the grain patterns will correspond.

The advantages to veneered doors are that they cost less than solid-wood units (or they should cost less), and the quality of the veneer grain is usually as good as or better than the best solid-wood doors. Although the market perception is that veneered panel doors are not as good as a solid-wood raised panels, they are in fact good doors for the money. But you do want to know which type you're buying.

wood door that you choose, be sure it has a conversion varnish or catalyzed lacquer finish. If the finish is "oven cured," that is even better because it will be harder and more durable. Steer clear of traditional lacquer finishes because they are nowhere near as durable as catalyzed versions. In addition, lacquer requires periodic waxing to keep it looking good. The newer generation of finishes needs just a spray-cleaner polish (something made especially for wood) to keep the cabinets looking spiffy.

CABINET REFACING

Cabinet refacing is a concept that caught on sometime in the 1970s, and it has become an increasingly popular kitchen remodeling option over the years. The quality and availability of refacing materials, as well as refacing skills, have evolved to a higher standard in that time. Refacing is now a reputable craft. The great attraction is that you get essentially a brand-new kitchen at less cost than having your old cabinets ripped out and replaced. The work is also less messy and can be done in less time.

If you are a homeowner with basic carpentry skills, refacing your own kitchen cabinets is a feasible do-it-yourself project. Here's how it works, in a nutshell:

Cabinet refacing involves replacing old doors and drawer fronts with brand-new ones. As part of the process, the cabinet sides—and sometimes the bottoms—are sheathed with a hardwood plywood finished to match the new doors. The cabinet faces are resurfaced with a flexible wood veneer (which, if properly applied, will stay in place for the life of the kitchen).

Before refacing, you can do a lot of things to improve the efficiency of your old kitchen, as well as make it look brand new. Cabinets can be added to the kitchen, and old cabinets can be modified to improve access or accommodate new appliances. New drawers or slide-out shelves can be installed. You can also change the appearance of your kitchen to whatever new style you want. Does it sound like I'm big on refacing? Well, I am. I started offering cabinet refacing to my customers as an option six years ago, and the response has been overwhelmingly positive. Many of my cabinet refacing projects have been for customers who could easily have afforded completely new cabinetry, but they were attracted to the practical value of refacing.

If you want to do your own refacing, there are numerous suppliers that will make custom-sized doors, new drawers, and even extra cabinets if you need them. For how-to information, many reface suppliers offer instructional videos, help sheets, and technical phone assistance. See Resources on pp. 194-197 for a comprehensive how-to book on the subject.

The nice thing about doors that have a stain or clear finish is that minor surface damage is usually less noticeable than on laminate, vinyl, or painted wood doors. Scratches and dings can also be repaired more easily and successfully in natural wood. Looking long term, if you ever need to re-place a door or add a cabinet, any wood-working shop should be able to match a wood door style and color, but that may not be the case with vinyl or laminate doors. The color or pattern may not be available, or, even if it is, the old material may be faded noticeably compared to the new.

If you want to hire some-one to reface your kitchen cabinets, here are some things to consider:

■ Be wary of large franchise-type refacing outfits. Most send out well-trained sales-people, charge an exorbitant price, and offer a limited se-lection of door types. This isn't to say such companies won't do a decent job; it's just that there may be better alternatives.

■ Look for a local trades-person who has been re-modeling kitchens for years and offers refacing as an option. You want someone who is more of a multi-talented kitchen remodeler than a salesperson or refacing "mechanic." See pp. 33-39 for help on finding a reputable contractor.

■ Beware of the "plastic pitch." If your heart yearns for solid-wood doors in cherry (very nice), don't let the refacer sell you similar-style plastic-laminate doors with an imitation-wood-grain pattern. Some refacers don't offer wood doors because they are more trouble to deal with and more expensive than the plastic ones. They may say plastic is better be-cause it's more durable and easy to clean (true state-ments), but no plastic wood-grain door looks the same as real wood. Buy laminate doors if you want to, but don't be pressured into it.

■ Invest some time in get-ting prices, and compare the difference between refacing and replacing. On a very complex job, you may be better off remodeling with decent-quality new cabinets.

■ Most refacers apply ve-neer to the face of the frame only, but some cover the faces and then wrap the ve-neer around the inside edges of the frame. That way, when you open the cabinet door, your cabinet faces look com-pletely new, not just covered over. Though it may cost a bit more, wrapped veneer looks better and lasts longer.

■ Whatever wood you choose, if you opt for a light or natural finish, be sure to have doors made with a Select grade of lumber, which will have very few natural blemishes and a more uniform grain. If you decide on oak doors (proba-bly the most popular kitchen wood), northern-grown red oak is widely regarded to be better looking than southern-grown oak.

Door and drawer pulls

Pulls, also referred to as knobs or handles, are another style choice for you to make, but there are practical considerations also. Some people opt not to have pulls, but if you have wood doors, I strongly urge you to get some sort of grasp-and-open hardware. The alternative is the grope-and-open approach, which will leave dirt smudges and lead to fingernail wear around the edges. Even with pulls, it's common to get nail wear on the fronts after many years, but a good finish on the door will help to minimize the problem. Bright brass pulls look nice when new, but they may get tarnished. Some companies warranty the finish, and it's something to consider.

Some cabinet companies include pulls (or a selection for you to choose from) in the price of the cabinets, while others don't. If you have to supply the pulls, be sure to include the extra cost in your budget. The cost of pulls for an average kitchen can easily run over $100—a kitchen designer I know once had a client who spent $800 for pulls.

Accessories

Cabinet accessories are items inside cabinets that aid in organization or accessibility. Lazy Susans in corner cabinets have been a popular accessory for many years, and I think they're perfect for corner base cabinets. Slide-out shelves are equally useful in regular base cabinets because they make it easy to get at the items in the cabinet, especially things toward the back. A flip-down sink front with a tray on the back side makes use of an otherwise wasted space by providing a spot to stash sponges and scrub brushes. Slide-out trash receptacles and recycling bins are also very practical and useful. There are accessory racks of all kinds that can be added into cabinets: spice racks, knife racks, glass racks, towel racks, wine racks—if you want a rack for something, you can probably find it. Cutlery drawer organizers have become quite popular in recent years, too.

Accessories might come pre-installed from the cabinet manufacturer, but some stock lines may not have a wide selection. In any event, as helpful as accessories can be, they can also be somewhat expensive if they are pre-installed by the cabinet manufacturer. You can often save money by buying accessories through mail-order catalogs (see Resources on pp. 194-197) and at home centers for less than cabinet companies sell them for, and you can install them yourself when the kitchen is done. If you buy accessories for a contractor to put in, be sure to include this task in your job description (see pp. 26-29).

CHAPTER 11

COUNTERTOPS

We demand a lot from our countertops. Not only must they be attractive, but they must be exceptionally durable, sanitary, easy to keep clean, and affordable as well. For centuries, wood, stone, and tile were the only countertop choices. Before World War II, the modern countertop consisted of a sheet of linoleum laid on top of boards or plywood, with a chrome strip nailed over the edges. It wasn't until the building boom of the late 1940s and early 1950s that plastic laminate, under the brand name Formica, arrived on the scene. The stuff was practically an overnight sensation. Everyone had to have a Formica countertop and, before long, just about everyone did. Now, half a century later, most kitchens still have laminate counters—and with good reason.

The next significant development in countertops came in the late 1960s, with the advent of solid-surface material (Corian, by DuPont, was the first). This new plastic was much more durable than plastic laminate, yet it was not an immediate success primarily because of its high cost and limited range of colors (white and almond).

Now, on the brink of a new century, we find the choices for countertops have evolved, and at the same time, returned full circle. Plastic laminate still gets the largest share of the countertop market and has been improved in some ways. Solid-surface material has become a tad less costly, and there is a much broader choice of colors and patterns to choose from. There is even a new breed of countertops—solid-surface overlay, which has qualities of both laminate and solid surface. And natural stone, such as granite, and tile are experiencing a tremendous resurgence of popularity.

The good news (or the bad news—depending on how you look at it) is that you have a lot of countertop options to choose from. There is no single product that is beautiful to all people's eyes, affordable for all people's budgets, and at the same time, durable and maintenance free. There never will be. Your job as a remodeling homeowner is to consider the pros and cons of each counter material. My job as your advisor is to cut through the marketing hype and misconceptions that surround each of these materials so you can make the best possible choice for your own situation.

Keep in mind as you read through this chapter that all the countertops in your kitchen don't have to be made of the same material. Different materials can be combined in the same kitchen. Some materials are better suited to certain tasks than others (for example, stone is revered as a superior surface for rolling out dough). And some materials might simply be too costly to use for an entire kitchen, yet affordable for a short section of countertop.

This chapter will focus on the five most popular categories of countertop materials, starting with the most affordable: plastic laminate, tile, wood, solid surface, and stone.

ANATOMY OF PLASTIC LAMINATE

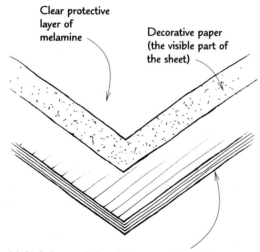

Clear protective layer of melamine

Decorative paper (the visible part of the sheet)

Multiple layers of phenolic-impregnated kraft paper (the dark-colored back of the sheet)

Plastic laminate

Many people are surprised to hear that a product referred to as plastic laminate is primarily a paper laminate. It consists of several layers of phenolic (plastic) saturated kraft paper (which make up the dark back of the sheet) topped off with a colorful top layer of paper (the visible top of the sheet); over that is a clear protective layer of melamine plastic (see the drawing below left). The materials are collated and fused into a solid sheet under heat and high pressure. To fabricate a countertop, the plastic sheets are glued over a wood underlayment. Plastic laminate is a remarkable product. For the price, there is no better value on the market.

Colors and textures

There are hundreds of different patterns, colors, and textures of laminate to choose from, so here's some practical advice to narrow down the possibilities. Dark solid colors will show dust and minor scratches more than light or neutral colors. Beyond colors, there are texture choices. The smoothest textures create a glossy surface. Then there are matte finishes and progressively deeper textures, ranging from small "crystal" surfaces to rough-grained "slate" faces. In the kitchen, I recommend a matte texture. Although gloss finishes are more appealing initially, they are not practical for work surfaces because they will show wear. Rougher textures are equally impractical because the "valleys" tend to collect grime, and they don't just wipe clean—you have to get after them with a soft bristle brush.

Durability

Plastic-laminate countertops will last a long time if they are properly cared for. I've seen inexpensive post-formed counters that were in almost pristine condition after 20 years of use, as well as more expensive custom counters that were so beat up after one year that they needed to be replaced.

One major concern, especially on white or light-colored tops, is staining. If left to soak in, ordinary liquids such as grape juice and coffee may discolor the laminate. Such stains should never be attacked with abrasive cleansers or undiluted bleach, which will damage the surface as they remove the stain. Instead, you should consult the manufacturer's instructions for care and maintenance.

More serious staining can be caused by hair dyes, or drain and oven cleaners. Surprisingly, even mild cleaning agents that are acidic or alkaline can lead to etching, if left on the surface for long. Blemishes left from such chemicals cannot be removed or repaired. Rust is another thing that can stain laminate, and it often comes from leaving steel-wool pads on the counter too long. All of these things are threats, but if you clean up spills quickly and keep harsh chemicals away from the laminate, it will continue to look great for many years.

Laminate is a tough material, but it is far from indestructible. If you place hot pans directly on it, the plastic may delaminate. A lit cigarette can burn the material, and knife cuts can scar it. Laminate can chip if you drop a heavy object on it. Thinner laminates are more prone to impact damage than thicker laminates. Trivets and cutting boards are a must with plastic-laminate countertops.

Laminate comes in three grades: vertical, horizontal, and post-form. The thinnest, vertical grade, is used on cabinet doors and sometimes cabinet sides, where impact is less of a problem. Post-form grade is the next thickest and is used to make post-form countertops (more about this on p. 128). Horizontal grade is the thickest of the three. If you have a counter custom made, you should specify that it be made of horizontal-grade laminate. Most professional fabricators do this as a rule, but I have heard that some use thinner materials.

As for resistance to abrasion and scuffing, you can get laminates that have a higher wear resistance. All laminate manufacturers offer a special high-wear laminate that's claimed to be five times more durable than their standard lines. This more durable material costs about 30% more. But, because the cost of laminate is only a fraction of the cost of having a custom top made, the upgrade is worth considering.

A completely different high-wear option is plastic laminate that has the color all the way through it instead of just on the top. By using colored papers and resins, it's possible to make a solid-color laminate (not to be confused with solid-surface overlays, which are discussed on p. 139). With these laminates, chips and scratches are less noticeable because there is no dark phenolic back to show through. And there is no black line along the counter edge. Solid-color laminates are available in only a limited selection of colors, and they are about three times more expensive than general-purpose laminate. They require more complicated fabrication procedures, and the seams are still somewhat evident.

The finished price of a solid-color laminate top is more than standard laminate and less than solid surface.

Post-formed counters

There are a few different ways that plastic-laminate countertops are made (see the drawing below), and of these, a post-formed counter will be your least costly option. It is made by heating a sheet of post-form-grade laminate and wrapping it around a particleboard core. The nicest thing about a post-formed counter is that one single piece of laminate covers the front edge of the countertop and backsplash; there are no separate pieces, and therefore no seams. On the down side, post-formed tops can be made only in straight sections, and when you need to turn a corner, two straight sections of counter will have to be bolted together and glued. The joints rarely line up perfectly and never look all that great. What's more, if you install a

post-formed counter on cabinets at a corner that is not perfectly square (and few are), it can be difficult, sometimes impossible, to get a good fit at the back wall while maintaining a tight joint in the corner. So I strongly recommend that if you have anything more than a straight run of cabinets, you should seriously consider a custom laminate top.

Custom counters

A custom laminate top is made to fit the unique layout of your kitchen. Instead of laminating over a premade postform underlayment, the underlayment is made to size using sheets of particleboard. The standard custom top will have a square front edge with plastic laminate on it. Backsplashes are not integral; they are made separately and attached to the counter (see the sidebar on the facing page).

Custom counters cost about twice as much as post-formed counters, but the cost

TYPES OF LAMINATE COUNTERTOPS

Post-formed counter

Custom counter

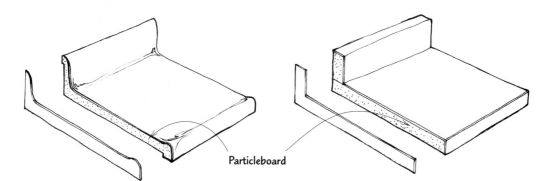

Particleboard

In a post-formed counter, there is no seam at the backsplash, and the edges are rounded.

In a custom square-edge counter, there are separate pieces of laminate on the edge, top, and backsplash.

A backsplash is a durable surface positioned at the back of a countertop, usually on or against a wall (see the drawing at right). Although the backsplash is a decorative element in the kitchen, it should also serve the practical purpose of protecting the wall from objects that might be pushed back against it, as well as seal the wall/counter junction against water penetration. The backsplash can be a few inches high, like the integral backsplash found on a post-formed countertop, or it can be extended all the way from the counter surface to the underside of the wall cabinets. Ceramic tile or a sheet of plastic laminate applied directly to the wall can make a durable and sensible backsplash.

Custom laminate tops often have an attached backsplash about 4 in. high that is made of plastic laminate glued over ¾-in. particleboard. The method of attachment is important. Backsplashes should be fastened directly to the counter, not glued to the counter and wall with silicone adhesive caulk. Glued backsplashes rarely hold up over the long haul, and a gap usually opens up at the counter, allowing water to seep in (especially behind the sink) and really do a job on the particleboard. One of the best ways to have a backsplash put on is with backsplash clips. Fabricators who use these swear by them. But many fabricators don't use them because they either don't know about them, don't realize the value of using them, or don't want to spend the little bit of time and extra money to put them on.

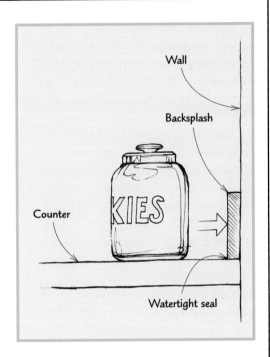

Solid-surface counters can have an attached backsplash or an integral backsplash. The attached backsplash is glued on with silicone, and the joint is caulked. Eventually, it will probably need to be re-caulked. An integral backsplash (sometimes referred to as a cove splash) is glued and formed directly into the counter. A solid-surface cove splash is preferable to a silicone-attached backsplash, but it is also more expensive.

Never use wood for a backsplash behind a sink. Rarely does the wood look good after a few years of exposure to water, no matter how well it's finished.

is still affordable to most budgets and you do get a better fitting product with a thicker laminate. Custom edges on the counter is another option (which I'll discuss shortly).

Because a custom counter is made just for you, you can specify exactly how you want it to look. It's worth spending some time thinking about seams, front overhangs, and custom edges now, during the planning stage, to get exactly the detailing you want.

Seams Seams in a custom top are only between pieces of laminate, not between whole sections of countertop. With the power tools and experience that fabricators now have, today's laminate seams can be made tighter and less conspicuous than on older counters and certainly better looking than seams between sections of a post-formed top (see the drawing below). Even so, the ideal is to avoid seams. The largest piece of general-purpose laminate that can be purchased is 5 ft. by 12 ft.; if your countertop fits within that size, you won't need a seam. For example, if

your counter is L-shaped with a 12-ft. leg and a 5-ft. leg, no seams will be needed. Of course, depending on the counter layout, laminate material will sometimes be left over when a big sheet is used, but that's okay; it's worth buying a little extra material to avoid a seam. If you anticipate this size restriction for making seamless laminate tops early in the kitchen design process, it might be possible to come up with a cabinet layout that allows all your countertops to be made with no surface seams.

If a seam can't be avoided, it should be put in an inconspicuous place—not, for example, directly through an eat-at peninsula countertop. I try to position seams through a sink or cooktop where only a couple of inches of the joint will show. Some fabricators avoid seaming in these places because they've had problems with water seeping into the seam and swelling the particleboard. That is a possibility, but if the seam is made tight and has plenty of glue under it, water penetration shouldn't be a problem. I've been seaming

THE FEWER SEAMS, THE BETTER

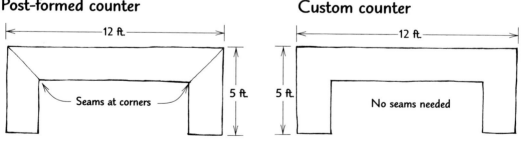

Post-formed counter

12 ft.

Seams at corners

5 ft.

Post-formed counters are made only in straight sections, so seams are unavoidable if the counter changes direction.

Custom counter

12 ft.

5 ft.

No seams needed

If the base-cabinet section doesn't exceed 5 ft. by 12 ft. overall, any shape can be cut out of a single large sheet of laminate.

through the sink area on countertops for nearly 20 years without any problems (that I'm aware of). In any event, the placement of seams is something to discuss with your fabricator.

Front overhangs With custom countertops, you can have a sizable overhang at the front edge of the cabinets. Countertop depth on the average post-formed counter is 25 in., which is only 1 in. deeper than a standard cabinet. But door and drawer fronts often project ⅞ in. from the front of the cabinet, and that means spilled liquids often drip down the face of the doors. Knowing that, if you make an overhang of 1½ in. to 2 in. (see the drawing at right), you will give the fronts better cover and even increase the total working surface of your counter by a couple of square feet. The added depth does not look odd or obvious.

If you have an extended overhang (12 in. to 14 in.) on an eat-at counter, have the fabricator reinforce under the cantilevered area with a solid piece of ¾-in. plywood that extends back over the top of the cabinets. It will make all the difference in the world in the stiffness of the counter. Another support option for counter overhangs is a decorative bracket underneath.

Edge treatments A square front edge of plastic laminate is referred to as a self edge. On a custom laminate counter, you also have the option of a wood front edge or a bevel-edge laminate molding, or even an edge of solid-surface material.

Wood has a practical advantage over laminate. If it is banged into, it will only dent, whereas laminate may chip. Dents in wood are less noticeable and can be repaired; in laminate, dents can't be mended. If you opt for wood edges, they will have to be periodically resealed. And if the wood is applied by butting it up to the laminate, the top joint is prone to water damage. A more practical wood edge approach is to have the fabricator

OVERHANGS

A generous overhang will protect the door and drawer fronts below from spills.

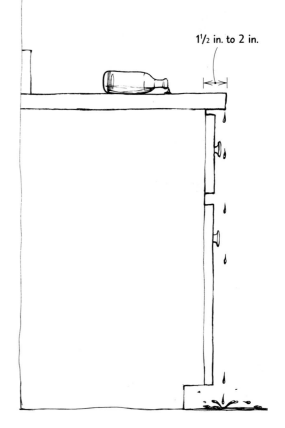

1½ in. to 2 in.

WOOD EDGE OPTIONS FOR LAMINATE COUNTERS

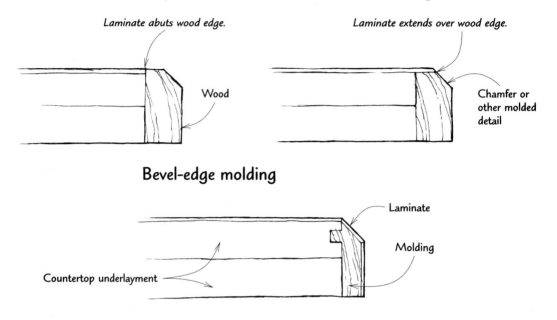

Flush-butted wood edge

Laminate abuts wood edge.

Wood

Laminate over wood edge

Laminate extends over wood edge.

Chamfer or
other molded
detail

Bevel-edge molding

Laminate

Molding

Countertop underlayment

put the piece of wood on before the laminate, run the laminate over the wood, and use a router to shape the edge (see the drawing above).

Bevel-edge moldings are used to create bevel-edge countertops. Besides the more stylish look of the bevel edge, the molding eliminates the dark phenolic stripe that comes with a self-edge top. Laminate patterns with a bevel have a monolithic appearance and can sometimes resemble solid-surface counters.

A bevel edge is a nice laminate upgrade, but there are two important things to be aware of and discuss with your fabricator. First, some laminate fabricators glue the molding on with contact cement, because

it's convenient (no clamping necessary), but that is not considered proper. The edges should be attached with a water-resistant wood glue, which is stronger than contact cement. Second, the edges of the molding must meet up to the counter with great precision to avoid revealing any dark phenolic paper. Occasionally that degree of precision is not entirely possible, and the phenolic may show as a very thin line in a spot or two. This is purely an aesthetic issue, and it's apparent only with light-colored laminates. A dark-colored top with a light-colored bevel, or vice versa, will mask any dark lines.

132

Solid-surface edges, which are relatively new, come as moldings, and, like bevel-edge moldings, are applied using a special adhesive supplied by the edge manufacturer. The moldings cover the dark core of the laminate and allow a lot more edge design possibilities than laminate because different profiles can be routed into the solid-surface edge. Solid-surface material is durable and not affected by water, so it is a practical alternative to wood.

Tile

For only a little more money than laminate (and sometimes less), you can give your kitchen an upscale custom countertop by using tile. Tile has a lot going for it. The material is very durable, waterproof and easy to clean. You can set hot pots directly on tile—no trivets, no burn marks. Tile is hard, but not indestructible. If you drop a cast-iron skillet on a tile countertop, you may break or chip a tile, but the damaged tile can be removed and replaced (that's why you should order a little extra tile and grout, and keep them on hand).

Another nice thing is that tiling a countertop is not too difficult. Most homeowners can do a decent job of it even if they have never worked with tile before—as long as they take the time to educate themselves (see Resources on pp. 194-197). The big concern with a tile countertop is the grout between individual tiles.

After tiles are glued in place, the gaps between them are filled with grout, which has a bad reputation for staining. However, if the thought of using tile on your countertop appeals to you, there are ways to reduce the risk of stained grout (see p. 134). But first, let me help you select the tile.

Choosing tile

Not all tiles are suitable for kitchen work surfaces because they are not all equally hard and durable. In terms of materials, your choices are ceramic, porcelain, and stone.

Ceramic tile When people think of tile, the first thing that comes to mind is ceramic tile. Common ceramic tile has a hard, fired-on surface glaze over a much softer clay base (called the bisque). The glaze is the protective finish, but some glazes are thicker and more durable than others, and it goes without saying that you want the thickest glaze on a work surface. Another concern is the gloss of the glaze. Just as with laminate, tiles come in different degrees of gloss and texture. High-gloss tiles on a work surface will show the effect of wear, but if you want a gloss tile, some have a more durable finish than others. The salesperson at the place where you buy your tiles should be able to steer you toward tiles that are acceptable for a counter. Nonetheless, if you question the durability of a tile, don't hesitate to take home a sample and do some tests. Scrape some pots and pans over the surface and then inspect the tile for wear. While you're at it, see how easily dried coffee or grape-juice stains can be wiped off.

Porcelain tile Solid porcelain tiles are probably the hardest and most durable tiles you'll find. There is no soft clay bisque; the porcelain is solid, and the color is homogenous. That means that even if you do manage to chip a tile, the defect won't be so noticeable. Porcelain tiles with a gloss surface are particularly resistant to dulling.

Stone tile Granite, marble and slate are cut into tiles as well as slabs (see p. 140). There are also all-clay tiles that have no surface glaze on them. The hardness and durability of natural stones will depend on the natural properties of the material; a granite tile will be substantially harder than unglazed clay. Stain resistance will also vary accordingly, but you will need to seal natural stone tile with an appropriate sealer at least once a year. No natural stone surface will have the stain resistance of ceramic glaze.

The problem of grout stains

The tacky look of stained grout lines and the thought of spending hours trying to scrub them clean often put the kibosh on tile as a countertop material. Grout stains because it is porous and readily absorbs liquids that come in contact with it. But before you cross tile off your wish list, you should know that there are ways to reduce staining.

Grout comes in a powder that is mixed with water into a muddy slurry, which is packed into the spaces around the tile. If the grout is mixed with a special latex additive instead of water, it will be much more resistant to staining. Furthermore, if the grout lines are then sealed with a top-quality grout sealer (one that is acceptable for food contact) according to the manufacturer's directions, the grout will be even less porous. Not all grout sealers are equally effective. You want the best-quality grout sealer you can find, and an established tile supplier will be able to advise you on sealer selection.

The hands-down best way to lessen, if not eliminate, the chances of grout staining is to use an epoxy grout. Epoxy grouts are rated as having a 0% absorption rate, and they do not require further sealing. They are fairly expensive and a bit tricky to use (working time is short and clean-up is a tad difficult) so I wouldn't recommend them to an amateur tile setter, but there is nothing better for a kitchen counter.

There are other ways to reduce the risk of staining. You can use larger tiles; you can make the grout joints smaller (about ⅛ in.); and you can fill the joints so the grout is level with the top surface of the tile (avoid deep, concave grout lines). Using any grout color besides white will also help.

Installation

Aside from your choice of tile and grout, there is the important matter of how the tiles are applied—the type of adhesive used and the underlayment they will be glued to.

Adhesives Tile adhesives come in organic or thinset versions. Organic adhesives come in a can and are premixed and ready to use. Thinset is a dry powder that you mix with water as needed. Organic adhesives are ideal for wall tiles in an area that will not get a lot of water, such as on a backsplash. But for a countertop, thinset should be used because it is stronger and more resistant to water. Thinset fortified with a latex additive has superior strength and moisture resistance, and the additive should definitely be used. There is also an epoxy tile adhesive that is perfectly suitable, but is more expensive and more difficult to work with and, unlike epoxy grout, probably overkill on the average countertop.

Underlayment For a successful ceramic-tile installation, the tile must be glued to a suitable underlayment. A lot of people who are doing minor remodeling wonder if you can tile directly over an old square-edge plastic-laminate countertop. The answer is yes, as long as it's sound. The tile book I recommend in Resources on pp. 194-197 details the proper steps to take when tiling over laminate. In most instances, however, you will want the work done over a new substrate, which is better anyway.

The recommended construction specifications for countertops are to make the substrate with a ¾-in. underlayment-grade plywood base, topped with a layer of ½-in. or ¼-in. cementitious backer board (see the drawing at right). Backer board is made specifically as a tile underlayment; two common brand names are Durock and Wonderboard. The material won't rot and has better dimensional stability than plywood. You can save some money by eliminating the backer board and gluing the tile directly to ¾-in. underlayment-grade plywood, but this isn't the best approach for long-term quality. Do not tile countertops directly on top of thinner plywoods, such as ¼-in. lauan. The thin surface veneers of the wood are inadequate, and the glues used on the plies don't have the necessary water resistance. For ceramic tiles that are glued onto a wall, such as a backsplash, drywall is fine as an underlayment.

A TILE COUNTER WITH THINSET ADHESIVE

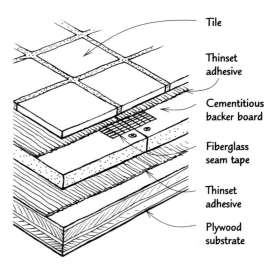

Tile

Thinset adhesive

Cementitious backer board

Fiberglass seam tape

Thinset adhesive

Plywood substrate

Edgings

The edges of a tile countertop can be finished with tile or wood (see the drawing on p. 136). Special tile pieces made especially for the edges are ideal. Alternatively, a strip of hardwood set flush with the tile makes a durable and inexpensive edge. However, because wood needs protection from water, it's a good idea to have the wood strips sealed on all sides with a good-quality polyurethane finish before they are installed. When the work is done and you are using the counter, you'll need to wipe up spills promptly; don't let them sit for long on the vulnerable tile/wood joint.

EDGE OPTIONS
FOR TILE COUNTERS

V-cap tile

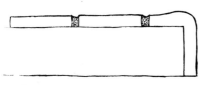

Surface-bullnose tile

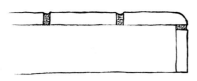

Quarter-round tile

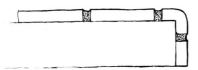

Wood

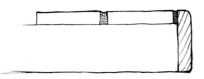

Wood

Nowadays, wood as a kitchen work surface usually takes the form of butcher block, which is made from glued-together strips of hardwood, usually hard maple. Like anything else, a wood countertop has its pros and cons. You can chop and cut on it without dulling knife blades, but the cutting edges do leave marks. And staining of the counter is inevitable, even if you seal the wood regularly.

The look of a worn and stained butcher-block top is perfect for some kitchens. I once had a 5-ft. section of butcher block in my own kitchen and loved it. I didn't mind that it was stained and marred until I remodeled the kitchen and decided I wanted a cleaner look. So I put in a laminate top, but I do miss having a counter that I can use (and occasionally abuse) with equanimity.

Because it is susceptible to water damage, butcher block is not recommended for counters adjoining the sink. And because it is porous, some people think it is not as sanitary a surface as the other countertop materials.

Butcher block can be purchased at any home center in premanufactured lengths. It costs more than custom laminate but less than solid-surface material.

Solid-surface material

Solid surface may well be the closest thing there is to a perfect countertop material—at least from a practical standpoint. It typically looks something like natural stone, yet it is more stain resistant and usually not as expensive. Cigarette burns and knife scratches can be buffed or sanded away. Chips and other damage can be repaired. And pieces of solid-surface material can be bonded together seamlessly.

In terms of custom styling, solid-surface material is truly amazing. It can be fabricated with an integral sink bowl of the same material (see the discussion on p. 146), and it's even possible to have drainboard grooves routed right in the surface of the counter adjacent to the sink. What's more, fabricators can do some incredible things with edge styles and decorative inlays.

A standard solid-surface counter will cost you about three times as much as a standard custom square-edge laminate countertop. Solid colors are the least expensive, followed by small particulate matrixes and then the larger aggregate patterns, but the difference in prices between brands and "flavors" (a term sometimes applied to all the different colors and patterns) is not usually substantial. Yes, it costs more, but you do get a lot of advantages over plastic laminate, and when it comes to the resale value of your house, solid-surface material in the kitchen is a big plus.

The biggest functional drawback to solid-surface materials is that they have an aversion to extreme heat. It's not a huge problem (especially if you are mindful of it), but most fabricators can tell you about counters cracking when their customer put a hot pan directly on the surface. Solid-surface material will usually take the heat, but occasionally the thermal stress of cooling back down is occasionally too much, and the counter

simply cracks—sometimes with an audible popping sound. Even crock pots and electric skillets elevated on legs above the counter have been known to put out enough heat on the bottom to stress solid-surface material. Seams between adjoining pieces of solid surface are, for the most part, invisible (fabricators prefer to call them "indistinguishable" or "imperceptible") but they are considered more susceptible to heat cracking. The redeeming value of the solid-surface product, however, is that if it ever does crack, a certified fabricator can repair it with a filler material or by gluing in a patch.

Solid-surface materials will definitely stain. In fact, I think some of them stain more readily than plastic laminate, but unlike plastic laminate, you can take after solid surface with an abrasive cleanser and a plastic cleansing pad and scrub the spot out. Virtually any stain will come clean because solid-surface material is not porous. Even still, solid surface has the tendency to look dowdy after a while because of grease, grime, hard-water deposits, and fine scratches that accumulate on the surface. The countertop will need to be renewed periodically, but you can usually do this yourself by scrubbing the entire surface down with a plastic abrasive pad and abrasive cleanser. If there are a lot of noticeable scratches, the surface can be resanded with an orbital sander and extra-fine sandpaper.

The chemical resistance of solid-surface material is higher than most other countertop materials, but the plastic is not entirely impervious. Solvents such as paint thinner will soften solid-surface material if allowed to stand for long. There are other substances, primarily strong acid solutions, that could also do harm, but they are rarely a concern in the kitchen.

Discoloration from heat or physical shock will occasionally be a problem. If you drop a heavy pan on the counter, besides causing a chip or dent, it could "shock" the color out of the impact area. This effect is noticeable, I'm told, even on non-colored solid surfaces like white. Sometimes such spots can be sanded out, and sometimes they can't.

Knife slice marks can be sanded out, but that doesn't mean you should make a habit of cutting directly on the counter; knife cuts don't look that great and sanding them out isn't necessarily a breeze. It's better to have a separate cutting board of the material (or another material, like wood). Make sure the fabricator makes a cutting board for you out of the sink opening cutout. You will want the leftover material anyway because it will have the same lot number as the counter, and that would be important if any future repairs are necessary.

You can have solid-surface countertops buffed to a high gloss. The finish has a lot of eye appeal but absolutely no practical value on a work-surface kitchen countertop because the sheen will dull rather quickly. A satin (matte) finish will require considerably less maintenance to remain looking good for a long time. And it is the matte that you can easily renew yourself, as I explained a few paragraphs back.

Choosing a brand

Various brands of solid-surface material are on the market (see Resources on pp. 194-197), but they are not all the same. Almost all the products are made by mixing a natural mineral compound (typically aluminum trihydrate) with a resin binder. Polyester and acrylic are the two kinds of resin used. Polyester is a harder resin, but acrylic is more flexible and less susceptible to cracking and chipping. Scratches on acrylic show white, while scratches on polyester don't (this might be a concern if you are considering a dark color). Acrylic is unaffected by the destructive ultraviolet (UV) rays in natural light, but polyester solid surface must have ultraviolet inhibitors in its mix. Some people argue that the UV blocking agents don't hold up long term and can lead to fading. Proponents of polyester say that fading, if it does occur, can be sanded out.

There is a lot of debate and occasional mudslinging about brands and product quality, but I think the proof is not so much in the "pudding" as it is in the warranty. Almost all manufacturers warranty their product for 10 years, but some cover only replacement materials, while others will pick up the tab for labor, too. Some warranties are transferable (usually with written notification), and others aren't. If it comes down to making a choice between different solid-surface products, your biggest concern will probably be finding a color or pattern that you like, and that's fine, but if you can find that pattern from a company with one of the better warranties, that's even better. A knowledge-able solid-surface fabricator can be a big help when it comes to comparing warranties and products (see the sidebar below).

Solid-surface overlays

Solid-surface overlay, sometimes called solid-surface veneer, is a thin sheet of homogenous material glued over a solid particleboard underlayment. This process is similar to a plastic-laminate installation; the difference is that the solid-surface overlay is thicker than laminate and it can be scrubbed with abrasive cleansers. Seams between sheets are fused like solid surface instead of butted together like laminate. Some solid-surface overlays can be fabricated with an integral solid-surface sink bowl.

Most overlay materials are just thinner versions of the same natural mineral and resin solid surface used on regular solid-surface counters. but one company (Formica) makes an overlay out of PVC plastic. My opinion is that solid-surface materials have better performance standards than PVC.

As I write this, solid-surface overlays are relatively new on the market and are still somewhat unproven. Although thick solid-surface materials have a good overall reputa-tion, the concept of gluing thin sheets of the product to a particleboard underlayment con-cerns some fabricators; there is debate about the long-term viability of the adhesive con-nections. If you want to explore this option, take a close look at the prices and war-ranties of the various overlay countertop products, and also compare them to the prices and warranties offered on the thicker solid-surface materials. Generally speaking, overlays cost about 30% less than thick solid-surface counters and like them, must also be installed by certified fabricators.

Stone

Cut slabs of natural stone can be used for countertops, and this option has become more popular in recent years. Marble and granite are the most common choices, and of the two, granite is by far the more practical surface. It is less porous than marble, which is easily stained and even etched by acidic foods. The surface of granite can also be damaged by mild acids, but not nearly as readily. Granite is about five times harder than marble; in fact, some granites are almost as hard as diamond. Polished to a high gloss, granite is strikingly beautiful, and the gloss finish is not dulled with normal use, as is the case with a gloss laminate or gloss solid-surface material. There are no bad consequences from setting hot pans directly on granite.

But granite does have a few drawbacks. For one, it is very costly. Prices can range from less than solid-surface material to twice as much. If your budget is ample enough to consider solid surface, then you should definitely check into granite as well, and compare the costs. If are looking to save money, keep in mind that granite tiles will be substantially less expensive than a granite slab.

Because of its extreme hardness, granite (or any stone, for that matter) has no mercy when glasses or dishes are dropped on it; they will assuredly break. If you drop something hard and heavy enough (such as a cast-iron skillet), you may even damage the stone. Chipped or cracked granite can be repaired fairly well with a colored epoxy patch by a skilled stone fabricator.

Granite slabs for countertops are 6 ft. to 9 ft. long. When two pieces of stone are joined, they are butted together with silicone caulk between them. The seams are obvious.

As hard and dense as granite is, the stone is still porous and can be stained, especially by hot oil. So a sealer appropriate for granite should be applied once a year. If stains do occur, they need to be removed with a poultice; a stone professional could help you with that. Cleaning of granite (and other stone surfaces) must be done with cleansing agents that are compatible with the stone. Many regular household cleaners can do damage, particularly if they are not pH neutral. Again, a stone pro can advise you.

If you do decide on granite, go to the stone shop or quarry and hand-pick your slabs. There are over 100 different kinds of granite, and the patterns and colors of grain are unique. Slabs are typically ¾ in. or 1¼ in. thick. The latter is less prone to cracking, though it will, of course, be more expensive.

CHAPTER 12

SINKS

The sink and faucet you choose for your new kitchen will have a decided effect on the finished appearance of the room. And just as with all the other remodeling choices you face, there are practical elements beyond appearance and style that should go into your buying decision. By explaining the many sink and faucet options, this chapter will go a long way toward helping you make informed choices and avoid unreasonable expectations. Let's start with sinks.

Sink materials

There are plenty of things to consider when deciding on a sink. The first question is usually what the sink will be made of. You can buy sinks made of stainless steel, porcelain enamel over a metal base, or solid-surface material. Of the three, there's no clear winner or loser, but the choices do offer different qualities that may be better in terms of style and durability.

Stainless steel

Stainless steel is probably the most durable sink material there is. It won't chip or crack, and that's why it is used in commercial and institutional kitchens. However, stainless steel can dent, especially when made of thinner gauges of metal, and it can sound "tinny" (e.g., when dishes are being washed) compared to other sink options, even if the bottom is sprayed with a layer of sound-deadening material.

Gauge Generally speaking, stainless-steel sinks are your least expensive option, but, depending on style and quality they can get quite costly. There are various thicknesses and grades of metal, as well as many different styles. The cheapest versions are often made with 23-gauge steel, which in my opinion is just a step above tinfoil. If you buy a stainless-steel sink, don't go any thinner than 20-gauge steel (the smaller the gauge number, the thicker the metal). Most sinks I install, including the one in my own kitchen, are 20-gauge steel—18 gauge is even better, but such sinks are more expensive.

Chromium content and finish Look for a sink with at least 18% chromium content. Chromium is what keeps stainless steel from rusting, and it also makes it gleam. Cheap stainless-steel sinks have a low chromium content and start to look shabby before long. You should be able to find the chromium content in the manufacturer's literature unless there is very little chromium, in which case the manufacturer might not include the information.

Stainless steel comes with a high luster or a brushed satin finish. Brushed satin will be easier to maintain and won't show minor scratches as readily.

Care and maintenance Stainless steel is tough, but, like any sink material, it still requires specific care and maintenance. Minor scratches are to be expected in the bowl and are not usually a concern, but if the rim or deck is scratched with a sharp object, the blemish may be obvious and objectionable—and it usually can't be removed. Over time, the chlorine in bleach and other kitchen cleansers may pit or corrode stainless steel. You can use such cleansers, but they should not be allowed to sit on the surface for long and should be thoroughly rinsed off. Iron and minerals in water can leave spots on the sink, too. To keep your sink looking like new, manufacturers recommend rinsing it and wiping it down with a dry cloth every time you use it. I don't know many people who are that fastidious. Most people just rub out the stains and water marks with an abrasive (or non-abrasive) cleanser and a plastic scrubber pad. Steel wool is not recommended because it leaves tiny

steel particles in the small pores of the sink, and when they rust, it will look like the sink is rusting.

Porcelain enamel

Porcelain enamel is essentially a glass coating that is fused to a metal base. Porcelain is less porous than stainless steel and can be made in a full spectrum of bright colors. No other kind of sink can give you the color and glassy, bright finish that you get from porcelain enamel. The material is smooth, hard, and durable, but it isn't as tolerant of abuse as stainless steel.

Porcelain enamel can be bonded to either a thick and heavy cast iron, formed from molten iron poured into a sand mold, or to a much thinner, lighter sheet steel that has been pressed into a sink shape (see the drawing on the facing page). Porcelain-steel sinks cost about the same as stainless-steel sinks, but porcelain cast-iron sinks cost about twice as much—and they have certain advantages. Cast iron is more solid than sheet steel, and not as noisy when pots and pans bang against it. Cast-iron sinks also have a much thicker enamel coating, which results in a finish with a notably greater depth of gloss. It can also be argued that a thicker coating of enamel will provide a longer service life.

This isn't to suggest that enameled steel sinks are no good—they can be. You can get plain enameled-steel sinks, but the better-quality ones (and the only ones I recommend) have a thick plastic resin bonded to their back side. The backing insulates the bowls and muffles the tinny sound that is traditionally associated with sinks made of thin steel. Looking at the two, you could

PORCELAIN-ENAMEL SINKS

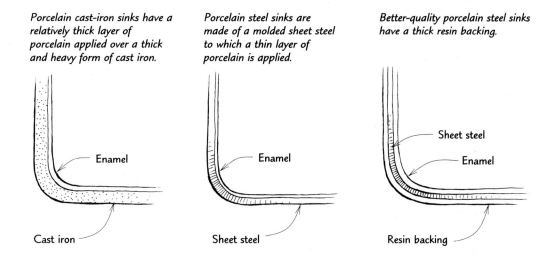

Porcelain cast-iron sinks have a relatively thick layer of porcelain applied over a thick and heavy form of cast iron.

Porcelain steel sinks are made of a molded sheet steel to which a thin layer of porcelain is applied.

Better-quality porcelain steel sinks have a thick resin backing.

Enamel

Cast iron

Enamel

Sheet steel

Sheet steel

Enamel

Resin backing

actually mistake a resin-backed steel sink for cast iron. Besides price, the obvious difference is in the weight of the sink (cast iron weighs at least twice as much).

In terms of durability, porcelain enamel is porcelain enamel—the material is equally durable regardless of the base metal it's applied to. However, one drawback to porcelain enamel is that a hard, concentrated blow to the surface can cause it to chip. This is not necessarily a major problem—of all the old enameled sinks I've replaced, the unchipped ones outnumber the chipped ones. Manufacturers disagree about the impact resistance of porcelain enamel on cast iron vs. steel, but there really isn't that much difference. A thick enamel coating may be denser than a thin coating, but the thin coating will absorb more shock before it breaks. Damage to porcelain enamel can be repaired reasonably well with an epoxy paint; just match the color carefully.

You can use abrasive cleansers on porcelain, but they should be used with restraint or they will eventually dull the original gloss. Rust, fruit juices, and other kitchen substances can stain porcelain, but when this happens, the stain can be removed. You might want to consult with the sink maker or contact the Porcelain Enamel Institute for stain-removal guidelines (see Resources on pp. 194-197).

Solid surface

Solid-surface sinks are made of the same mineral and resin formulations used to make solid-surface countertops (see pp. 136-139), and they have all the same advantages and disadvantages. In short, solid-surface sinks are durable, unaffected by most household chemicals, and easy to keep clean. The choice of solid-surface sink colors is not as great as for counters, and the sheen of the sinks is never glossy, only matte.

When you look at sinks in showrooms and home centers, you realize there's a lot more to decide on besides the material. Sinks come in a bewildering array of designs and configurations. Here are a couple of important issues you'll need to consider before you make your final decision.

SINGLE VS. DOUBLE BOWL

What about sink size and the configuration of bowls? The basic choice is between single and double bowls, but sink manufacturers don't make it easy by offering so many variations (a few of which are shown in the drawing at right).

Traditionally, double-bowl sinks have been used to wash dishes on one side, while stacking them to dry in a dish drainer on the other side. But two equal-size bowls are a tad small for washing big pans and cookie

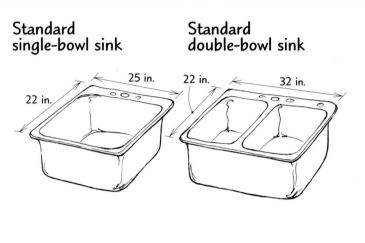

Standard single-bowl sink

22 in. 25 in.

Standard double-bowl sink

22 in. 32 in.

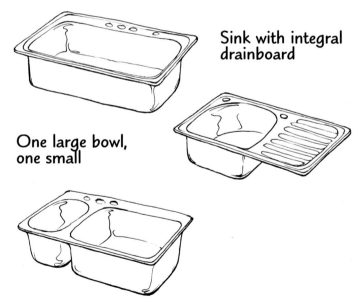

One large bowl

Sink with integral drainboard

One large bowl, one small

sheets. If you have a dish-washer in your kitchen, you might want to get a sink with a single large bowl. That will give you plenty of room for soaking and washing big pans. A nice compromise could be a two-bowl sink with one large bowl and a second smaller bowl. Three-bowl sinks are also available.

BOWL DEPTH AND CURVATURE

Another thing to consider is the depth of the sink bowl and the curvature of the bowl where the sides meet the bottom. Most people find a deep bowl more useful, but I've had a few customers who wanted shallow bowls because the deep ones were a strain on their back. A bowl depth of 7 in. to 8 in. is con-sidered average. Some bowls have sides that are a bit straighter than others and a tighter curve where the side and bottom join. Straighter sides and a tighter radius are preferred because the sink will have a greater capacity, especially across the bottom (see the drawing at right).

One thing I should point out about bowl sizes is that a cast-iron sink typically has a slightly smaller bowl capacity than a comparable sink in porcelain steel or stainless steel, and to a lesser degree, solid surface. This is because of the thickness of the sink material as well as the curva-ture of the bottom. I noticed the difference when I re-placed the enameled cast-iron sink in my own kitchen with a stainless-steel unit; big pots that didn't quite fit be-fore are no longer a problem.

Bowl design and capacity

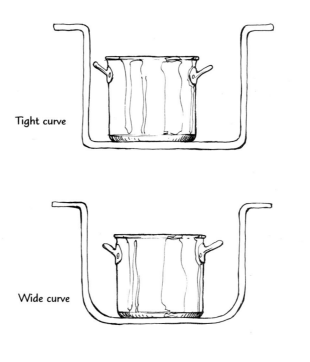

Tight curve

Wide curve

The niftiest thing about solid-surface sinks is that they can be fabricated right into a solid-surface countertop with no ridges or seams showing (see p. 148). Integral solid-surface sinks are easily your most expensive sink option. But you can get some solid-surface self-rimming (drop-in) style sinks for about the same price as enameled cast iron. Drop-ins have a rim around them that fits on top of the counter (see the next section). I've installed several solid-surface drop-in sinks in plastic-laminate countertops, and my customers have been pleased with them.

Sink installation options

Sinks are available as self rimming, flush mount, integral, and undermount. It's important to work closely with your contractor regarding this choice. Not all sinks come in all versions, and your choice will have a definite bearing on cost.

Self rimming (drop-in)

Self-rimming, or drop-in, sinks are the least expensive option and the easiest to install—they just drop into a hole cut in the counter. Most drop-in sinks are held in position with small clamps (called clips) under the sink, but cast-iron sinks are so heavy that only adhesive caulk under the rim is needed to hold them in place.

With self-rimming sinks, you need to be aware of the height of the rim and how tightly it fits to the counter (see the drawing at right). A stainless-steel rim will fit very tightly

SELF-RIMMING SINK STYLES

Stainless steel and porcelain-enameled steel

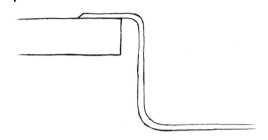

Rim fits tight to counter and sticks up about ¼ in., with tapered transition from sink to counter.

Solid surface

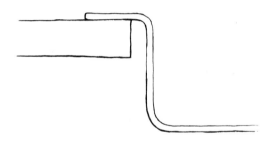

Rim fits tight to counter and sticks up about ⅜ in.; transition is abrupt.

Porcelain-enameled cast iron

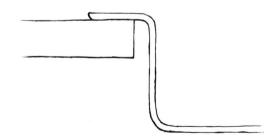

Rim does not fit snug to counter; sink is sometimes a bit warped and bottom of edge is rounded. Rim is about ½ in. high and and must be caulked; transition is abrupt.

to the counter and typically stick up about ¼ in. In addition, the profile of the rim is usually tapered so the transition from counter to rim is gradual. Porcelain-enameled steel sinks are usually profiled similar to stainless-steel ones. Solid-surface drop-in sinks seat tightly to the countertop, and are about ⅜ in. high.

Self-rimming cast-iron sinks usually have a rim that stands about ½ in. proud of the counter surface, and the transition is fairly abrupt. Because the rim is rounded a bit on the bottom, it won't fit tight to the counter surface, and a bead of caulk, which will be visible, is required to seal the joint. If the sink rim was slightly warped in the casting process, the sink will not seat perfectly flat on the counter, and a bit more caulk will be needed. A nice bead of caulk can look just fine (as long as it's color-matched to the sink), but usually it will discolor over time and need to be reapplied. If the sink is not properly caulked, a condition known as rim rust may result from water seeping under the rim. Rust will gradually creep under the porcelain-enamel coating and cause it to chip off.

Flush mount

Flush-mount sinks are installed flush with the countertop. This style is available only with cast iron and comes in a couple of different versions (see the drawing at right). A tile-in model has a square rim that is designed to have ceramic tiles butt up to it. The top surface of the tile is then flush with the rim of the sink, so you can sweep crumbs and scraps off the counter directly into the sink. Another model has a separate stainless-steel rim that covers both the countertop cutout and the rim of the sink. Clips on its underside hold the sink in place. With this arrangement, the sink and countertop are flush, and the rim that spans the joint sticks up just a bit.

FLUSH-MOUNT CAST-IRON SINK STYLES
Tile-in sink

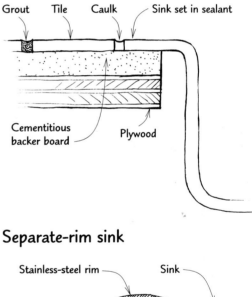

Grout   Tile   Caulk   Sink set in sealant

Cementitious backer board

Plywood

Separate-rim sink

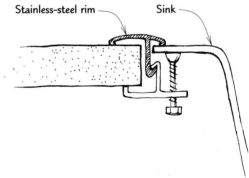

Stainless-steel rim   Sink

INTEGRAL AND UNDERMOUNT SINK STYLES

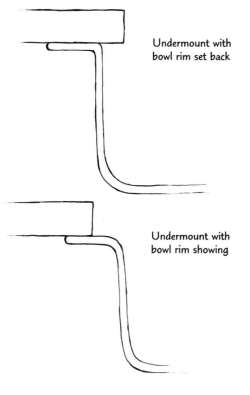

Integral sinks of solid-surface material are fused to the counter. Drainboard grooves can be routed directly into the countertop in various patterns.

Undermount with bowl rim set back

Undermount with bowl rim showing

Integral

Integral sinks have no projecting lip around them and no visible seam between the counter and sink; the countertop and bowls flow into each other. This is an arrangement that is very easy to keep clean and work around (see the top drawing at left). Sink manufacturers make stainless-steel counter-top sections, or stainless-steel sinks with at-tached drainboards that have integral bowls. But most often, an integral-bowl sink is fabri-cated from solid-surface materials fused into a solid-surface countertop. This is a practical feature and, as is the case with solid-surface material in general, there are plenty of unique style options. Some solid-surface overlay materials can be fabricated with inte-gral solid-surface sinks, too.

One slight disadvantage to an integral solid-surface bowl is that if for some reason it cracks (this is rare but occasionally hap-pens), it will be very messy and difficult to replace the bowl. But, unlike any other sink or countertop material, a remarkably good repair can be effected.

Undermount

Undermount sinks are fastened to the under-side of the counter and are available in all sink materials. Undermounting is done on countertops of solid surface, stone, and sometimes tile, but never over plastic lami-nate. As shown in the middle and bottom drawings at left, an undermount sink can be attached so the counter overlaps the bowl, in which case there is no visible joint or seam to clean. Alternatively, the counter can meet the bowl on the top of its mounting rim.

Faucet and accessory holes

When you buy some types of sinks, you need to specify how many holes will be needed in the counter or on the sink ledge to accommodate the faucets and any accessories. Porcelain-enamel sinks (both cast iron and steel) must be ordered with the proper hole drillings because they have to be made that way at the factory—drilling them on site isn't recommended. Stainless-steel sinks are also ordered with specific hole configurations, but when another hole is needed, it's not too much of a problem to punch one out with an electrician's hole-punch tool. With stone and solid-surface sinks, holes can be cut by the fabricator as needed.

Basket strainers

All sinks require a basket strainer to hold water in the bowl, channel it into the drain, and prevent chunks of food from escaping down the drain and plugging it up. However, sinks do not come with a basket strainer. This essential item is considered an accessory, so you'll want to include a strainer for each sink bowl in your job specifications. Baskets can be plastic, thin plated steel, or cast brass with a heavier metal plating. Cast-brass baskets cost more but they won't break the bank, and I recommend them. Cast brass doesn't rust, has a longer-lasting surface plating and is less prone to leaking. Baskets with a rubber stopper on the bottom are common, but I've installed spin-in baskets without a rubber seal for years with good results—unlike the rubber seal, they never wear out.

Strainers with a brass finish are available, but they tend to discolor and look bad in a short time, as do white and colored strainers. Chrome plating makes a more durable finish, and a chrome strainer looks perfectly fine in a white-colored sink.

Faucets

The kitchen faucet used to be a humble and unassuming kitchen fixture, but that is no longer the case. The once plain faucet is now sleek and stylish (see the drawing on p. 150). Beyond appearance, faucet performance has been improved in several ways, although not all faucets will satisfy your expectations. Two faucets can look very similar but be vastly different in price. Why does one faucet cost more than another? What features are most important to consider when buying a faucet? Those are the questions I'll answer here.

There are three major criteria to consider when shopping for faucets: material construction, valve technology, and warranty. First, if you want a faucet that will perform admirably for the life of your kitchen, avoid materials such as plastic, steel, and pot metal. Tubular brass is better, but solid cast brass is the hands-down best faucet material you can get. It's more expensive than other options, but if you choose a standard style of cast-brass faucet instead of a "designer" model, the faucet will be much more affordable. You can't tell a cast-brass faucet by its appearance; you have to check the manufacturer's literature and maybe ask some

FAUCET STYLES

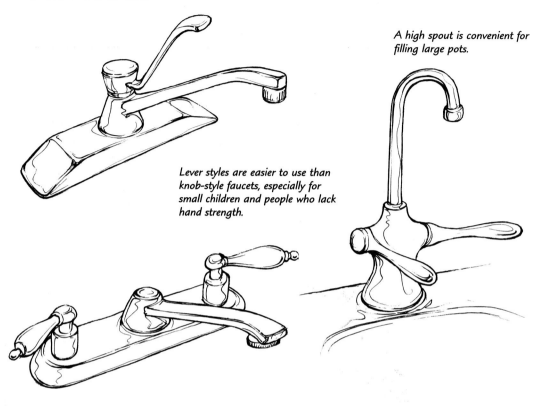

A high spout is convenient for filling large pots.

Lever styles are easier to use than knob-style faucets, especially for small children and people who lack hand strength.

questions. But you can tell a lot by the heft of the fixture—cast brass is noticeably heavier than other materials.

Faucets with old-fashioned washers are still available but not recommended, because the washers wear out relatively quickly and are a nuisance to replace. Newer types of washerless valve mechanisms last longer and are easier to replace when they finally do start to leak. Washerless faucets employ various proprietary gizmos to regulate water flow, but the newest technology uses two discs made of a super-hard ceramic. The discs are perfectly flat and slide against each other to seal the water out or let it through when holes in the discs align. Ceramic discs are purported to be so hard that they are unaffected by minerals or bits of grit in the water that would quickly wear out or damage other types of faucet valves. As you might expect, ceramic-disc valves are supposed to give trouble-free service for a lot more years than other washerless options—and for the most part, they do.

On a faucet with a pull-out sprayer spout, the spout doubles as the handle of the sprayer; you pull it out and push a button or flip a switch on the handle to turn on the spray (see the drawing below). Such sprayers work a lot better than a separate sprayer, but the faucets are not constructed of solid brass (the handle is typically plastic).

If you are considering a faucet with a sprayer spout, be sure to compare different models. Hold them in your hand and see how convenient the switch or button is to operate, and see how solidly the handle fits into its holder. I've had a sprayer-spout faucet in my kitchen for about six months and I like it a lot, but it doesn't strike me as a device that will hold up as long as the conventional-spout faucet that I removed (it was 11 years old and still worked fine). But I did buy my new faucet from a reputable manufacturer, and it came with a lifetime warranty. Time will tell.

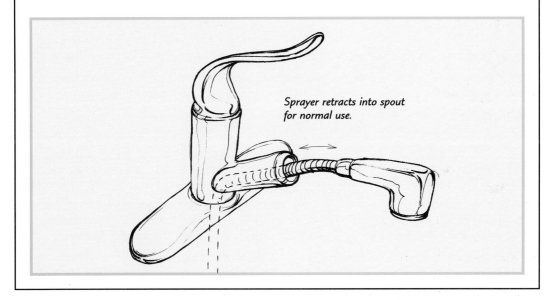

Sprayer retracts into spout for normal use.

Warranties should be considered an important issue when buying a faucet, and I recommend that you buy a name-brand product that carries a lifetime warranty on parts. A few companies have incredibly good warranties that cover just about everything, including the valves. When a valve starts to leak, you can get a replacement free (sometimes by just calling a toll-free phone number and explaining what you need). However, don't base your decision on warranty alone—I know someone who bought a $20 plastic faucet with a lifetime warranty and, although the company did supply free valve replacements, he was replacing them at least twice a year. With better-quality faucets, that won't be the case.

Faucets are available with chrome plating, brass plating, epoxy coating, or an enameled color coating—usually white. I like chrome because I think it holds its clean, bright appearance better than anything else. Brass-finish faucets are usually a poor choice because they can spot and tarnish rather quickly, and tarnished brass looks terrible. However, recent developments in plating technology look promising. One company I know of (Delta) offers a brass finish that's guaranteed not to tarnish; other companies, I expect, will follow suit.

Steer clear of chrome faucets that have clear plastic knob-type handles (often referred to as "crystal" handles). Although the plastic is attractive when new, it doesn't take long for mold and grime to collect inside the handle, where it is clearly visible but impossible to clean unless the handles are removed. What's more, plastic is simply not as resistant to minor scratching and wear as a good chrome finish.

Besides collecting literature from the companies listed in the Resources on pp. 194-197, you should go to a showroom that offers several different brands and styles of faucets. Compare the size of spouts between different faucets. Some are longer and taller than others and would be more useful for filling tall pots. Also look at the handles. Whether you get a single-handle lever-style faucet or a double-handle knob-style faucet is a matter of personal preference. Many "seasoned" citizens prefer lever handles because they are

easier for arthritic hands to operate. Single-handle units also have only one replacement valve to change when that times comes.

Do you want a faucet sprayer attachment? Some people don't like them because the little holes clog up or the end leaks and drips water into the cabinet below. One way to eliminate the separate sprayer hose is to get a faucet that has a retractable sprayer spout with a hose attached (see the sidebar on p. 151).

One last thing to think about when buying a faucet is how easy it will be to keep clean. Water or mild cleanser is the only thing you should ever use on a faucet—never an abrasive cleanser. Water spotting is removed by wiping the surface with a dry cloth. Hard-water deposits can usually be removed with white vinegar. A faucet style with simple lines and gentle curves will be easier to keep clean than a faucet with many surfaces and tight joints where grime can collect.

Other sink accessories

Thus far we've looked at the essentials: the sink itself, the basket strainer, and the faucets. There are a host of optional accessories available as well, including water dispensers, water-purification systems, and lotion and soap dispensers. You'll see these at the showrooms you go to, and probably other devices as well.

Instant hot-water and chilled-water dispensers are installed underneath your sink and have an outlet on the sink rim near the faucet. I'm not overly excited about either option because I think they are unnecessary clutter and just something else that can

THE SINK THAT HAS EVERYTHING

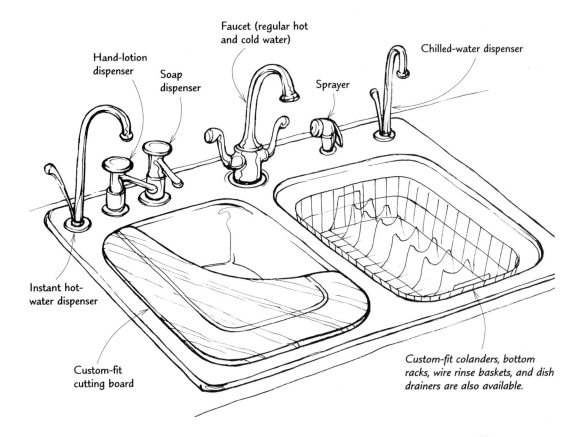

Hand-lotion dispenser

Soap dispenser

Faucet (regular hot and cold water)

Sprayer

Chilled-water dispenser

Instant hot-water dispenser

Custom-fit cutting board

Custom-fit colanders, bottom racks, wire rinse baskets, and dish drainers are also available.

break down the road, but that's just my opinion. Some people rave about their hot-water dispensers. More valuable, to my mind, and something you might want to consider in your plans, would be some sort of a home water-purification system with a separate outlet near the sink faucet.

A lotion or soap dispenser can be installed on your sink by the faucet. Most people find these to be a nice convenience. If you stack dishes to dry in one particular bowl of a double-bowl sink, it's a good idea to install

the soap dispenser on the opposite bowl so you have easy access to it at all times.

Sink manufacturers often offer a selection of accessories that custom-fit into their sinks, such as cutting boards and strainers. Such items can be a nice convenience and are worth checking into.

CHAPTER 13

FLOORING

A kitchen floor takes a lot of abuse. We spill things on it and drop hard objects on it. When we walk in from outside, we track in mud, grit, and tar. Small children are another problem for the floor, as are pets—from long toenails on the dog to furballs from the cat. It all figures in.

It's not pleasant to think that the gorgeous kitchen floor of your dreams will ever be anything but fresh and new, so durability is something to consider—some flooring materials will look fresh and new longer than others. Comfort is another consideration. And cost, not only of the flooring itself but also of installation, is yet a third thing to factor in. So is the ease of installation, particularly if you will be doing the work yourself. Finally, maintenance is an important concern. With all those thoughts in mind, in this chapter we will take a close look at four of the most popular kitchen flooring choices: wood, ceramic and stone tile, vinyl, and plastic laminate. In the end, you will have the information you need to choose the flooring that's best for your kitchen and your lifestyle.

This chapter falls near the end of the book because you will want to have your flooring installed near the end of the remodel. If it's installed too soon, the finish will almost certainly suffer premature wear or even accidental damage while the room is being worked

WHAT ABOUT CARPET?

If you look at kitchen magazines, you may find a certain number of rooms with carpeting on the floor. The look may appeal to you, but don't be seduced. Carpeting is warm and soft underfoot, but it is not a good choice for a kitchen because it collects and holds onto dust, mold spores, and moisture. Cleanliness should be a prime concern in a room where food is prepared. But even with frequent vacuuming and shampooing—and who wants to be burdened with that?—carpeting remains inherently dirty.

on (unless elaborate protective measures are taken). Unless the floor is unfinished wood that will need to be sanded and finished in place (see p. 159), the floor should go in after the cabinets and countertop, but before the baseboard moldings. The moldings will fit over the edge of the floor to finish it off, and with some types of flooring, they serve to hold down the edges. Any painting in the room is best done before a finished floor goes in.

Wood

If chosen wisely, installed correctly, and maintained properly, wood can be very satisfactory as kitchen flooring. I wouldn't go so far as to say it is the best choice for every kitchen, because I wouldn't put a wood floor in my kitchen. It wouldn't even be my first recommendation to you, for reasons that should become obvious as you read on.

The biggest concern with wood flooring is its reaction to water, and the joints between boards are especially vulnerable. When you spill a glass of juice or your new puppy piddles on the floor, it's not a problem if you wipe up the mess quickly, but it's another matter if the dishwasher springs a big leak or the icemaker connection on the back of the refrigerator drips unnoticed for a few months. Water that seeps into the joints will swell the wood, possibly buckle the floor, and probably destroy the surface finish. This is a worst-case scenario, but it does sometimes happen.

The more immediate moisture concern is not liquid water, but water vapor in the air, commonly known as humidity. Humidity has

a profound effect on wood because long after the floor is laid, wood cells will continue to absorb and release moisture to maintain equilibrium with atmospheric conditions. When wood cells absorb water, they swell,

SUBFLOORING AND UNDERLAYMENT ARE NOT THE SAME THING

Subflooring and underlayment are terms that are sometimes used interchangeably, but they are not the same thing. Subflooring is the "skin" that is fastened over the floor joists when the house is framed; it is a structural element. In older houses, the subfloor typically consists of individual boards nailed alongside each other. In newer homes, the subfloor is plywood or oriented strand board (OSB). The subfloor should be at least ¾ in. thick; a thicker subfloor makes for a stronger and more solid finish floor.

Underlayment is a material that provides a suitable substrate for the finish flooring. Underlayment may contribute stiffness and structural strength to the floor, but it doesn't always. Particleboard was once a popular underlayment but is not used much anymore (and is not recommended under any flooring in the kitchen). With vinyl flooring, ¼-in. plywood is often used as a underlayment. Cementitious backer board is a common underlayment for ceramic tile.

F or a flat and gap-free floor, unfinished strip and plank flooring should not be installed until the moisture content (MC) of the wood is the same as the relative humidity of your home. And if you live in an area of the country where atmospheric humidity levels fluctuate significantly from season to season, it's best to install the flooring when its moisture content is closest to that in the driest season of the year (winter).

In upstate New York, where I live, a wood floor will have a winter MC of about 7%, and a summer MC of up to 11%. This means that each $2\frac{1}{4}$-in.-wide oak strip in a floor will fluctuate in width about $\frac{1}{32}$ in., a distance roughly equivalent to the thickness of seven pages of this book held together. Obviously, you don't want your floor to gap apart that much, and to avoid the situation, you and your installer need to take preventive measures.

The ideal way to ensure a gap-free installation is to store the wood in your house for several weeks and put it down during the dry winter season, but that's seldom practical. The next best thing is to have the flooring delivered to your home at least five days before it will be put down. It must be stored inside. The temperature should be at least 70° and dry (any plastering, or finishing of drywall, should be completed because such operations put high levels of moisture in the air). A dehumidifier would prove beneficial. The pieces should be spread about so air can get to them.

Under these conditions, the moisture content will usually drop down to acceptable levels. In the

and the wood gets bigger. When wood cells release moisture, they shrink, and the wood gets smaller. This expansion and contraction can wreak havoc with a wood floor, but fortunately, there are ways to deal with the problem (see the sidebar above).

Depending on the species (and the finish), wood can be a relatively durable flooring, roughly on a par with good-quality vinyl flooring. Oak has for years been a popular wood for flooring because it is so dense, and it is also the most reasonably priced species. The other old standby is maple, but maple doesn't have oak's distinct grain patterns or

naturally golden color. Beech, ash, and pecan are also hard and practical choices for a kitchen floor. Avoid pine and cherry—these woods can be beautiful but they are relatively soft, and even with the best of surface finishes, they will suffer damage more readily than the other species. Each species is available in various grades.

The best way for you to make up your mind about wood flooring is to visit one or two suppliers to look at samples. Always take samples home (wood or otherwise) and lay them on the floor in your kitchen to get a better idea of how they will look. Whether the

humid South, 10% moisture content at installation is considered good; in the dry Southwest, 6% is good. For the rest of the country, 8% or 9% is acceptable. Moisture content is measured with a hand-held moisture meter, a device that most flooring contractors and many woodworkers own.

When the flooring is installed, a ½-in. to ¾-in. open space should be left around the perimeter of the floor to allow for seasonal dimensional movement. Floors installed tight to the wall can swell and buckle for lack of the perimeter space. If the floor doesn't buckle, the walls will be pushed out of alignment; expanding wood is a surprisingly powerful force. The open space is covered over with baseboard molding, and usually a base shoe molding (see the drawing below).

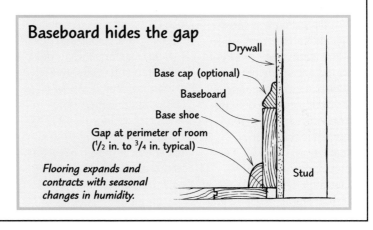

Baseboard hides the gap

Drywall

Base cap (optional)

Baseboard

Base shoe

Gap at perimeter of room
(½ in. to ¾ in. typical)

Flooring expands and contracts with seasonal changes in humidity.

Stud

room is done (or even started) doesn't matter so much as just getting the samples into your own "space" where you can better contemplate the possibilities.

Unlike other flooring materials, a wood floor can be refinished, and that's a big plus. In some instances, you can lightly sand the existing surface finish and brush on another. If the floor is really beat up, you can sand off the old finish along with a thin layer of wood, and then refinish the whole thing. A properly maintained wood floor can last for generations.

If you have an old house, the possibility exists that there is already a hardwood floor there, underneath a layer or two of worn vinyl flooring. If that's the case, you might be able to salvage it by tearing up the vinyl (see the sidebar on p. 158). Such floors are often diamonds in the rough, and I've seen some amazing reclamations.

Prefinished wood floors should be installed after the cabinets and countertops, but unfinished wood floors that need to be sanded and finished in place should be installed before the cabinets and final trim work. Why? Sanding machines are heavy

Old vinyl flooring can be removed fairly easily if it was glued over a thin underlayment—the flooring and the underlayment can be torn out together, in one operation. But if the vinyl was glued directly to hardwood flooring, getting it up will require hard work, vision, and determination. The vinyl itself will usually come up relatively easily; the problem is the mastic used to glue it down. Sanding it off is not recommended because the mastic will quickly gum up the sandpaper, and it may contain asbestos fibers. (See the sidebar on pp. 174-175 for information about asbestos concerns with vinyl flooring.)

There are various home-grown ways to get recalcitrant mastic off an old floor. Towels soaked with scalding-hot water and placed over small sections will often soften the glue enough so that it can be scraped off. Goop brand hand cleaner is purported to do the same thing in some instances. A third method is to put dry ice in a pan and slide it over the surface, freezing the material so it can be chipped off.

Wresting the mastic skin off a "hidden" hardwood floor is a tedious job that you will probably have to undertake yourself because few contractors will touch it, and the labor cost would be too much anyway. Once you got into the job, you would probably wonder why you didn't just opt for another layer of floor over the old (which is always possible). But if you persevere, you'll be justifiably proud of your efforts when the newly un-covered hardwood floor is sanded and finished.

and bulky; they sometimes bang into the wall and do minor (though repairable) damage. Also, sanding is a dusty process. After sanding, the floor should be carefully covered over with a layer of taped-together cardboard. When the cabinets are in and the painting is done, the cardboard can be removed and the wood floor coated with an appropriate finish (see the sidebar on pp. 160-161). That's the ideal order of events, but for one reason or another, things may not be able to work that way on your job. In any event, give the subject some thought and discuss the best course of action with your contractor.

The difficult and often confusing part about choosing wood flooring is that it's available in so many different forms. There are three styles (strip, plank, and parquet) and three installation methods (nail-down, glue-down, and floating). You also must decide whether to get prefinished flooring or unfinished flooring (and have it finished after installation). Finally, you must select a finish. No other type of flooring presents so many different choices and requires so many decisions. But if you want a wood floor, these are all things you'll need to understand in order to make the right choices.

BLIND-NAILED STRIP FLOORING

Nail

T&G joint

Roofing paper

Plywood
subfloor

Floor joist

Nails angled through the tongues into the subfloor hold the floor boards in place, and you don't see the nails from above.

Unfinished strip flooring

Unfinished strip flooring is the most commonly used form of wood flooring. It is also the most difficult and time-consuming type to install. Strip flooring consists of narrow boards that typically measure 2¼ in. wide and ¾ in. thick, with a snug-fitting tongue-and-groove (T&G) joint milled along the edges and ends. Each piece of flooring is fastened down with nails driven through the tongue (see the drawing above).

A T&G strip floor can be installed over any flat, solid subflooring that is at least ¾ in. thick, usually at right angles to the joists. To help prevent moisture from migrating into the underside of the floor and to reduce the likelihood of squeaking, 15-lb. asphalt-coated roofing paper is typically installed under the new flooring. Because of concerns over excessive moisture, strip flooring is not recommended for installations that are below grade (below the exterior ground level).

Strip flooring can be installed over concrete, but only if special measures are taken. If your contractor isn't familiar with the construction details, the books listed in Resources on pp. 194-197 will point you in the right direction.

Special consideration should also be given to wood-floor installations over a crawl space. If the area under the floor is not ventilated and a plastic vapor barrier is not installed on the ground, high moisture levels under the floor could cause each strip of wood in your nice new floor to swell on the bottom and cup on the top—it's not a pretty picture. Hardwood floors over radiant heating (see the sidebar on p. 73) can also be problematic. In such instances, a floating floor (see pp. 164-165) should be used instead of a nail-down or even glue-down wood floor.

Lengths of unfinished strip flooring never go together perfectly flush on the top. The floor when first laid will be uneven. This is a condition known as "overwood" (see the drawing on p. 163), and the cure is sanding. After sanding, the floor will be perfectly flat and at that time, the finish can be applied.

The finish on a wood floor is the sacrificial front line against attack by water and grit. Of all the floors in the house, the kitchen floor is where the hottest battles rage. If your floor is to prevail against the enemy, it must have only the best of finishes, and you must be vigilant in your daily maintenance (see pp. 165-166). Okay, at ease. Now let's survey the troops.

WAX

Waxed floors in kitchens are a bad idea. Wax is dangerously slippery when wet, and it is not very hard. What's more, for a waxed floor to stay looking good, it has to be completely rewaxed at least once a year. The process involves stripping the old wax off by dissolving it with a solvent, applying new wax, and then buffing the floor. Wax finishes are beautiful and they have their place, but not in the kitchen.

URETHANE FINISHES

A basic oil-based or water-based urethane (often called polyurethane) is the best finish for most site-finished kitchen floors. Oil-based urethanes go on thicker and bring out the rich, golden color of a wood like oak. But oil-based finishes will yellow over time, each coat takes eight hours to dry, and the solvent used in these products can be terribly noxious.

Water-based urethanes (also referred to as "water clear") don't yellow with age. This is a good thing over light-colored woods like maple, but with oak, some water-based finishes can leave the wood looking anemic. Water-based urethanes dry in two or three hours, and their odor is not nearly as obnoxious as the stench from oil-based products. Water-based finishes are a touch more fussy to apply, and because they go on thinner than oil, an extra coat is necessary to make up the difference (for a kitchen floor, three or four coats of

Prefinished strip flooring

Compared to unfinished flooring, strip flooring that has been prefinished at the factory is a breeze to install because there is no sanding or finishing to do. Prefinished strips are available in two versions: solid wood and engineered. Solid wood is just that, lumber as it's sawn out of a tree. Engineered flooring is, essentially, a plywood base with a thick top-surface veneer (see the drawing on the facing page). In most instances, moisture content is not a big issue with prefinished flooring.

Prefinished products still need to acclimate for a couple of days in the area where they will be installed, but moisture content is more closely regulated in the factory, and packaging helps to maintain optimum low moisture content.

Engineered flooring has considerably more dimensional stability than solid lumber and can usually be used in below-grade installations. What's more, the pieces are typically straighter and go together more easily than solid wood. Engineered wood is often

oil-based urethane or four or five coats of water-based urethane are recommended).

As long as you buy a good-quality product, oil-based and water-based finishes are equally durable. Generally speaking, price is indicative of product quality with finishes, and this is not a place to cut costs. If you go to a store that specializes in paint supplies or wood flooring, you will find some top-quality finishes and get good advice about applying them. An experienced flooring contractor will also know which floor finishes are the best. As a rule, water-based finishes cost more than than oil-based finishes. My recommendation is to use a water-

based finish; see Resources on pp. 194-197 for a few manufacturers.

You have a choice of gloss or semigloss (satin) sheen on the floor. High gloss will show wear faster than semi-gloss. Many professional floor finishers like to put on gloss base layers and top them off with a layer of semi-gloss because it makes for a clearer finish.

In addition to oil- and water-based urethanes, there are also acid-cure and moisture-cure urethanes. These finishes are exceptionally durable, but they have a very strong odor and are more difficult to apply properly. They should be put on by experienced applicators.

The best-factory applied finishes are superior to the best site-applied finishes because they can be put on under carefully controlled conditions. Urethanes that have a high solids content and are cured under ultraviolet light are considered the Cadillac of finishes (and are priced accordingly). If you are comparing factory finishes that aren't quite so "high end," you will want to consider film thickness (i.e., how thick a layer of finish is). A thickness of 2 mils or better is recommended. This information should be in the product information literature.

glued down, instead of nailing or stapling (though nailing is sometimes an option). Some engineered wood floorings can even be glued over an existing vinyl floor without the need for a new layer of plywood underlayment. Another possible advantage to some prefinished products, both solid wood and engineered, is that they are one-third as thick as the usual unfinished strip flooring.

However, despite the advantages, prefinished strip flooring does have a few drawbacks. When prefinished floors are nailed

ENGINEERED FLOORING

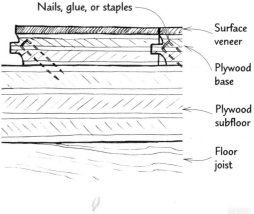

Nails, glue, or staples

Surface veneer

Plywood base

Plywood subfloor

Floor joist

The thickness of a flooring (and any necessary underlayment) is always something to take into account in a remodeling project. This small but significant added height can cause problems for the job if you don't plan for it. The added height of a new floor will often mean that the bottoms of interior passage doors opening into the kitchen need to be trimmed. If new doors are part of your project, they should be installed after the flooring. If they have to be installed first, they can be shimmed up so trimming won't be necessary. However, the bottom of existing entrance doors can't usually be trimmed because they are either steel clad or would no longer seal properly at the threshold (see the drawing below). The typical solution is to get a new door unit (see pp. 81-83) and install it a bit higher.

Unfinished wood flooring that's installed before the cabinetry is typically run just underneath the edges of where cabinets are to go. When the flooring is installed after the cabinets are in, it's advisable to shim the cabinets up the height of the finish flooring so the toe kicks won't be shortened and the area made harder to clean. If the flooring isn't too thick (½ in. or less), shimming up the cabinets might not be necessary.

Dishwashers pose a particular problem. Flooring is best run under the dishwasher, but sometimes the additional thickness of new flooring in an existing kitchen could make the opening between the floor and the underside of the countertop too short to accommodate the appliance. But if you don't run the new floor under the dishwasher, the flooring may prevent the removal of the dishwasher should it need servicing. In a case like this, there are two solutions: shim up the cabinets or choose a thinner flooring.

New floor, old exterior door

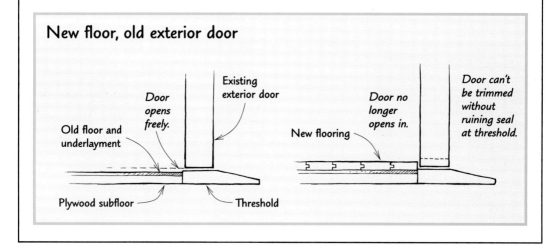

Door opens freely.

Old floor and underlayment

Existing exterior door

Plywood subfloor

Threshold

New flooring

Door no longer opens in.

Door can't be trimmed without ruining seal at threshold.

down, they are susceptible to installation damage: little dents and scratches that would typically not be a concern if the floor were yet to be sanded and finished. Because engineered wood has a thin top veneer of wood, it might not allow for future sanding and refinishing. How much wood a future sanding will remove depends on the condition of the floor and the skill of the person doing the work. Typically, however, machine sanding removes about $\frac{1}{16}$ in. of wood, so the veneer thickness is something to keep in mind when shopping for engineered flooring. Most engineered flooring will allow for at least a couple of sandings.

Another concern with prefinished floorings is overwood (see p. 159). Prefinished flooring pieces are milled to join together with surprisingly good precision compared to unfinished boards, and the overwood will be very minor, but it will always be there to a degree. Most people don't mind the occasional and barely perceptible unevenness, but some are disappointed if the floor isn't as flat and smooth as a traditional strip floor that's been sanded and finished in place. Some manufacturers mill a small chamfer along the edges of each board to deal with the situation (see the drawing below). This solves the visual problem of overwood, but it leaves small grooves between the boards. The grooves can be a nice-looking feature, but they aren't necessarily practical in a kitchen because dirt can collect in the crevices. The shape of the grooves also funnels liquid spills down into the flooring.

ACHIEVING A FLAT FLOOR

Unfinished strip flooring

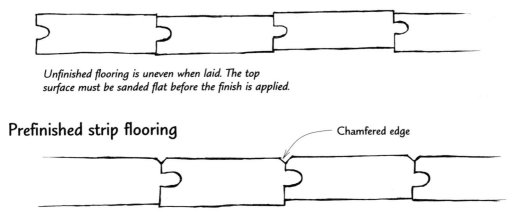

Unfinished flooring is uneven when laid. The top surface must be sanded flat before the finish is applied.

Prefinished strip flooring

Chamfered edge

Prefinished flooring with chamfered edges looks relatively level, even if the boards themselves don't form a perfectly flat surface.

Plank and parquet flooring

Floor boards wider than 3 in. are called planks. Like strip flooring, planks can be either unfinished solid wood or prefinished versions of solid and engineered wood. Planks can be glued or nailed (or glued and nailed) in place. Wide solid-wood planks have a tendency to cup, so screws are often driven through the top face of the board and the heads are covered with plugs.

Parquet flooring is made of many pieces of wood joined together in a geometric pattern (four typical designs are shown in the drawing at right). These days, most parquet flooring is sold as preassembled tiles (9 in. square or bigger) that are simply glued down, similar to ceramic tiles. Parquet tiles are available in thicknesses from $\frac{5}{16}$ in. to $\frac{3}{4}$ in. You can find them in combinations of engineered, solid, prefinished and unfinished wood.

Floating floors

Floating floors look like any other wood floor once they are put down, but their installation is radically different. Instead of being glued or nailed to a subfloor, the pieces are joined to each other in a solid mass that is independent of the structure of the house (see the drawing on the facing page). The usual floating-floor system consists of a layer of $\frac{1}{8}$-in. foam underlayment that is simply rolled out on the subfloor. Over that, T&G engineered wood flooring panels are placed and glued to each other. The foam keeps excess glue from adhering to the subfloor, and it cushions the new floor. The wood panels are about 8 in. by 48 in. and fit together tightly.

WOOD PARQUET

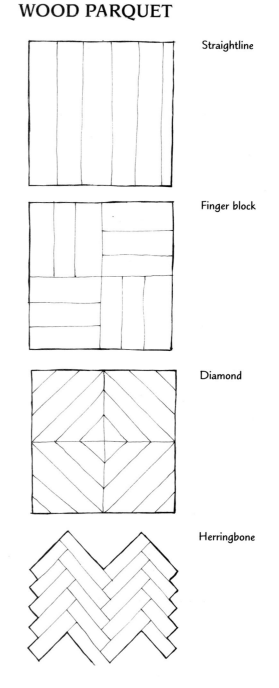

Straightline

Finger block

Diamond

Herringbone

There are no grooves, and overwood is minimal. Most panels have a top surface made up of several strips of wood joined to resemble strip flooring.

The great thing about a floating floor is that it is relatively thin (about ½ in.) and goes down fast and easy. It expands and contracts freely as a whole unit, so gapping between boards doesn't occur (which is why floating floors are considered the only kind of wood flooring that should go over a radiant heating system). The foam underlayment gives the floor resiliency and comfort. The surface veneers of a floating wood floor are thick enough to be sanded at least a couple of times.

Floating wood floors have been popular in Europe for decades, but they are still something of a novelty here. Too bad. I installed my first floating floor eight years ago and fell in love with the whole concept. Disadvantages? Some people are turned off by the "give" of the floor, and I've heard complaints that it makes a "different" sound when walked on. Besides that, floating floors are relatively expensive. But they come prefinished and are easy to install, which is a big plus.

Maintenance of wood floors

The finish on wood floors takes a certain amount of effort to maintain. Spills should be cleaned up immediately. The surface should be swept daily and damp-mopped almost as often. If you want to use a cleaning solution, get one that is made specifically for the finish on your floor, and make sure it doesn't contain any wax (see the sidebar on pp. 160-161). Any amount of wax on the flooring will prevent adhesion of another coat of urethane, and it can't be removed without sanding the finish to bare wood. For flooring with a factory finish, consult the manufacturer's maintenance instructions. The bottoms of table and chair legs should have soft felt glides, which you can get at any home center. The glides should be replaced when they wear out.

FLOATING FLOOR

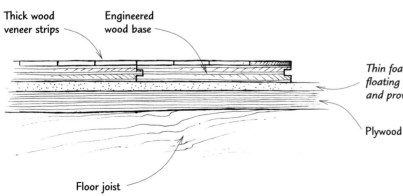

Thick wood veneer strips

Engineered wood base

Thin foam underlayment isolates floating floor panels from subfloor and provides resiliency.

Plywood subfloor

Floor joist

In time (typically two or three years), the finish will show enough wear that it should be recoated. An old urethane finish can be cleaned, lightly sanded, and "refreshed" with another coat of finish of the same type (oil- or water-based) that was originally applied. For a factory-applied finish, check with the flooring company for refinishing instructions (it's a good idea to do this before you purchase the floor).

A urethane finish that is carefully maintained and recoated periodically will look good for many years. A finish that is abused beyond repair can be sanded off and completely refinished.

Stone and ceramic tile

Tile makes a durable and easily maintained kitchen floor, but on the down side it can be cold and lacks resiliency. Glassware dropped on a tile floor will most assuredly break. Much of what I said in Chapter 11 regarding tile countertops also applies to tile floors. In terms of materials, your choices are stone of various kinds (granite, slate, marble), porcelain tiles, glazed ceramic tiles, and unglazed clay tiles, which are collectively referred to as quarry tiles. When shopping for tiles, I recommend that you go to a store that specializes in tile and tile supplies. Such places usually have the largest selection and offer the best technical advice.

Because stone and quarry tiles are porous, they require periodic sealing and are susceptible to staining. On the other hand, there is no kitchen flooring I know that can match glazed or porcelain tiles for their durability and ease of maintenance.

As with a tile countertop, it's essential to have a properly prepared substrate and to use the right installation procedures and products. Floor tiles need a solid floor frame and stiff underlayment because excess flex will lead to failure of the installation. Deflection of the subfloor at the middle of the floor joists should be no more than $1/360$ of the joist length. I don't know any tile installer who actually measures and does this calculation; the more common approach is to walk across the floor and bounce up and down on it a bit. If there is noticeable movement or if dishes in the cupboard rattle alarmingly, the floor needs stiffening. In addition, the floor under tile should be flat—no dips or undulations.

Part of a floor's stiffness comes from its subfloor, and in the case of tile, usually from the underlayment too (see the sidebar on p. 155). Although it isn't the best underlayment, tile can be glued to a clean plywood subfloor (see the drawing on the facing page). When this is done, the total thickness of the wood-floor substrate should be a minimum of $1\frac{1}{8}$ in. If you have a subfloor that is $3/4$ in. to start, you'll want to add a new layer of $5/8$-in. underlayment-grade plywood over that. CDX plywoods and $1/4$-in. lauan are not considered suitable materials to tile over.

A better underlayment for tile is cementitious backer board (see p. 135), using a method known as thin-bed tile installation. A layer of $1/2$-in. backer board installed over $3/4$-in. plywood is considered adequate for most tile installations. If you have a thicker wood subfloor, thinner backer board can be used.

THREE WAYS TO TILE OVER WOOD

Tile directly over a plywood subfloor

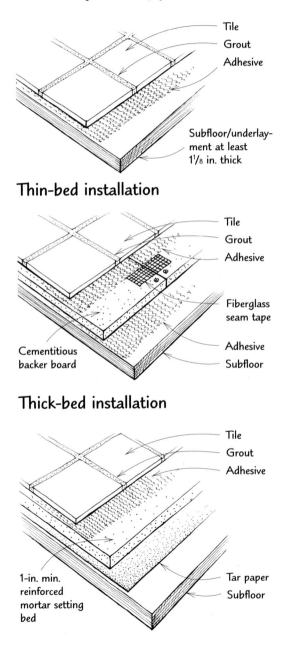

- Tile
- Grout
- Adhesive
- Subfloor/underlayment at least 1⅛ in. thick

Thin-bed installation

- Tile
- Grout
- Adhesive
- Fiberglass seam tape
- Adhesive
- Subfloor
- Cementitious backer board

Thick-bed installation

- Tile
- Grout
- Adhesive
- Tar paper
- Subfloor
- 1-in. min. reinforced mortar setting bed

Yet another underlayment option is a thick mortar bed. Mortar (a mixture of sand, water, and cement) is leveled out over the floor. The mortar is reinforced with wire and is typically at least 1 in. thick. Mortar dries to a strong, flat surface (thick beds are perfect for installations over uneven floors) that is excellent for tile. A thick-bed tile installation is considered superior to other methods. Of course, it is also usually a more expensive option, and not a lot of contractors are experienced at putting down a thick bed.

The adhesive used to bond the tiles should be compatible with the tile and the underlayment you use. In most instances, you will want a latex-fortified thinset adhesive, not an organic mastic. Thinset is a powder that's mixed as needed, while organic mastics come ready to use in a can.

For grout, a sanded floor grout should be used. The epoxy grout recommended on p. 134 for countertops is an option, but not so essential on the typical kitchen floor. The grout powder should be fortified with a latex additive, and the finished grout lines should be sealed with an appropriate sealer. If you choose earth-tone colors rather than white tiles and grout, you shouldn't have much problem with the grout on your floor.

Maintenance of a ceramic- or porcelain-tile floor is as simple as sweeping and occasionally mopping. Waxes or special treatments are usually not required.

The guidelines in this section should get you started. For more detailed information, you should consult the sources listed in Resources on pp. 194-197 or seek the counsel of a tile specialist.

Resilient vinyl

Resilient vinyl in sheet or tile form is by far the most popular flooring used in kitchens. Like its predecessor, linoleum, it is durable, comfortable underfoot, and impervious to water. Vinyl flooring is generally more affordable than most other flooring materials. It comes in a vast selection of colorful patterns, and a new installation does not add much height to a floor (about ⅜ in., including new underlayment).

Standard sheet vs. inlaid flooring

Standard sheet vinyl flooring is made of several layers of material bonded together (see the drawing on the facing page). There is a bottom backing of paper or vinyl, which bonds with the glue during installation. On top of that is a spongy vinyl core, which gives resiliency to the floor. Above the soft core is where the floor's decorative color and pattern are printed. Then comes a clear vinyl wear layer—the thicker the wear layer, the more durable (and expensive) the vinyl will be. On top of the wear layer is a thin surface layer. The surface layer provides a barrier of protection for the wear layer and gives the floor its gloss (some vinyl floorings are made without a gloss finish, but vinyl is a floor covering where gloss is pretty much expected). Different manufacturers have their own proprietary surface-layer formulations and, of course, they all tout their own as superior to everyone else's. No doubt, some surface layers are better than others but, in general, if you get a floor with some sort of urethane top layer, you're getting a good product.

A true inlaid vinyl floor is made completely differently from standard sheet vinyl. Instead of a soft vinyl core and a clear vinyl wear layer, inlaid vinyl is made by piling up layers of different-colored vinyl granules and bonding them all together with heat and

LINOLEUM

Some people make the mistake of referring to vinyl flooring as linoleum, but linoleum is a product from a bygone era. Developed in the 1800s, it reigned supreme until the 1950s, when it was dethroned by vinyl, which requires less maintenance. The only similarity between the two is that they are both sheet floorings. Linoleum is made of all natural substances, including wood pulp, cork, and linseed oil, while vinyl is a petroleum derivative. The two look radically different as well: Vinyl is bright and colorful, while linoleum can be bland and dull. It's interesting to note that linoleum was impossible to get a few years ago but is now being produced once again to meet the increased demand for environmentally friendly products.

If having an old-fashioned floor like your grandmother had in her house (and maybe still does) appeals to you, then check out Resources on pp. 194-197 for sources for linoleum. Your local flooring store is unlikely to carry the stuff.

VINYL FLOORING

Standard sheet vinyl

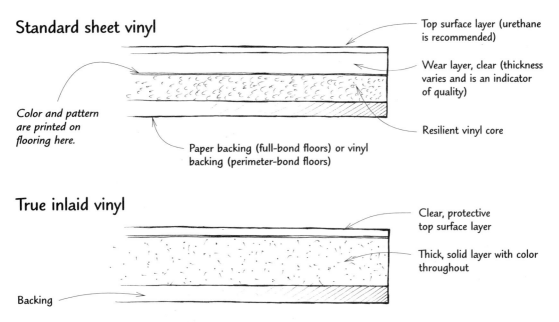

Color and pattern are printed on flooring here.

Top surface layer (urethane is recommended)

Wear layer, clear (thickness varies and is an indicator of quality)

Resilient vinyl core

Paper backing (full-bond floors) or vinyl backing (perimeter-bond floors)

True inlaid vinyl

Clear, protective top surface layer

Thick, solid layer with color throughout

Backing

pressure. The result is a dense vinyl with the color all the way through. Inlaid vinyl is very durable and, although it lacks the softer resiliency of standard vinyl, the inlaid product is not as prone to denting, punctures, and tearing as standard vinyl. True inlaid vinyl also has a different look from standard vinyl, and it costs about twice as much as a better-quality standard product.

You might have sensed from my use of the word "true" inlaid that some inlaid floors aren't inlaid in the commonly accepted sense of the word, and that is correct. Some manufacturers will refer to versions of their standard floorings as being "inlaid," but what this usually means is that there are occasional specks of colored vinyl suspended in the clear vinyl wear layer. The inlaid specks are

for visual effect, and the flooring is not constructed at all like true inlaid vinyl, nor does it have the practical qualities of true inlaid flooring.

Full-bond vs. perimeter-bond installations

There are two methods for installing resilient vinyl flooring. The traditional full-bond method is to glue down the entire sheet. In recent years, a new perimeter-bond installation system has come on the market. With a perimeter-bond floor, only the outside edges of the sheet and the seams are glued. Sometimes the edges are simply stapled down and covered with base molding. The flooring is specially designed to shrink taut and lie flat after it's put down. You can distinguish full-bond flooring from perimeter-bond flooring by looking at the backing. A paper backing is found on full-bond flooring; perimeter-bond flooring has a smooth vinyl backing.

Perimeter bonding was originally promoted as a way of quickly applying a new layer of vinyl over an old layer without the need for any new underlayment, saving the trouble of gluing down the whole sheet. However, most professional installers still like to install vinyl flooring over a plywood underlayment because they think it makes for a better-looking and longer-lasting job. The way I see it, the disadvantages of perimeter bonding outweigh any advantages. It costs more that the full-bond method, and because the flooring is not completely bonded to the floor, it is more susceptible to damage. I know this because I once snagged and ripped a perimeter-bond floor when moving an appliance. Furthermore, if the perimeter bond fails at some point, the floor will shrink back several inches away from the edge, and

I've seen this happen too. Of course, if the floor fails, it is a whole lot easier to replace, and I guess that's some consolation. I would never use perimeter bonding on sheet vinyl flooring, but with true inlaid floors, which are stiffer and heavier, it seems to work just fine.

Full-bond floors must be installed over a clean, new layer of plywood underlayment. For years, the accepted underlayment was ¼-in. lauan plywood, but because of delamination problems with the top layer of veneer (this occurs with lesser grades of lauan) the vinyl flooring industry is now encouraging the use of a special ¼-in. underlayment plywood with thicker surface plies (see the drawing below). It's also recommended that the underlayment be pneumatically stapled down rather than nailed. Staples hold tight, automatically set below the surface, and don't need to be puttied over. If nails are used, the heads must be set and puttied. Then, if the nail moves, the putty bulges, and the lump shows clearly through the flooring.

UNDERLAYMENT FOR VINYL FLOORING

Three-ply ¼-in. lauan plywood with a thin surface veneer is no longer recommended.

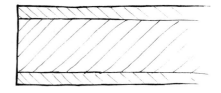

Three-ply ¼-in. flooring underlayment has a much thicker surface veneer.

If you put down your own flooring, you will want to follow the manufacturer's installation recommendations to the letter; not doing so could void the warranty. Some flooring manufacturers will not warranty their products unless they are installed by a recognized professional.

Getting the most for your money

Standard vinyl flooring comes in 12-ft.-wide rolls, from which any length you want is cut off. Inlaid-vinyl rolls are only 6 ft. wide. Seams will almost always be necessary in a kitchen when you use inlaid vinyl, but that isn't necessarily the case with the standard material. But try to avoid having seams, even if it means buying extra flooring. Seams in standard vinyl have a reputation for gapping apart, peeling up, and otherwise looking bad after a few years. The joints in inlaid flooring seem to fare much better.

Vinyl flooring is priced by the square yard, whereas most other floorings are priced by the square foot. When comparing costs, remember to convert to the same measure (one square yard equals nine square feet).

When you shop for vinyl flooring, you will find that each manufacturer offers three grades of standard sheet vinyl: good, better, and best. Inlaid flooring has only one grade, which I guess we could say is better than the standard best. If you shop only one brand, selecting the flooring is simply a matter of finding a pattern you like in the best quality you can afford. But if you shop across brands, you will also want to compare the thickness of the wear layers and the qualities of the top finishes. Another thing to compare is warranties.

Flooring stores typically stock several rolls of standard vinyl flooring for you to choose from, and if you can find one you like in stock, it will usually cost you less than ordering from a showroom sample. Inlaid vinyls are almost never in stock and will need to be ordered.

If you don't find a flooring you like in stock, it usually pays to look at a few other stores. Each will have a different selection, and you might find a particularly good price on a particularly good grade of vinyl that you really like. You should also check the remnant section. Remnants can be quite large and are typically a good value. You might luck out.

Maintenance of vinyl floors

I'm sure you've heard the term, "no-wax floor." It's something of a selling point to say your product requires no wax; the inference is that less maintenance is required. That's true, but what many people don't realize is that is that all the residential sheet-vinyl flooring sold these days is no wax. No wax just means that you should apply something other than wax when the flooring needs maintenance.

Vinyl is impervious to water but not to staining. Foods like mustard and some fruit drinks can permanently discolor the flooring if they are not wiped up quickly. Petroleum-based products, such as oil from the surface of an asphalt driveway, are another threat. I'm not referring to black tar marks (though they aren't good either) but little "invisible" particles that transfer to people's shoes and are deposited on the floor. If this happens over a period of time, you will notice a yellow staining (that doesn't come off) in the main

VINYL TILES

Vinyl in the form of 12-in. by 12-in. tiles has many advantages, especially for the do-it-yourself installer. Like sheet flooring, vinyl tiles come in a selection of grades, with the difference primarily in the wear layer. Some of the top-quality tiles can be very nice and quite expensive.

Many vinyl tiles have a peel-and-stick backing that is a whole lot easier to use (less messy) than spreadable mastic from a can. Also, tiles are more manageable than a big sheet. If you make a bad cut, you ruin only one little tile, instead of a big floor-size piece. If the floor becomes damaged at a later date, you can remove the tile and easily replace it in a few minutes (sheet vinyl is repairable, but it's a job for a pro and the patch requires seaming; the cure is sometimes worse than the sickness). The final advantage to vinyl tiles is that you buy individual square-foot pieces of flooring. You can get just what you need, with little waste (but do be sure to get a few extras for future repairs).

With all of the advantages, I sometimes wonder why vinyl tiles aren't more popular. The reason, of course, is due to the one big disadvantage to tile, and that's all the seams. A vinyl-tile floor won't hold up to standing water like a sheet-vinyl floor.

traffic areas of the floor. Walk-off mats inside the door will go a long way toward keeping your floors clean of asphalt residue as well as dust, sand, dirt, and other forms of grit. But even walk-off mats have been known to cause staining—avoid the kind with rubber bottoms.

If you take care of your new vinyl floor by sweeping it daily and mopping it when needed, it will look nice for a very long time without additional maintenance. If you use any cleaning products other than water, make sure they are approved by the flooring manufacturer. Many off-the-shelf products will harm the vinyl and void the warranty. Chairs and tables should have soft felt glides on the bottom of the legs.

In time the vinyl surface layer will lose its gloss, and the floor will need to be stripped and refinished. How long before this happens depends on the quality of the flooring you bought and how well the floor is cared for. When you refinish a floor, you will want to use the proper products as supplied by the maker of the flooring. The stripper is a deglosser; it removes any remaining shine and prepares the surface to accept the new finish. Once the floor is stripped, the new finish is mopped on. It fills in all the little scratches in the surface and leaves a nice new gloss. The only problem is that the new finish will never be as durable as the original. It may be years before you have to strip and recoat your new floor, but once you do, the process will need to be repeated two or three times a year from then on.

Laminate flooring

Laminate flooring was developed by a Swedish company, Perstorp, which introduced its product line, Pergo Original, a few years ago in the United States. Today, the brand name Pergo is used by some people for any laminate flooring. But laminate flooring has become so popular that there are now more than 50 companies worldwide that manufacture the product.

Laminate flooring consists of a decorative plastic-laminate top surface bonded to a ¼-in. core of particleboard or MDF. On the underside of the core is a moisture-resistant layer of paper or laminate (see the drawing below). Flooring pieces vary somewhat in size, depending on the manufacturer, but they are usually about 8 in. wide and 4 ft. long. The pieces are joined together on the floor with a tongue-and-groove joint and glue over a thin foam underlayment sheet. Laminate floors are floating floors just like wood floating floors (see pp. 164-165). And like a wood floating floor, the pieces go together quickly, easily and precisely. If you are a moderately handy person, you can confidently tackle the job yourself.

Laminate flooring has many advantages. It can be installed over your current kitchen floor (even if it's concrete), providing that the floor is flat. And because laminate flooring is only about ¼ in. thick, it doesn't add much more height to a floor than vinyl. Another advantage to laminate flooring is its density— some promotional literature claims that it won't be damaged by stiletto heels (which would mar a wood or vinyl floor). The surface finish of a laminate floor is purported to be from 10 to 20 times more resistant to scratching and damage than average countertop laminate. Unlike countertop laminate, laminate flooring is virtually stainproof, and it can't be burned by cigarettes.

Most laminate flooring is imprinted to resemble wood strip or plank flooring, but some companies also make pieces that resemble stone tiles. The look is remarkably realistic because the printed papers used to make the laminate patterns are taken from photographs of real wood and stone.

If you are a purist and feel you must have genuine wood (or stone) products in your home, then you won't like laminate flooring.

LAMINATE FLOORING

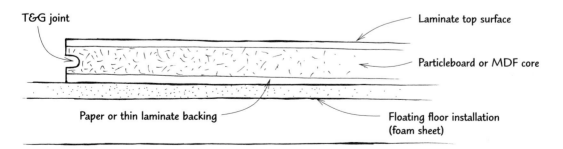

T&G joint — Laminate top surface — Particleboard or MDF core — Paper or thin laminate backing — Floating floor installation (foam sheet)

Vinyl floor coverings (sheet or tile) that were installed before 1987 probably contain asbestos in the backing and in the mastic adhesive that was used to glue the flooring down. Breathing asbestos fibers is dangerous to human health. If you have, or suspect you might have, old vinyl flooring that contains asbestos, the situation is not a cause for panic. But you do need to be aware of how the presence of asbestos can affect your remodeling job.

Asbestos in building materials is found in two forms: friable and nonfriable. Friable means the asbestos material can be reduced to powder under hand pressure. Non-friable means the asbestos fibers are locked in the matrix of another material, and they do not become airborne unless subjected to cutting, sanding, grinding, or mechanical abrading. The asbestos in flooring and flooring mastic is nonfriable. It does not present any hazard until you rip it out.

Regulations regarding the removal and disposal of residential vinyl flooring that contains asbestos are confusing and somewhat contradictory. The Environmental Protection Agency (EPA) does not regulate nonfriable asbestos removal in single-family homes (or apartment buildings with fewer than than five units). But the Occupational Safety and Health Administration (OSHA) does have regulations that apply to workers. In addition, each state has its own asbestos regulations that are, in some instances, more strict than OSHA standards. For example, in my state (New York) only state-licensed asbestos abatement contractors are allowed to take care of asbestos removal, and such contractors must meet special requirements.

In some states, having asbestos flooring removed according to state and federal regulations can cost thousands of dollars because

However, if you want a convincing wood look on a product with more durability than real wood, then laminate will fit the bill nicely.

Drawbacks? Yes, of course. As you know from reading the rest of this book, water and particleboard (or other particulate composite woods) are not a good combination. Standing water can seep into the joints and cause swelling, and if that happens, the pieces will need to be replaced, and the fix is almost never as good as the original. Laminate floors fit together remarkably well, but in my experience there is always a little gap here and there. You may not notice it as you look down, but it's big enough for water to seep into. So you need to be especially vigilant about water with laminate flooring. The cleaning routine is sweeping and damp-mopping.

of the precautions that must be taken: negative-pressure plastic work enclosures with with multiple airlocks, the use of high-tech respirators, continual monitoring of air quality, and the need for special refuse-disposal bags. In other states, the process can be simplified greatly by following OSHA's "revised recommended work practices for the removal of resilient floor covering," but the process is still more involved and costly than just ripping the stuff up and throwing it in a dumpster.

The irony in all of this is that, as far as I have been able to ascertain, all of the different regulations make an exception for homeowners who work on their own home. You can remove flooring with asbestos any way you want, but the typical general contractor isn't allowed to do the same thing.

So what does all of this mean? Several things. One, the easiest solution to the problem is to leave the old flooring in place and, depending on the new flooring you choose, either install an appropriate underlayment or the new floor itself right over the old flooring. If you do wish to remove the flooring and want it done by the book, start by calling your state Department of Health. You could also look in the Yellow Pages under Asbestos for abatement contractors and testing services.

If you decide to remove your own nonfriable asbestos, you can get a free booklet on OSHA's revised procedures from the Resilient Floor Covering Institute (see Resources on pp. 194-197). Fortunately, most landfills classify nonfriable asbestos as construction debris and disposal presents no problem, but you should check just to be sure. You need not treat the removal of old vinyl flooring like it's the ebola virus—just be aware of the hazards and use some common sense in dealing with it.

Although laminate flooring is admirably tough, it is not impervious to wear and damage. Sections of flooring can be repaired, but only with difficulty and special tools, and the fix will be costly. When laminate flooring becomes worn, the surface is not renewable, and you certainly can't sand and refinish the floor. When laminate flooring looks worn out, you just replace the whole floor.

Laminate flooring isn't cheap. You will find that it costs as much as many hardwood choices and the better grades of vinyl, but prices vary between different laminate products. The more expensive floorings will have longer warranties (the range is 5 to 20 years) and be of better quality. Choose a laminate style you like from a company you feel you can trust to honor the warranty. This is important because the long-term performance and longevity of laminate flooring are largely unproven.

CHAPTER 14

Major Appliances

It's hard to imagine a kitchen without a cooktop, oven, and refrigerator. Indeed, each of these items is a necessity. To that list of essentials, many homeowners would add a microwave and a dishwasher. In the past 10 years, technology and consumer demand have led to developments that make each of these major appliances vastly more convenient, useful, and economical to operate than ever before. This chapter will give you a general understanding of the features and choices that are available. If you read this before you go appliance shopping, you will be better informed than most of the buying public.

If you are doing budget or minor remodeling (see p. 8) and are planning to keep at least some of your old appliances, you might be surprised to hear that they can be spray-painted to achieve a fresh new look, and the color can be changed to coordinate with any new appliances (see the sidebar on the facing page). But if you are doing major kitchen remodeling and your appliances are a few years old, I recommend that you get

new ones. Checking out appliance options should be an important part of your pre-design planning (see p. 18). All appliances should be selected, clearly specified in the job specifications, and, if you are supplying them, on site when remodeling starts—or at least at the appliance store ready for delivery.

Cooktops

The average cooktop is 30 in. wide, has four heating elements and fits into an opening cut into a countertop. Cooktops that are 36 in. wide are also relatively common, and have the advantage of providing more room for big pots. Some 36-in. cooktops have five cooking surfaces, or four with a griddle cooking plate set in the middle. Beyond these two most common configurations, you will find plenty of other sizes and shapes. The style and placement of the burner controls will vary from brand to brand and from model to model.

Major kitchen appliances can be successfully repainted. This is typically done when, for example, you buy a new black range and want your old almond-colored refrigerator to match. I've seen appliances repainted by homeowners with aerosol spray cans of enamel appliance paint, and the results looked surprisingly good. But you are more assured of getting a good finish (and it's just a whole lot easier) if you hire a professional, with professional equipment, to do the job for you. If done properly, the finished job will look like new.

You should be able to locate an appliance refinisher by looking in the Yellow Pages under "Appliances—Painting and Refinishing." Or you can call an auto-body repair shop; if the shop doesn't paint appliances (many do), you can probably get the name of someone who does. Usually, the appliance must be moved out into the garage for painting, but I've heard that some refinishers will do the job right in the kitchen without making a mess. In any event, you can expect to pay roughly one-quarter of the cost of a new appliance to repaint your old one.

One thing you can't repaint successfully is an enameled cooktop surface because there is no paint that will hold up to the high heat of a cooktop. So, to refinish a cooktop (including those on ranges) you must have it re-enameled. The process is simple and surprisingly inexpensive, but only if you live near a place that does this sort of work. You can contact the Porcelain Enamel Institute (see Resources on pp. 194-197) for the name of the place nearest you and decide if re-enameling is feasible in your situation.

Changing the color of a dishwasher front panel may be easier than you realize. Most of the appliances have four different-colored panel sheets stored in the door. If you simply remove the metal edge around the door with a screwdriver, you will find the panels, which can be changed with no problem.

Gas or electric?

One of your biggest choices with a cooktop is whether it will be fueled with gas or electricity. Most residential cooktops are electric, primarily because electricity is easier and more economical to hook up than gas. And the electric cooktop itself is typically less expensive than a gas version. However, there is little debate about the desirability of gas vs. electric burners—gas is the hands-down favorite of professional chefs. With gas, the cook can see the flame and regulate it with greater precision, and the heat responds more immediately than an electric coil. A gas flame will also efficiently heat cooking containers that don't have flat bottoms, while that is not the case with electric heating elements.

COOKTOPS AND BURNERS

Typical gas cooktop

Typical electric cooktop

Glass cooktop (smooth surface)

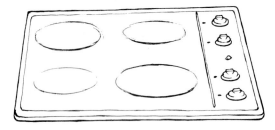

However, gas does have a couple of drawbacks. If natural gas cannot be piped directly into your home from a utility company, you will have to use LP (liquefied propane) gas, and that will require that a storage tank be installed somewhere in your yard. The installation usually isn't difficult, but the tank itself is something of an eyesore. Also, LP gas doesn't burn quite as hot as natural gas. Beyond those things are issues of indoor-air quality. The combustion of either gas produces small quantities of nitrous oxide, nitrogen dioxide, and carbon monoxide. These potentially noxious chemicals can aggravate or even cause respiratory ailments in people who are sensitive to them. That's why a ducted exhaust fan is essential with a gas-fueled cooktop (see pp. 100-101).

Gas cooktops

Gas cooktops are not what they used to be. Older gas appliances have a pilot flame that consumes a small amount of gas 24 hours a day. But most newer gas appliances have electronic ignition instead of a pilot, so the fuel requirements of such cooktops are substantially less. You can expect a fuel savings of 25% or better.

Another innovation is the sealed burner. Standard old-style gas burners have a circular opening around them and usually a removable drip pan. Cooking spills end up in the drip pan and frequently migrate into the burner box under the cooktop. The cooktop hinges up so you can clean out the gunk. Sealed burners are enclosed right up to the burner (the flame is not sealed), so spills remain on top of the cooktop, where they are more easily dealt with.

Gas cooktops are made of porcelain-enameled steel or a specially developed glass. Both are practical and durable, but the glass tops look more stylish. One drawback to glass tops is that most of them are flat; there is no raised-up rim around the unit to contain spills, as is usually the case with an enameled steel top. A glass cooktop with sealed burners will typically cost twice as much as a porcelain-enameled steel top with open burners.

Gas burners come with different heat outputs, as measured in Btu ratings—the higher the rating, the hotter the flame. The average maximum output for a gas burner is 6,500 to 7,500 Btus, but output varies among brands and models, and even the burners on a single cooktop will vary. If you do a lot of canning or wok cooking or anything else that requires high heat, you might want to get a cooktop with a high-capacity burner rated at 12,000 to 15,000 Btus. Appliance manufacturers use names such as Power Burner and Maximum Output Burner to describe their high-capacity burners. Some stoves also have low-output "simmer burners" that can be throttled down lower than a standard burner. Keep in mind that advertised Btu ratings are always for natural gas; LP gas will not burn as hot. Appliance specification sheets will list both LP and natural-gas ratings.

Gas cooktops have removable grates that fit over and around each burner. Larger, heavier grates provide a more stable surface for cookware. The best grates are cast iron (usually with a porcelain-enamel coating), not steel.

Electric cooktops

The traditional electric "burner" is actually called a coil element. Coil elements have worked well for years; they are dependable and simple to repair when they go bad. Coil elements are surrounded by removable drip pans, and the appliance lid hinges to allow cleaning of the burner box. Just as with gas cooktops, glass surfaces are now quite popular. On electric cooktops, however, the glass-surfaced tops are completely flat, and the heat elements are sealed underneath the glass.

With a flat glass top, there are no nooks and crannies for food spills to hide. Cleaning is a bit unconventional—manufacturers recommend that dried food deposits be removed with a razor scraper. The surface is relatively easy to clean, but a special glass-top cleaning paste must be be used; it not only cleans but also leaves a protective coating.

In lieu of the coil element, glass cooking surfaces have radiant, halogen, or magnetic-induction heating elements. Radiant coils (sometimes called ribbon elements) work similar to the old-style coil element, and they are relatively inexpensive. Halogen elements are essentially high-heat light bulbs. Halogen elements heat up faster than radiant coils, but they are expensive to buy and repair. Magnetic-induction elements produce high-frequency magnetic fields that agitate the ferrous metal molecules in a cooking container, which in turn causes the metal to heat up and cook the food. The heating quality of magnetic induction is supposed to be more similar to gas than any other electric option. For induction to work, you need steel or cast-iron cookware—no aluminum. As you might guess, this "space age" technology costs a bundle compared to the standard radiant element.

When cooking on an electric cooktop, it's recommended that the size of the cooking surface match as closely as possible the size of the pot or pan you're using. Most cooktop elements are available only in 6-in. and 8-in. diameters. If you often cook with large pots,

MODULE COOKTOP

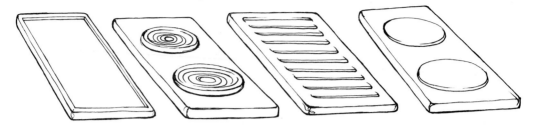

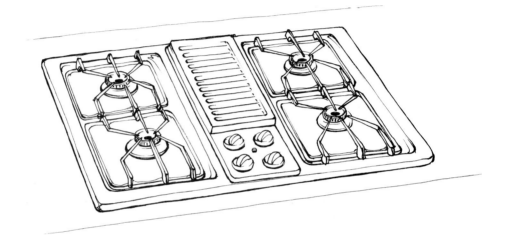

COMMERCIAL-STYLE COOKTOP

you will get better performance from smooth-top surfaces with a dual element that can be adjusted to deliver a 6-in. or 9-in. cooking base. Dual elements are not found on all cooktops.

One disadvantage to smooth-top cooking surfaces is that they look the same when hot as they do when cold. When an element is on, it glows an obvious red, but once turned off, the glow goes and the high heat stays (it slowly dissipates). It's a situation that has led to many people being accidentally burned. Old-style coil elements can stay hot for a while too—but they aren't as deceptively innocent looking as a smoothtop. So, if you buy a smoothtop cooking surface, be sure to get one with a hot-surface warning light that stays on until the cooking surfaces have cooled down to a safe temperature.

Module cooktops

Some gas and electric cooktops are made with removable cooking sections called cartridges, or modules (see the top drawing on the facing page). With these units you can remove a module having standard heating elements and install a grill or griddle module. Most module cooktops have a downdraft exhaust fan (see pp. 107-108). If the module concept sounds appealing, ask yourself if you will really go to the trouble of using it that much. The modules are not usually difficult to change, but the process isn't as easy as just setting a griddle pan on the existing burners. I once remodeled a kitchen that had a module cooktop, and the grill and griddle modules were packed away deep in the cupboards—apparently they had never been used. I suspect this is a fairly common situation.

Commercial-style cooktops

Commercial-style cooktops are all the rage these days, and having one in your kitchen has become something of a status symbol. These beauties are made of stainless steel, gas fueled, and usually 36 in. or 48 in. wide. Commercial-style cooktops are 8 in. to 9 in. thick and rest on top of a shortened cabinet; the countertop abuts the appliance on either side (see the bottom drawing on the facing page).

Commercial-style cooktops are equipped with high-rated burners (typically 15,000 Btu) and usually accept grill and griddle modules. Because of the high heat generated by these units, a stainless-steel heat shield is often required on the back wall and an appropriately sized overhead ventilation system is absolutely necessary (see p. 109). None of this comes cheap; a commercial-style cooktop and the ventilation system to go with it will cost you thousands of dollars more than any domestic setup. Few home cooks really need such a system.

Ovens

Like cooktops, ovens present the prospective buyer with a lot of choices in terms of type of fuel, placement in the kitchen, kind of cooking action, and so on. In this section we will take a look at "conventional" ovens; microwave ovens are discussed on pp. 185-187.

Electric or gas?

Most people prefer an electric oven to a gas oven. Electric heat is better suited to oven cooking because it is more even and, in this particular application, electric heat can be thermostatically regulated better than gas. With gas combustion, a continual flow of fresh air into the oven compartment is required, and this tends to dry out the food. Air does not need to circulate in an electric oven, so the food dries out less.

Placement

Ovens can be mounted in a wall or under a countertop, or they can be part of a range. The standard width is 30 in., but wall ovens and undercounter ovens can be had in 24-in. and 27-in. widths. The interior capacity of to-day's ovens exceeds that of older ovens because of improvements in insulation efficiency; thick insulated walls are no longer necessary.

Wall ovens can be installed in a wall (either singly or stacked one above the other), but they are more often fit into an oven cabinet). In any event, it's a nice design

WALL OVEN

solution because the oven is located at a convenient height (see the drawing below left) and base-cabinet storage space is freed up elsewhere in the kitchen. However, a wall-oven cabinet is not recommended for a small kitchen because it robs valuable countertop space. And besides, a large, bulky oven cabinet can be an overwhelming presence in a small room.

Radiant ovens

The conventional electric oven that you're probably familiar with is often referred to as a radiant oven. It has two electric heating elements, one at the top and one at the bottom of the oven compartment. The elements heat up, and the oven gets hot—it's as simple as that.

Convection ovens

A convection oven has electric elements, along with a fan. Convection means "heat transfer by the circulation of currents from one region to another," and that's what the fan does—blow hot air around inside the oven cavity. The circulating hot air cooks foods more quickly and more evenly. For example, you can roast meat 30% faster in a convection oven than in a conventional oven. Baked goods don't necessarily cook faster, but they will brown more uniformly. And you can bake several tiers of cookie sheets at once and the cookies will all come out evenly done—no burned ones on the bottom pans. Obviously, reduced cooking time adds up to greater fuel efficiency and dollar savings.

Many convection ovens are convection/radiant, which means they allow you the option of either cooking mode. Convection ovens that have an additional heating element surrounding the fan are often referred to as "true" convection ovens. Their performance is said to be noticeably better.

One disadvantage to convection cooking is that the time and temperature settings in recipes are typically geared to radiant cooking, and they will have to be adjusted for convection cooking. Some convection ovens have a computer-programmed feature that is supposed to make automatic adjustments in cooking times. Another drawback to convection cooking is that the fan is sometimes a bit noisy.

All convection ovens are electric. Gas ovens are sometimes referred to as natural convection cookers, because of the fresh air that flows through the oven to support gas combustion, but the cooking effect and energy savings are not as great with gas as they are with an electric convection oven.

Features to look for

Among the features you might want to consider for your new oven are electronic controls (see the drawing below). Touch pads are easier to clean than old-style rotary control knobs, and temperature settings can be entered into a computerized control system with considerably more accuracy than a dial setting. They are also easier to use if your fingers lack dexterity or strength. Furthermore, electronic controls are programmable for a variety of specific cooking functions. As one example, some ovens come with a meat probe that the oven-control sensor reads. The oven will automatically shut down when the meat reaches the desired degree of doneness.

An oven light and window in the door are not standard features on all ovens but they are a great convenience. The number of cooking racks and rack positions will vary from model to model; more of both means greater cooking flexibility. And yet another convenient oven option worth considering is a self-cleaning feature. In self-cleaning mode, the oven heats up to about 900°F for a couple of hours. At that temperature, any baked-on cooking spills are reduced to an ash, which can be wiped off without the need for chemical cleaners. Self-cleaning ovens are mostly electric, but there are also some gas models with this feature.

OVEN CONTROLS

Electronic control center

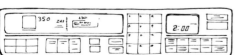

Old-style knobs

Ranges

When you combine a cooktop and an oven into one appliance, you have a range. Ranges come in three basic versions—freestanding, slide-in, and drop-in units (see the drawing on the facing page). A fourth option, for kitchens with plenty of space and people with plenty of money, is the commercial-style range.

Freestanding units

Freestanding ranges have a raised integral backsplash, and they fit between two separate sections of cabinetry or at the end of a run of cabinetry. Roughly 75% of American kitchens have ranges for cooking, and most are freestanding. A freestanding range is the least expensive to buy of any cooktop/oven option.

Everything I've said thus far about the features of cooktops and ovens applies to ranges, too. In addition, freestanding ranges usually have a storage drawer underneath (as do slide-in units). Some of the lower-priced gas ranges, however, have a separate broiling drawer in place of the storage drawer.

Some freestanding ranges have heat-control knobs located on the raised back-splash, while other units have the controls on the front. Controls at the back are not as convenient as on the front because you have to reach over the cooktop. However, controls at the back are out of the reach of small children. Slide-in and drop-in ranges always have controls on the front.

The disadvantage to freestanding ranges is that there is a joint where the range and countertop meet. In a good kitchen installa-tion the gap is small, but it is still a crud-catching area and a conduit for counter and range-top spills.

Slide-in units

Slide-in ranges have a storage drawer underneath and fit into a cutout in the countertop. They have an overhanging top edge that rests on the countertop, eliminating the gap between the appliance and the base cabinets. Countertop sections on both sides of the range are connected by a small strip of counter along the back wall. What this means is that the countertop, as well as the cutout, are more difficult to make. So a slide-in installation will cost you more than a free-standing one. The appliance itself will also be more costly—and it doesn't even come with finished side panels.

Drop-in units

A drop-in, or set-in, range fits into the countertop like a slide-in unit, but, instead of having support legs and a storage drawer, it hangs directly on the counter and has no drawer. The bottom of the oven must be fin-ished off with a range base panel, which is nothing more than a horizontal board with a cabinet-matching toe kick built into it. Drop-in ranges have a more built-in look than the other range choices. But, again, it is a more complicated and costly installation than a freestanding range.

Commercial-style ranges

Commercial-style ranges have become a must-have item in many high-end kitchen re-modeling projects. Typically 36 in. or 48 in. wide, these sleek and costly behemoths are

THE RANGE AT HOME

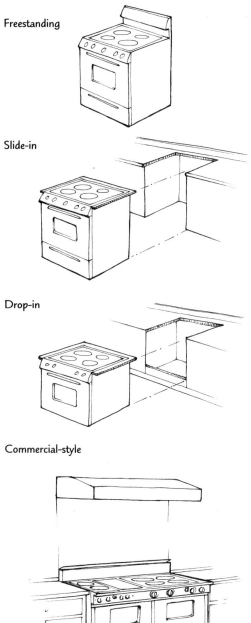

Freestanding

Slide-in

Drop-in

Commercial-style

all stainless steel and usually have an electric convection oven. The 48-in.-wide models have two ovens. It's worth noting here that the combination of a gas cooktop and electric oven (known as dual fuel) is an option with commercial-style ranges, but not normally available in regular domestic ranges.

Microwave ovens

Microwave ovens work by generating electromagnetic waves that agitate the water molecules in the food, causing them to heat up. The singular advantage to a microwave oven is speed. Although few cooks use the microwave for serious cooking, many people consider it indispensable for thawing frozen food and reheating leftovers.

Because the microwave oven is a relatively new appliance, it can usually be found in older kitchens sitting on the countertop or off to the side on a microwave cart. If this is the case in your old kitchen, you will want to free up counter space by integrating the microwave into your new kitchen plan (see the drawing on p. 186). One good placement option is in the cabinet above a wall oven. Another might be over the range or cooktop. Microwave units with a ventilating exhaust fan in them have become popular (see the sidebar on p. 109), but the ventilation efficiency of the fans is not great. Or the oven can be integrated among the wall cabinetry of a kitchen by using a shelf or a special microwave-oven cabinet. Another option that's less common but still workable is to have the oven built in below the countertop. When deciding on the placement of a microwave, keep in mind that almost all

MICROWAVE INSTALLATION OPTIONS

In the cabinet above a wall oven

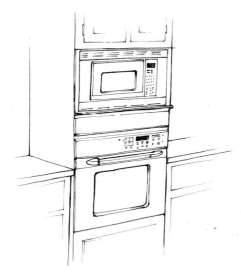

Over a range or cooktop

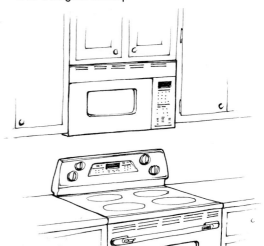

Under a wall cabinet

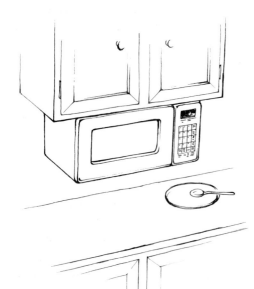

Built in below the countertop

microwave-oven doors hinge on the left side. A few models hinge downward, like a regular oven door.

Microwave ovens are sized according to the oven capacity, measured in cubic feet. You can get anything from a relatively tiny 0.5-cu.-ft. unit that mounts under a wall cabinet (another placement option), to a 1.5-cu.-ft. model that fits over a wall oven. The power of an oven is directly related to how quickly it heats. Power is measured in watts, with 1,000 watts the current maximum. Higher-wattage ovens are naturally more expensive than lower-wattage units. Options and features also have a bearing on price. At the high end, microwaves have cooking probes and sensors, rotary turntables (for more even cooking), and programmable cooking modes.

If you plan on using the microwave for actual cooking (baking and roasting), you should probably get a combination microwave/convection oven. The convection feature consists of a fan and an electric radiant-heat element that browns and crisps the food and makes it more appealing—something microwaves alone don't do.

Refrigerators

In the early 1800s folks preserved their fresh food by putting it in an insulated box cooled by big chunks of ice. In the early 1900s, ice boxes became obsolete when the first electric cooling boxes arrived on the scene. Curiously, those early refrigerators worked the opposite of an ice box, by removing heat instead of adding cold. A motor and compressor pump circulated refrigerant between a condenser and evaporator coils, and heat was removed from the box. Today's refrigerators work pretty much the same way. What has changed a lot, especially in recent years, is the style and convenience of the refrigerator, as well as its energy efficiency.

Freestanding units

One of the fundamental considerations when choosing a new fridge is how the unit will be installed. You have three choices: freestanding, built-in, and boxed-in installation (see the drawing on p. 188). Freestanding units are typical, and they are usually placed among the cabinets with the sides of the appliance at least partially visible.

Freestanding fridges are usually from 30 in. to 36 in. wide and 64 in. to 71 in. high (smaller units are also available). The depth of the box (including the door) will range from 27 in. to 32 in., which means the appliance will stick out past the cabinets quite a bit (base cabinets are usually 24 in. deep).

Virtually all freestanding refrigerators have two doors, one for the freezer compartment and one for the fresh-food compartment. Technically, such refrigerators are refrigerator/freezers but these days, when you say refrigerator, it's implied that there is a freezer compartment too. The freezer section may be above (top-mount), below (bottom-mount) or next to (side-by-side) the fresh-food compartment. Most homes have top-mount refrigerators, but from an efficiency point of view, top-mounted freezers don't make sense. This is because the fresh-food section gets a lot more use than the freezer, and kitchen efficiency studies have found that the most accessible shelf space in a refrigerator is between 22 in. and 56 in. off the floor.

REFRIGERATORS

A freestanding fridge juts out past the face of the adjoining cabinetry.

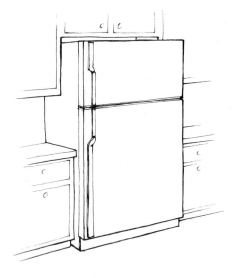

A built-in unit aligns with the cabinetry and takes up less floor space than a freestanding fridge.

A boxed-in unit is a freestanding fridge that fits into an enclosure sized to hold it.

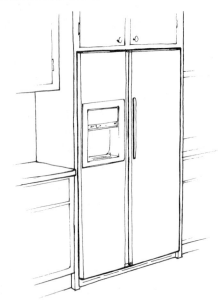

Knowing that, a bottom-mounted freezer should be more efficient. Such appliances aren't common, but everyone I know who has one gives it higher marks than the top-mount freezer they previously owned. I recently bought a bottom-mount freezer for my own home, and I like it a lot better, too.

Side-by-side refrigerators (freezer on the left, fresh food on the right) get mixed reviews from people I know who own one. Some people don't like them because the storage shelving on both sides is narrower than a full-width compartment, and big items can be difficult to fit in. And the lesser-used freezer area consumes valuable fresh-food storage area in that convenient 22-in. to 56-in. height range. But other people love their side-by-side fridges because everything is more convenient to get to.

Built-in units

When you are perusing all the beautiful pictures of kitchens during the predesign stage of your kitchen planning, take note of the refrigerators. You'll discover that many kitchen pictures don't even show a fridge (especially in cabinet sales brochures), and if you do see one, nine times out of ten it will be built in. That's because built-ins blend in better with the cabinetry.

A built-in refrigerator is only about 24 in. deep, so it doesn't stand proud of the cabinet fronts and take up as much floor space in the kitchen as a freestanding fridge. In addition, built-ins have stylish front-panel trim kits that allow you to attach panels of sleek stainless steel, glossy colors, or even cabinet-matching wood. Most built-ins have side-by-side doors, and they come in 36-in., 42-in., and 48-in. widths. The wider versions are spacious, and because the appliance is shallower than a conventional fridge, the contents are right at your fingertips. In addition, built-in fridges are 84 in. tall. Some of that height is taken up by a grille on the top that covers the unit's compressor and condenser coils, but there is still more vertical storage space compared to a freestanding unit. However, a 36-in.-wide built-in fridge generally has less total storage space than a 36-in.-wide freestanding unit.

Built-in refrigerators look great in a kitchen and have many practical advantages, but the bad news is that they are downright expensive. As with a commercial-style range, you can expect to pay thousands of dollars more for a built-in fridge than you will for a top-quality freestanding unit.

Boxed-in units

If you want the look of a built-in fridge without the cost, consider a boxed-in unit. Here's how it works. You design your kitchen with a cabinet over the fridge that is slightly wider than the fridge and 24 in. deep, and then place 24-in. side panels (or deep cabinetry) on either side of that cabinet, thereby creating an enclosure that a freestanding fridge can be slid into. But unlike a true built-in, there is air space at the sides and top of the appliance, and the refrigerator will project past the face of the cabinets into the room.

A refinement on the boxed-in approach is to custom-size the opening to the refrigerator you buy, and/or recess the unit back into the wall behind. Many times, I've gained an extra 4 in. of depth by removing the layer of drywall and studs in the wall directly behind the fridge (this isn't always possible though). In my own kitchen, I was able to set the fridge back 6 in. more than usual by removing the wall behind and sliding the unit back under an enclosed stairway. If you custom-size the opening, though, you have to take into account the manufacturer's recommended air clearances at the sides, top, and back (¾ in., 1 in., and 1 in., respectively, are typical). What's more, I've found that the sides of freestanding refrigerators usually bow out a bit in the middle. These are things that need to be accounted for during the design stage of your project, not after remodeling work starts.

Hybrid units

A more recent fridge design is a hybrid freestanding "built-in" appliance. One such unit is standard height but only about 24 in. deep.

It is engineered so that very close side and top clearances are acceptable. Furthermore, it has an optional matching trim kit that can be used to cover the gap at the sides and top. And the doors will accept stylish front panels just like a built-in appliance. You get the look of a true built-in refrigerator for a lot less money.

Features to look for

One of the biggest buying decisions you face with a new fridge is the size of the unit. Kitchen planners recommend 8 to 10 cu. ft. of fresh-food storage for a family of two, and 1 cu. ft. more for each additional family member. For the freezer section, 2 cu. ft. per

WHAT GOOD IS A FRIDGE IF THE DOOR WON'T OPEN?

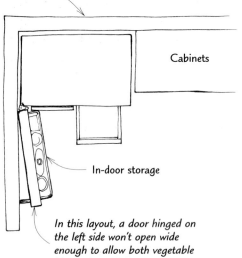

Wall

Cabinets

In-door storage

In this layout, a door hinged on the left side won't open wide enough to allow both vegetable bins to be pulled out.

person is suggested. My advice is simply to get at least a 32-in.-wide single-door free-standing fridge. And if you go the double-door route, don't get a fridge less than 36 in. wide. Even if you don't think you need all the room, it's nice to have, and better for resale value.

The refrigerator is an appliance you use many times a day, so convenience is critical. Go to a well-stocked showroom and open the doors of several different models. Take a really close look at the arrangement of shelves and bins and at the in-the-door storage capabilities (doors that hold gallon containers are a real plus for a family with children). How accessible are the commonly used items—butter, eggs, milk, vegetables? Where will the platters of leftovers go after Thanksgiving dinner? You will discover that refrigerators differ quite a lot in their interior design and storage capacity. If you are looking at side-by-side models, you want to be especially conscious of the configuration of storage space as it relates to your needs.

Also look at door swing. Side-by-side doors always hinge left side left and right side right. Single-wide refrigerator doors can typically be hinged left or right unless the appliance has an in-the-door ice or water dispenser. In that case, there is no reversing the door swing; you must buy with the proper swing in mind.

Another concern is how far the door can open or needs to open. If your fridge is located close to a wall or other obstruction that will prevent the door from opening far enough to pull out the vegetable bins, you may have a problem (see the drawing at left). In most instances, the door will have to open more than 90°. Little details like this need to be anticipated in the planning and buying stages of your remodeling project.

Refrigerator options worth considering are ice makers and in-the-door ice and water dispensers (these require plumbing work, as described in Chapter 6). There are also drawers for meat that keep their contents several degrees cooler than the rest of the fridge, and crisper drawers with lowered humidity that are good for lettuce and celery. Glass shelves with raised edges are a nice feature for containing spills. Some refrigerators have a special quiet-running feature that might be appealing. Automatic defrosting is a real convenience.

Energy efficiency

Today's refrigerators consume much less energy than the refrigerators of the 1970s and early 1980s, but there is still a relatively wide range of efficiency among the various makes and models. Refrigerators are major electricity users in the home, so it is a good idea to compare the distinctive yellow and black energy-guide labels that are displayed prominently on every new appliance. A refrigerator that uses less electricity will have a more efficient cooling system and/or better insulation. The large-sized dollar amount shown in the center of the sticker represents the estimated yearly operating cost of the appliance. Your actual cost will most likely vary, but this number is an excellent indication of the energy efficiency of one model relative to another. Chances are that a higher-efficiency refrigerator will cost more than one with lower efficiency, but you will almost assuredly recoup the extra cost in savings on your electric bill.

Freezers

Because the freezer compartment of a refrigerator is often too small for the average family's needs, a separate freezer is commonly found in most homes. Unless it's quite big, the typical kitchen doesn't have a freezer in it. Freezers are used so infrequently and take up space that could be put to better use, so they are often put in the garage or basement. There is nothing wrong with that, but if the unit has an automatic defrost system, it must be in a room where the temperature remains above 60°F. Below that temperature, the appliance's cooling system will not operate properly. And below 38°F, the cooling system may shut down completely, and food in the storage compartment, ironically, will thaw.

If you want to incorporate the freezer into your kitchen, there are full-size built-in models and smaller built-in models that will fit under a countertop, in amongst the cabinets. But built-in freezers can be pricey. Otherwise, you have the choice of upright freestanding freezers, which look pretty much like refrigerator/freezers but with only one door, or chest freezers, which are about 36 in. high and from 2 ft. to 6 ft. wide and have a lid that lifts up. Chest freezers are more energy efficient because cold air doesn't spill out the door every time you open it, but they, too, are usually relegated to the garage or basement.

Dishwashers

Have you ever heard of an electric sink? That's the name the Kohler Company gave to its first automatic dishwasher in 1927. It was part of a large cast-iron kitchen sink, and an oddity. These days it's the kitchen without a dishwasher that's the oddity. Most people who have dishwashers really appreciate them, but there are a few who rarely use them. One thing is for sure, however: When it comes to selling a home, kitchens with a dishwasher are more appealing .

Almost all dishwashers are designed to fit in a 24-in.-wide opening between two cabinets and underneath a countertop. There are also 18-in.-wide units, as well as dishwashers designed to fit under a sink. It's also possible to get a portable unit that you roll over to the sink and connect to the sink faucet with a hose, but these are not normally installed in remodeled kitchens, since one of the primary objectives of remodeling is to create an organized work environment.

If you currently have an older dishwasher, you will be pleasantly surprised by the improvements that have come to the appliance in recent years. Mid- and higher-priced dishwashers wash better than ever. Instead of just blasting a lot of water around inside the washer compartment, less water is used, and the effectiveness of the appliance has been improved through careful engineering.

With optimum cleaning efficiency in mind, some dishwashers have an internal water-heating option that boosts the temperature of incoming hot water to a more effective cleaning temperature. Another improvement found on new dishwashers is an integral food-filtering system, which helps to clean the wash water. Some dishwashers even have a small food grinder and disposal system integrated into the wash cycle. With all of these improvements, you rarely have to rinse off the dishes before putting them into the dishwasher.

Older dishwashers can be annoyingly noisy, but that problem has been engineered away on the newer washers. If you pick a model that touts its superior sound insulation, it's likely to be significantly quieter during operation than models whose sales literature doesn't mention this feature.

When you shop for dishwashers, you'll find plenty of convenient options, starting with shelves and racks that are designed to hold more dishes as well as handle many different sizes. Electronic controls allow you to program a delayed start. Some computerized models actually "read" the turbidity, or cloudiness, of the wash water and adjust the cleaning cycles as needed. And electronic touch-pad controls are easier to wipe clean than old-fashioned buttons and dials. For fast drying, some dishwashers have an optional convection action (heat and a fan). The more expensive dishwashers now have stainless steel "tubs." The bright metal interior has an appealing look, but the less expensive plastic tubs also can be expected to last as long as the rest of the machine—about 10 years.

Making your purchase

When you are ready to buy your appliances, deal only with established retailers, and look for the best features at the lowest price that you can get. If you start far enough ahead, you can save money by waiting for sales promotions. But along with features and price, don't neglect to compare warranties (see the sidebar on the facing page). Ideally, the place where you buy your appliances can also provide parts and repair service.

A lot of people think that a brand-new appliance will work perfectly for years to come. That may very well be the case, but there's a pretty fair chance that something will go wrong before the warranty expires. Knowing that, it's wise to be prepared for the problem if something does go awry.

To get the full benefit of warranty protection, the Association of Home Appliance Manufacturers (AHAM) recommends taking the following actions:

■ Keep the sales receipt so you can provide proof of the date you bought the appliance. My wife and I keep appliance receipts in the kitchen with the operating manuals.

■ Try out all the features and controls on the appliance as soon as possible after buying it. Warranty-protection coverage starts on the date you bought the appliance, and most product defects show up during the first few uses.

■ Always contact the dealer and/or manufacturer about a problem before your warranty expires.

■ Keep records. Put your complaints in writing, and keep copies of correspondence and service receipts. Request a receipt even for servicing that didn't cost you any money; some companies will handle appliance problems that occur shortly after warranty expiration if proof exists that the problem started before.

■ Note details, such as when the problem was discovered and when it was reported. Keep a written record of the servicing history, including the name of the person who serviced the appliance, and what was done when.

If you keep your paperwork in order, problems should get resolved to your satisfaction. But if they don't, you have recourse through the Major Appliance Consumer Action Program (MACAP). Sponsored by AHAM, one of MACAP's primary purposes is to "provide consumers with unbiased mediation of their unresolved major appliance complaints." See Resources on pp. 194-197 for contact information.

Before you close the deal on an appliance, be sure to discuss delivery. Some retailers charge for this service and some don't. In either event, if you can pick up the appliance yourself, saving them the trouble, you might be able to save some money. If you or your contractor will not be installing the appliance, you will need to discuss the details and costs associated with having the store take care of the installation.

Many retailers will take your old appliance off your hands for no cost; others will charge a fee. Of course, if the old appliance is still functional, you may want to sell it through a classified ad in the newspaper or give it away to a charitable organization.

RESOURCES

The key to successful kitchen remodeling is knowledge properly applied. To that end, I have endeavored to provide you with lots of pertinent data and my own professional opinion. But every remodeling project is different, and there are practical limitations to how much information can be crammed into a book like this. That's why we have Resources, which is organized roughly to correspond with chapters in this book. The listing is by no means comprehensive, but should serve as a starting point for your research.

In the predesign stages of your remodeling, when you are investigating various products and design features, take a few minutes to look at the books and contact some of the companies and trade associations listed here. Most of them have toll-free phone numbers, so it won't cost but a few minutes of your time. They also have specialists who can advise you on technical details. If you have a computer and are on-line, you can do a lot of product research by looking at web pages, as well as request information.

Kitchen design and planning

National Association of the Remodeling Industry, 4900 Seminary Rd., Suite 320, Alexandria, VA 22311; (800) 440-6274; www.nari.org
(Information for homeowners about project planning, budgeting, choosing a contractor, and contracts. NARI also has a professional remodeler certification program and can direct you to contractors in your area who are NARI members.)

National Kitchen and Bath Association, 687 Willow Grove St., Hackettstown, NJ 07840; (800) 410-NKBA; www.nkba.com
(Contact this organization for information on where to find a Certified Kitchen Designer, or CKD, in your area.)

Remodeling magazine's Cost Vs. Value Report can be requested by calling (202) 452-0800 for a small charge (at this writing, $7.95 plus $1.50 shipping and handling), or you can read the report in Remodeling Online at www.remodeling.hw.net.

Edic, Martin and Richard. *Kitchens That Work.* Newtown, Conn.: The Taunton Press, 1997.

Thomas, Steve. *This Old House Kitchens: A Guide to Design and Renovation.* New York: Little, Brown and Co., 1992.

Contractors, money, and contracts

American Association of Architects, AIA Documents, 1735 New York Ave., NW, Washington, DC 20006; (202) 626-7359; www.aia.org
(Source for several different forms of owner/contractor contract documents)

American Homeowner's Foundation, 6776 Little Falls Rd., Arlington, VA 22213-1213; (800) 489-7776 or (703) 536-7776
(For a small fee this organization will provide a five-page contract you can use for your remodeling.)

Council of Better Business Bureaus, 4200 Wilson Blvd., Suite 8000, Arlington, VA 22203; (703) 276-0100; www.bbb.org
(This group can direct you to your closest BBB office and send you general information about what the BBB does. If you have problems with a contractor, the BBB can provide arbitration services.)

Smart Consumer Services, 2111 Jefferson Davis Highway 722, N. Arlington, VA 22202; (703) 416-0257; www.uha.org.
(For $25.95, this company offers homeowners an "advocacy review" of remodeling contracts, with an eye toward heading off potential problems. The company also sells a sample remodeling contract.)

Levine, Mark, and Stephen M. Pollan. *Stephen Pollan's Foolproof Guide To Renovating Your Kitchen.* New York: Simon and Schuster, 1997.
(Pollan is an attorney and offers advice on contracts that only an attorney can.)

Rusk, John. *On Time and On Budget.* New York: Doubleday, 1996.
(Rusk is a high-end remodeling contractor in New York City and has good insights on how to avoid problems when working with contractors and designers.)

Construction how-to books

Bollinger, Don. *Hardwood Floors: Laying, Sanding and Finishing.* Newtown, Conn.: The Taunton Press, 1990.

Byrne, Michael. *Setting Tile.* Newtown, Conn.: The Taunton Press, 1995.

Cauldwell, Rex. *Safe Home Wiring Projects.* Newtown, Conn.: The Taunton Press, 1997.

Cauldwell, Rex. *Wiring a House.* Newtown, Conn.: The Taunton Press, 1996.

Ferguson, Myron. *Drywall: Professional Techniques for Walls and Ceilings.* Newtown, Conn.: The Taunton Press, 1997.

Hemp, Peter. *Installing & Repairing Plumbing Fixtures.* Newtown, Conn.: The Taunton Press, 1994.

Hemp, Peter. *Plumbing a House.* Newtown, Conn.: The Taunton Press, 1994.

Kimball, Herrick. *Making Plastic-Laminate Countertops.* Newtown, Conn.: The Taunton Press, 1996.

Kimball, Herrick. *Refacing Cabinets: Making an Old Kitchen New.* Newtown, Conn.: The Taunton Press, 1997.

Savage, Craig. *Trim Carpentry Techniques: Installing Doors, Windows, Base, and Crown.* Newtown, Conn.: The Taunton Press, 1989.

Tolpin, Jim. *Building Traditional Kitchen Cabinets.* Newtown, Conn.: The Taunton Press, 1994.

Plumbing and radiant-floor heating

Easy Heat, 31977 US 20 E, New Carlisle, IN 46552 (800) 537-4732 or 219-654-3144; www.easyheat.com
(Radiant-heating systems that are designed to go under tile and stone floors and remove the chill)

Heatway, 3131 W. Chestnut Expwy., Springfield, MO 65802; (800) 255-1996; www.heatway.com
(Electric and hydronic floor-heating systems)

Holohan, Dan. *How Come? Hydronic Heating Questions We've Been Asking For More Than 100 Years.* Published by Dan Holohan Associates, 63 North Oakdale Ave., Bethpage, NY 11714; (800) 853-8882; www.danholohan.com
(A book and web site for people with an interest in radiant-heat)

In-Sink-Erator, 4700 21st St., Racine, WI 53406; (800) 558-5700; www.insinkerator.com
(Instant hot-water dispensers)

Studor, 2030 Main St., Dunedin, FL 34698; (800) 447-4721; www.studor.com
(Studor mechanical vent)

Wirsbo, 5925 148th St. W, Apple Valley, MN 55124; (800) 321-4739; www.wirsbo.com
(PEX plastic plumbing)

Windows and doors

Andersen Corp., Bayport, MN; (800) 426-4261; www.andersen-corp.com
(Windows)

Blaine Window Repair Service, 2410 Linden Lane, Silver Spring, MD 20910; (301) 565-4949
(This company has a catalog featuring obsolete, hard-to-find, discontinued, and current replacement hardware for windows.)

Marvin Windows & Doors, PO Box 100, Warroad, MN 56763; (800) 346-5128; www.marvin.com
(Windows and doors)

Pease Industries, 7100 Dixie Hwy., Fairfield, OH 45014; (800) 883-6677; www.peasedoors.com
(Entrance doors)

Pella Corp., Pella, IA 50219; (800) 847-3552; www.pella.com
(Windows)

Pozzi Wood Windows, PO Box 5249, Bend, OR 97708; (800) 257-9663; www. pozzi.com

Stanley Door Systems, 1225 E. Maple Rd., Troy, MI 48083; (800) 521-2752; www.stanleyworks.com
(Entrance doors)

Therma-Tru Corp., PO Box 8780, Maumee, OH 43537; (800) 537-8827; www.thermatru.com
(Entrance doors)

Velux-America, PO Box 5001, Greenwood, SC 29648; (800) 283-2831; www.velux.com
(Skylights)

Lighting

American Lighting Association, World Trade Center, Suite 10046, PO Box 420288, Dallas, TX 75342; (800) 274-4484; www.americanlightingassoc.com

Lightolier, 631 Airport Rd., Fall River, MA 02720; (800) 544-LYTE; www.lightolier.com
(Lighting fixtures)

Seagull Lighting, 301 W. Washington St., Riverside, NJ 08075; (609) 764-0500
(Miniature low-voltage track lighting)

Ventilation

Broan Manufacturing, PO Box 140, Hartford, WI 53027; (800) 548-0790; www.broan.com
(Vent hoods)

Fantech, 1712 Northgate Blvd., Sarastota, FL 34234; (800) 747-1762
(Remote-mounted exhaust-fan systems)

Nutone, Madison and Red Bank Rds., Cincinnati, OH 45227; (800) 543-8687
(Vent hoods)

Tamarack Technologies, PO Box 490, W. Wareham MA 02576; (800) 222-5932; www.tamtech.com
(Difficult-to-find products that deal with indoor-air quality in the kitchen and throughout the home)

Vent-A-Hood, PO Box 830426, Richardson, TX 75083; (214) 235-5201
(Vent hoods)

Cabinets

AristoKraft, PO Box 420, One Aristokraft Square, Jasper, IN 47547; (812) 482-2527; www.aristokraft.com

Kraftmaid Cabinetry, 16052 Industrial Pkwy., Middlefield, OH 44062; (800) 654-3008; www.kraftmaid.com

Merillat Industries, PO Box 1946, Adrian, MI 49221; (517) 263-0771; www.merillat.com

Omega Cabinets, 1205 Peters Dr., Waterloo, IA 50703; (319) 236-2256; www.omegacab.com

Rev-A-Shelf, PO Box 99585, Jeffersontown, KY 40269; (800) 626-1126; www.rev-a-shelf.com
(Cabinet storage and organization accessories)

Rutt Custom Cabinetry, PO Box 129, 1564 Main St., Goodville, PA 17528; (800) 420-7888

Schrock Cabinet Co., 6000 Perimeter Dr., Dublin, OH 43017; (614) 792-4100; www.schrock.com

Countertops

Avonite, 1945 Highway 304, Belen, NM 87002; (800) 428-6648; www.avonite.com
(Avonite solid-surface material)

Bally Block Co., 30 S. Seventh St., Bally, PA 19503; (610) 845-7726
(Maple butcher-block countertops)

DuPont Corian, Chestnut Run Plaza, Wilmington DE 19880; (800) 426-7426
(Corian solid-surface material)

Formica Corp., 10155 Reading Rd., Cincinnati, OH 45241; (800) FORMICA; www.formica.com
(Surell solid-surface material, laminate flooring, and Formica plastic laminate for countertops)

Nevamar Decorative Surfaces, 8339 Telegraph Rd., Odenton, MD 21113; (410) 551-5000; www.nevamar.com
(Nevamar plastic laminate, Fountainhead solid-surface material)

Pionite, One Pionite Rd., Auburn, ME 04221; (800) 746-6483; www.pionitelaminates.com
(Pionite plastic laminate)

Ralph Wilson Plastics Co., 600 South General Bruce Dr., Temple, TX 76504; (800) 433-3222; www.wilsonart.com
(Gibraltar solid-surface material, laminate flooring, solid-surface veneer, countertop laminate, and bevel-edge moldings for plastic laminate counters)

The Swan Corp., One City Centre, Suite 2300, St. Louis, MO 63101; (314) 231-8148; www.theswancorp.com
(Swanstone solid surfacing and solid-surface veneer)

Sinks and faucets

Porcelain Enamel Institute, PO Box 158541, 4004 Hillsboro Pike, Suite 224B, Nashville, TN 37215; (645) 385-5357; www.porcelainenamel.com

American Standard, 1 Centennial Plaza, Piscataway, NJ 08855; (908) 980-2400
(Americast resin-backed enameled steel sinks)

Delta Faucet Co., 55 E. 111th St., Indianapolis, IN 46280; (800) 345-DELTA or (317) 848-1812; www.deltafaucet.com

Elkay Mfg. Co.; 222 Camden Court, Oak Brook, IL 60521; (630) 572-3192
(Stainless-steel sinks)

Kohler Co., Kohler. WI 53044; (800) 4-KOHLER; www.kohlerco

Moen, 25300 Al Moen Dr., North Olmstead, OH 44070; (800) 321-6636; www.moen.com

Sterling Plumbing Group, 2900 Golf Rd., Rolling Meadows, IL 60008; (800) STERLING; www.sterlingplumbing.com

Flooring and floor finishes

The Hardwood Council, PO Box 525, Oakmont, PA 15139; (412) 281-4980
(Brochures on how to use hardwood in different applications)

National Wood Flooring Association, 233 Old Merrimac Station Rd., Manchester MO 63021; (314) 391-5161; www.woodfloors.org

Resilient Floor Covering Institute, 966 Hungerford Dr., Suite 12B, Rockville, MD 20850; (301) 340-8580; www.buildernet.com/rfci
(Among other things, RFCI offers a how-to booklet on the proper removal of vinyl floor coverings that contain asbestos.)

Armstrong Corp., PO Box 3001, Lancaster, PA 17604; (800) 233-3823; www.armstrong.com
(Floor coverings)

Basic Coatings, 2124 Valley Dr., PO Box 677, Des Moines, IA 50303; (800) 441-1934; www.basiccoatings.com
(Urethane floor finishes)

BonaKemi, 14805 East Moncrieff Place, Aurora, CO 80011; (800) 574-4674; www.bonakemi.com
(Water-based urethane floor finishes and floor-care products for wood floors)

Bruce Hardwood Floors, 16803 Dallas Pkwy., Dallas, TX 75248; (800) 722-4647

Congoleum Corp., 3705 Quaker Bridge Rd., Mercerville, NJ 08619; (609) 584-3000; www.congoleum.com
(Vinyl flooring)

Crossville, PO Box 1168, Crossville, TN 38557; (615) 484-2110; www.crossville-ceramics.com
(Solid porcelain tiles)

DLW Gerbert Ltd., 715 Fountain Ave., Lancaster, PA 17604; (800) 828-9461
(Natural linoleum)

Forbo North America, PO Box 667, Hazelton, PA 18201; (800) 233-0475
(Natural linoleum)

Harris-Tarkett, PO Box 300, 2225 Eddie Williams Rd., Johnson City, TN 37605; (800) 842-7816
(Hardwood flooring, floating floors)

Mannington Mills, PO Box 30, Salem, NJ 08079; (800) 443-5667; www.mannington.com
(Vinyl and laminate flooring)

Miracle Sealants Co., 12806 Schabarum Ave., Bldg. A, Irwindale, CA 91706; (800) 350-1901
(511 Impregnator grout sealer)

Perstorp Flooring, 2809 Highwood Blvd., Suite 100, Raleigh, NC 27604; (800) 337-3746; www.pergo.com
(Pergo laminate flooring)

Major appliances

Appliance magazine has a "Consumer Connection" web site (www. appliance.com) that is useful to homeowners who are selecting new appliances.

Association of Home Appliance Manufacturers, 20 N. Wacker Dr., Suite 1500, Chicago, IL 60606; (312) 984-5800; FAX: (312) 984-5823; www.aham.org
(Sponsors of the Major Appliance Consumer Action Program, which mediates consumer complaints about appliances. MACAP may be contacted by phone at 800-621-0477 or on the Internet at www.aham.org/consumer/macapfaq.htm.)

Dimension Express, which can be reached by FAX at (702) 833-3600 or on the Internet at www.dexpress.com, will provide current size specification sheets for almost all kitchen appliances.

Amana Refrigeration, Subsidiary of Raytheon Co., Amana, IA 52204; (800) 843-0304; www.amana.com
(Amana)

Frigidaire, 6000 Perimeter Dr., Dublin, OH 43017; (512) 833-3250; www.frigidaire.com
(Frigidaire, Gibson, Kelvinator, Tappan, White-Westinghouse)

GE Appliances, Appliance Park, Louisville, KY 40225; (800) 626-2000; www.ge.com/appliances
(GE, Hotpoint)

Maytag Appliances, One Dependability Square, Newton, IA 50208; (800) 688-9900; www.maytag.com/index.cgi
(Admiral, Jenn-Air, Magic Chef, Maytag)

U-Line Corp., 8900 N. 55th St., PO Box 23220, Milwaukee, WI 53223; (414) 354-0300; www.u-line.com
(Built-in refrigerators)

Viking Range, 111 Front St., Greenwood, MS 38930; (888) 845-4641; www.viking-range.com
(Commercial-style cooktops and ranges)

Whirlpool, 151 N. Riverview Dr., Benton Harbor, MI 49002; (800) 253-1301; www.whirlpool.com
(Whirlpool, Roper, Kitchen Aid)

Wolf Range, 19600 S. Alameda, Compton, CA 90221; (800) 366-9653
(Commercial-style cooktops and ranges)

INDEX

Book Publisher: Jim Childs

Acquisitions Editor: Julie Trelstad

Assistant Editor: Karen Liljedahl

Editor: Ruth Dobsevage

Designer/Layout Artist: Lynne Phillips

Illustrator: Michael Gellatly

Indexer: Harriet Hodges

Typeface: Leawood

Paper: 70-lb. Utopia Two Matte, neutral pH

Printer: Quebecor Printing/Hawkins, Church Hill, Tennessee